A New Zen for Women

A New Zen for Women

Perle Besserman

First published in 2007 by
PALGRAVE MACMILLAN™
175 Fifth Avenue, New York, N.Y. 10010 and
Houndmills, Basingstoke, Hampshire, England RG21 6XS.
Companies and representatives throughout the world.

PALGRAVE MACMILLAN is the global academic imprint of the
Palgrave Macmillan division of St. Martin's Press, LLC and of
Palgrave Macmillan Ltd. Macmillan® is a registered trademark in the
United States, United Kingdom and other countries. Palgrave is a
registered trademark in the European Union and other countries.

ISBN-13: 978-1-4039-7214-9
ISBN-10: 1-4039-7214-1

Library of Congress Cataloging-in-Publication Data is available from
the Library of Congress.

Besserman, Perle.
   A New Zen for Women/Perle Besserman
      p.   cm
   Includes bibliographical references and index.
   ISBN 1-4039-7214-1, 978-1-4039-7214-9
   1. Religious life—Zen Buddhism.   2. Buddhist women—Religious
life.   3. Besserman, Perle.   I. Title.
BQ9286.B467   2007
294.3'927082—dc22
      2006050675

Design by Letra Libre.

First edition: April 2007

10 9 8 7 6 5 4 3 2 1

Printed in the United States of America.

Contents

*With fondest gassho to
Hetty Baiz, Brigid Lowry,
Jennie Martinez Peterson, Kathy J. Phillips,*

*and, most of all,
Manfred B. Steger,*

*without whom this book would
never have been written.*

Introduction

The Wandering Years

It is August, and winter in Australia, my new home. I am sitting at my desk in my half-furnished apartment looking out the window watching a flock of gulls swoop across the vast Pacific sky before briefly touching down on the highest branch of the gum tree in my neighbor's garden and flying off again. The nomadic gulls never seem to remain in one place for very long. They remind me of my own restless wandering, and the long journey that eventually led to my spiritual home in Zen. My memories of that turbulent past are in stark contrast to the peaceful place I find myself in today, and I am surprised to recall how angry I was as I embarked on my spiritual search. It was early in the seventies, and though most of the women I met on the path were as angry as I was, we hadn't yet admitted it to ourselves. It wasn't until the late seventies and early eighties that a growing number of feminists would dare to openly explore and justify that anger—brave spiritual pioneers like Mary Daly, foremost radical theologian of the women's movement—to assure us that our rage wasn't simply a "stage" in the process of women's liberation but the very essence of liberation itself.

I think of those heady years of second-wave feminism as—to steal a phrase from Dickens—"the best of times and the worst of times." "The best" was represented by the sexual, emotional, and professional liberation we spiritual feminists were achieving through consciousness-raising sessions, teach-ins, and nonviolent street demonstrations similar to the ones many of us had participated in during the civil rights movement of the sixties. Like our feisty sisters then taking their places in American boardrooms, laboratories, courtrooms, hospitals, and universities, we spiritual seekers, too, were educated, independent trailblazers carving new inroads for women.

"The worst" was represented by unresolved issues involving male hierarchy, authority, and power—the shady underside of the movement afflicting women in all social spheres, but especially those of us who were serious spiritual seekers. Though the new feminism infused our spiritual quest, our relationships with our male teachers were no different, really, from the male-dominated sexual politics of our secular life. But we were too insatiably hungry for "enlightenment" (whatever that was) to acknowledge the sexism we encountered, and we convinced ourselves that spirituality was somehow *different*. In the name of our spiritual quest even the avowed feminists among us surrendered to archaic patriarchal traditions (initially without complaint) by knuckling under and becoming handmaidens, caretakers, and/or concubines to our male teachers. Throwing away all our intellectual questioning and hard-won independence, impelled by the mistaken notion that we were "killing the ego," we bowed our heads and submitted our better judgment to the enlightened minds of our masters.

My own education in an Orthodox Jewish yeshiva for girls had alienated me early from what I had been told was my "natural" function—namely marrying, serving my husband, and bearing him sons—and I'd consciously abandoned the path of subservience as an eight-year-old girl in a long-sleeved blouse, long cotton stockings, and ankle-length skirt. Despite the daily bombardment of lessons in "modest Jewish womanhood," my patriarchal religious training had never prevented me from discovering how powerful women really were, and how much men depended on them:

1. *Intellectually:*
   Once I'd left the all-girls yeshiva and entered public school, I was so far ahead in my studies than most of the boys in my class that they were always pleading with me to let them copy my homework or move my paper over on my desk during exams so they could crib my answers.
2. *Financially:*
   Everyone in my family knew that my mother and her sisters were far better at earning and saving money than their hus-

bands, who were always "losing fortunes." Yet whenever the men gathered around our dining room table to "discuss business," the women were asked not to participate but to serve them tea and my mother's home-baked cakes.

3. *Emotionally:*
When my first husband's father died, not one of his four sons could bring himself to ride the mortuary elevator with his body and select his casket. (Two of them were medical doctors!) I ended up handling all the funeral details.

From my mother, I learned that all men were really babies and that it was a woman's job to protect them from the knowledge of their weakness, manipulate them from behind the scenes, and never openly compete with them—with ordinary men, maybe, but certainly not spiritual teachers. Spiritual teachers were fearless; they died sitting in perfect lotus posture with beatific smiles on their faces. Didn't they? The first crack in my idealized picture appeared when my celibate forty-eight-year-old Indian yoga teacher asked me for advice one day: should he give up the religious life for marriage and fatherhood? I was stunned when he took my advice and did just that. I was similarly amazed by the fragility of a world-famous Brahmin teacher in whose entourage I traveled for a while. His wealthy patroness decided everything for him, from the color of his ties to the amount of peas the cook put on his plate. This trail-blazing enlightener of thousands could do nothing for himself; he was as dependent on this woman as a toddler on his nanny. In India I witnessed limp-bodied gurus in loincloths being massaged, bathed, and otherwise pleasured by harems of female devotees. Tough Tibetan lamas drank themselves into a stupor and were supported onto university platforms all over America by golden-haired nymphs who translated their slurred speeches into intelligible English. Kabbalists left their wives for nubile beauties who dreamed of giving birth to the future Messiah. Sufi sheikhs sat on golden thrones weaving parables of divine union to chain-smoking male dervishes as their western women disciples—covered from head to toe in scarves and floor-length robes—brewed endless cups of coffee out of earshot in the kitchen.

"Surrender" was a word you heard a lot in spiritual circles in those days. Looking back, it seems that all the serious seekers I knew then—both women and men—were surrendering to a shared child-hood dream of melting into oneness with creation, of "transcending" the material world by cutting loose from the earth and soaring heav-enward. As a graduate student at Columbia, I remember hearing of an NYU sociology professor who quit his tenured job and surrendered everything he owned (including a Rolex watch) to his fifteen-year-old Indian guru before moving to the swami's ashram in New Mexico. Several friends of mine surrendered to drugs in hope of finding their childhood dream. Some of them were lucky enough to survive with their bodies and minds intact. Others were less fortunate. Like the brilliant physics student who took LSD and, thinking he could fly, leapt to his death from the window of his parents' Riverside Drive apartment. Or the prominent psychiatric drug researcher who jumped in front of a subway train. At a dinner party, I overheard my first hus-band (a strict Freudian psychoanalyst before becoming interested in alternative medicine) discussing the tragic suicide of our friend with a group of colleagues. They concluded that the search for higher con-sciousness that had led him to experiment with drugs was "deeply rooted in an infantile Oedipal desire to merge with his mother." But I was unconvinced. Pinning diagnostic labels on a profound spiritual yearning I myself had experienced since I was five years old struck me as facile. Only a few years later, many of those same psychoanalysts (my husband among them) would be heading East on their own spiri-tual journeys before returning home and incorporating the meditative techniques they'd learned into their therapeutic practice.

Pepperidge Farm Cookies and Antic Zen Masters

It was the second half of the twentieth century and the United States was teeming with Asian male spiritual teachers and Western female devotees. Take my friend "Jessie" (not her real name). Jessie was the kind of person who sent you letters even though you lived around the corner. Lately, she'd taken up practice with a Tibetan Rinpoche, so I would come home every day to find a picture postcard of some Buddhist shrine in my mailbox. I knew without even looking at the back that it was from Jessie. Sometimes she'd send me a Buddhist saying or a mysterious Zen koan. Her postcards were enigmatic, pedagogical, serious, and deep. I never felt worthy of them.

Jessie was a sculptor who had come to New York from Colorado. She was angular and lean and beautiful and quiet. Her manners were impeccable; yet she was sentimental to the point of bursting into tears over old snapshots of her movie-star handsome father who had died after a long time spent in the hospital as a helpless paralytic when Jessie was fifteen. I could sit with her for hours drinking tea and eating Pepperidge Farm cookies in her Soho loft, listening to her talk about her father, and how he'd taken her horseback riding in the mountains. Yet I always felt that Jessie was holding something back. She seemed to have some faraway child's secret locked up in a cave in the Rockies, a secret too fine and precious to share with a loud-mouthed Brooklyn girl like me.

I once dared to send Jessie a postcard of my own, depicting a pink and orange Miami sunset. "I am sick of searching," I wrote. "Help me find a teacher." I thought she of all people would know what I was talking about and would invite me to join her growing Tibetan *sangha* (Buddhist community). But all she did was send me one of her Buddhist shrine postcards with "When you're ready, your teacher will appear" scrawled across the back in aquamarine ink. In my mind I could follow Jessie to the mailbox on the corner as she approached it with her long, graceful stride; head lifted high; her thick black hair swinging in the wind—I could even feel in my nostrils the little sniff of satisfaction she'd given as the letter hit the metal. She'd probably banged the lid on the mailbox shut thinking, "Perle is too resistant to suffering. Life is suffering. I have known that from the beginning. But Perle fights it. She always has."

Though she'd chosen to practice with a Tibetan teacher, Jessie knew all sorts of Buddhists. It was she who indirectly, maybe even unwittingly, introduced me to my first Zen teacher. We were sitting in her loft drinking tea and eating Pepperidge Farm cookies one day when she started talking about the time she'd entertained her soon-to-be-ex-husband's Zen master in her home. She called the Zen master "antic," and said he was totally unpredictable. "Imagine, at two in the morning I woke up to find the roshi doing his laundry!"

I was immediately intrigued. What kind of spiritual teacher was this? None of the ones I knew even *did* laundry. They had armies of female slaves to do it for them. This antic Japanese roshi who got up in the middle of the night to do his own laundry was someone I would have to meet. And soon.

That was how, on a freezing sunny day in February of 1981, I found myself standing on the Mount of Olives in front of the traditional Arab sandstone building housing the Jerusalem Zen Center holding a box containing a gift for the roshi in one hand and a greasy brown paper bag stuffed with falafel pita sandwiches in the other. I knocked, and was surprised when the roshi himself appeared in the doorway; I had expected him to have an attendant monk. Jessie had described Dokyu Roshi as "a very traditional, very Japanese Zen master," adding that he'd been born into a temple family consisting of six generations of Zen monks. The black-robed man facing me in the doorway was tiny, about fifty-five. His head was as bald and shiny as a melon. His skin was golden and his eyes were fierce.

"What you want?"

"I'm . . . I came to say hello from your students in New York."

"Aaah . . . you Perle-san, yes? You come in for tea?"

Leading me to a tatami-covered room behind the *zendo* (meditation hall), the roshi motioned for me to sit down on a floor cushion at a low Japanese table and went to the kitchen. I noted that his robes were made of thin cotton and that he was barefoot despite the cold.

"No central heating," he apologized, returning with the steaming tea. "Only in lower belly, best central heating system." The roshi patted himself on the navel, crossed his legs, and without having to use his hands to balance himself, sat down.

Shivering, I opened the greasy bag and offered him a falafel sandwich. He took it and smiled.

"Four years is enough falafel for traditional Japanese monk. I now get word I go home to Japan and eat raw fish again."

I handed him the box. "For you . . . a gift."

The roshi put down his sandwich and clasped his palms together in thanks, then neatly unpacked the box. "Aaah . . . beautiful," he murmured, removing the cashmere sweater I'd bought him from the tissue paper wrapping and holding it up to the light. "Beautiful wine color, so young looking, my sister will say I become young boy again.

Very beautiful. Thank you very much, Perle-san." He made a little bow then continued to admire the sweater, smiling at me with the openness of a child, the fierceness in his eyes gone.

Suddenly, without thinking, I blurted, "Roshi, I want to see my face before I was born. That's why I've come here to you."

Pouring me a second cup of fragrant green tea, the roshi shook his head and purred. "No need to study with anyone. You sitting on your own diamond mountain and you run around the world looking for it. 'Where is my precious diamond mountain?' you cry. All the time right there with you. Only you dream you lost it. But it is right there," he pointed his finger at me.

I sipped the tea and felt my face grow warm. What was he talking about? A magic mountain? No, a diamond mountain. It didn't matter. All I wanted was to remain seated on the floor across from this little Japanese Zen master forever, watching him chew his falafel sandwich. But then our visit was over, and Dokyu Roshi did not say he would be my teacher. He didn't even invite me to come back and take tea with him again. As he led me out the door, he mentioned that he was planning to remain in Japan as vice abbot of his monastery, but he did not invite me to visit him there either. Instead, after handing me a piece of paper with the neatly typed names and addresses of two of his American students in Jerusalem, along with a small bronze Buddha and a book of Buddhist chants in Sino-Japanese with the English translation on facing pages, he encouraged me to start meditating with his Jerusalem students and then continue on my own in New York.

Walking downhill to the bus stop, I looked over my shoulder and saw the roshi standing in the doorway, waving.

So this is the way it happens, I thought, waving back at him. You travel around the world for years until you finally find your teacher . . . and he sends you back home.

Swinging-door Zen

That meeting with Dokyu Roshi in Jerusalem marked the official beginning of my Zen practice. But what first really drew me to Zen was Shunryu Suzuki Roshi's classic *Zen Mind Beginner's Mind*. I was standing on a crowded subway train reading the part about letting your breath move in and out like a swinging door when I suddenly felt my "self" disappear. I had no idea what was happening, but the feeling was so exhilarating that I started to laugh and cry at the same time. Accustomed to strange behavior on the New York subways, my fellow passengers took no notice of me. Besides, the experience lasted only for a few seconds. But when it was over, I knew without a doubt that Zen was the only practice for me. I can only describe the feeling as coming home and slipping into your most comfortable pair of slippers after years of traveling around the world in shoes that pinch your feet.

What I love most about Zen is its humor. (No other spiritual tradition I've come across has the comic spirit of Zen.) And its sparseness. Zen people don't have to spend hours praying or performing rituals, and best of all, there is no god threatening punishment for disobeying "His" laws or handing out rewards for good behavior—there's just sitting on a black cushion and following the swinging door of your breath. No magic. Nothing mystical about it. Zen is as direct as it gets. It emphasizes attending to the moon, not to the finger pointing at the moon. Like tasting a grapefruit or falling in love, you have to experience it for yourself; there is no understanding it from the outside. As I tell people who want to learn about Zen, there's no learning, there's only practicing. You can attend a thousand lectures on the subject, but until you sit yourself down on a cushion and meditate, you'll never know what Zen is. Experience is all. Then why write about it? Because the kind of Zen I like practicing best is based on stories—odd little anecdotes called koans, exchanges between teacher and student that bring the Zen experience to life. Because Zen stories are like no other kind of story telling I know. Because they pluck you out of time and space and land you right here in this very moment, "entwining eyebrows with the ancestors." And because those Zen ancestors were presumably all male, I want to tell a Zen story about women—a contemporary "WomanZen" story rooted in the ancient lineage of our recently discovered female Zen ancestors.[1] The following story is a perfect example of why I think focusing on women is so important.

I had been practicing in a Japanese Zen monastery and was traveling during a training period break when I met an American woman named Sally, the disciple of a young Japanese Zen master who'd been her fellow graduate student at a California university. When both had completed their graduate studies, they went to Japan—the young roshi as abbot of his monastery, and Sally as his Zen student, accompanied by her husband and children. There Sally was permitted to live at the roshi's monastery for three days a week; the other four days saw her playing housewife to her husband, mother to her children, and teacher of English on the side. For ten years Sally practiced *zazen* (sitting meditation) in that Japanese monastery, sleeping three nights a week on a narrow futon in a cell so far away from the meditation hall that she had to walk in the dark for a quarter of a mile wearing straw sandals with no socks in even the coldest weather before being granted the privilege of sitting behind a screen out of view of the male monks. All former traces of friendship and equality that had existed between Sally and her roshi when they were in graduate school were gone.

One day, prompted by Sally's example, a group of her Japanese female English students approached the roshi and asked to practice Zen alongside her. Much to Sally's surprise the gentle, modern, Westernized roshi she'd known in California was suddenly transformed into a fire-breathing dragon. Puffing himself up and getting red in the face, he screamed, "No Japanese women in my zendo!" The frightened women quickly made their bows and exited. What was okay for a loose, classless Western woman like Sally was clearly not okay for a virtuous, wellborn Japanese lady. You'd think that being a red-blooded American feminist, Sally would have complained. But she didn't. She just swallowed her humiliation, covered it up with a dose of good sportswomanship, and convinced herself that the roshi's outburst showed she was tough enough to be treated like a monk and should be grateful for the privilege.

The monks had a different story to tell. One talkative fellow I met at the monastery, a heavyset man in his twenties who had spent two years in Los Angeles with his Japanese Zen master, once confronted me during an after-supper break. "I don't understand you American women with your ideas about authority and freedom. You are all shopping for wisdom, as if in a supermarket, looking for enlightenment under your own ideal conditions, always looking for something you can use. Zen for self-understanding, Zen for better sex, Zen for developing a healthy body . . . You hate the discipline; all you want is immediate results. Why do you ask so many questions?"

"For the same reason you Japanese bow and do everything you're told," I said. "We're raised like that."

"But you women are completely wild. In the States you all set out to deliberately seduce the monks, as if the idea of celibacy sets you so much on edge that you must prove your power by defiling men."

I was too angry to answer him, for by then I had seen and lived through so much abuse of women by male spiritual teachers that it left me in a speechless rage just to think about it. In the States, where sleeping with your guru was an almost predictable part of spiritual training, I saw my friends, women who were otherwise selective in their relationships with ordinary men, submit themselves to concubinage when it came to servicing "a holy man's" sexual needs. They considered themselves "privileged" at having been chosen. All my life I had rejected such "privileges" as demeaning to women, and I wasn't going to stop just because I too had been allowed to live in a monastery and let myself be humiliated by pretending I was a monk.

WomanZen

Paradoxically (and Zen is full of paradoxes), decades of shared experiences with women like Sally have only deepened my commitment to the practice. It was, in fact, my love of Zen that prompted me to write this book. Not to rant and complain but to celebrate the strength, power, and insight of women past and present who have taken the Zen path. I want to "talk story" across the centuries with my dharma sisters—Asian and Western, nuns and laywomen, feminists and traditionalists. To give you a taste of what WomanZen is all about. To show you why, and how, it's (paradoxically) the same and different from the traditional monastic practice we inherited from the Zen patriarchs. I also want to dispel the notion that WomanZen is illegitimate because women supposedly had nothing to do with founding Zen. And I want to point out that it's not only feminist practitioners like me but Buddhist scholars, too, who are proving that false. For example, the recent discovery of medieval Japanese government documents no one ever knew existed shows that women were not only patrons and founders of the great Zen temples but that they were the first Japanese to be ordained as Buddhists.[2]

Some scholars go so far as to claim that by rejecting all words and scriptures and strictly insisting on meditation, patriarchal Zen itself isn't even really Buddhist! Others argue that the lineage charts tracing the relationships of the patriarchs all the way to the Buddha were fabricated by Chinese monks and are totally inauthentic.[3] But most still agree that—however radical a departure—Zen has its origins in ancient Indian Mahayana Buddhism. This means that, along with all the wonderful things Buddhism had to offer, Zen, sadly, inherited its sexism as well. Several excellent books have been written on the subject of Buddhist attitudes toward women, but I will only be referring to Buddhism as it pertains specifically to the stories of women practitioners encountering and responding to its male-dominated monasticism. How we coped with its built-in sexism. How we adapted to, or transformed, traditional meditation, rituals, lineage, and the transmission of certification giving—or denying—us the right to teach. How we integrated our practice professionally and in our private lives— particularly with regard to our sexuality, our religious and social engagement, and our relationships with our teachers.

I hope our women's version of a centuries-old story told by men will not only give you a new perspective on the Zen life but that it will engage and entertain you as well.

Part One

1

Dragged Around by Zen

Sesshin

Three months after meeting Dokyu Roshi in Jerusalem and returning to New York, I received a blue airmail letter marked with a Japanese postage stamp and no return address. Even before opening it I knew who it was from.

> *Perle-san:*
>
> *I will be London beginning of June till end of July. (Chalk Farm . . .) If you want to take sesshin (Zen meditation retreat) please come anytime. During sesshin everybody stay in zendo. Please bring your own sleeping bag or blanket. . . .*
>
> *Dokyu*

"When you're ready, your teacher will appear." I finally understood what Jessie meant and no longer resented her elliptical reply to my plea. It didn't take me a second to decide what to do next. I bought an open-ended plane ticket to London as soon as I had finished reading the *roshi*'s letter.

The earliest I could get out of New York was July 3, and my flight was delayed, so I didn't land at Heathrow until midnight. It was one o'clock before I arrived at the zendo, a narrow row house on a shabby cul-de-sac with a pub on the corner. The lights were out and everyone appeared to be sleeping. I gave one quick jab at the doorbell, and a slender silent figure I took to be male opened the door and led me through a narrow hallway up three flights of stairs into a spacious, tatami-floored room with only a futon and several floor cushions for furniture. Depositing my bags on the floor alongside me, my escort walked out of the dimly lit room. I wondered if I was meant to unpack and lie down on the futon. Adjusting my eyes to the gloom, I looked around. There, in front of a lamp covered with a towel, sat Dokyu Roshi! I jumped and let out a little cry. His bald pate shining in the glow cast by the lamplight behind him, the roshi had been transformed from a puckish elf into a slit-eyed samurai with a gash for a mouth and a square iron jaw.

"You sit down here," he growled, pointing at a *zafu* (round black meditation cushion) in front of him.

My skirt was too narrow for me to cross my legs without revealing my underpants, so I opted for sitting on my cramped knees Japanese-style, my body and mind numbed by jet lag.

"We face each other again!"

Why is he talking so loudly? Does he want to wake up the whole house?

I caught my breath. "Yes. It's been five months since we last met in Jerusalem."

"No, I do not mean Jerusalem. It took you a century to come. Finally, your karma has brought you here."

Fearing I might burst into tears, I bowed my head.

"Sesshin is very hard, very painful," the roshi continued in the same loud voice, his left hand resting on his right in his lap, palms-up, like the Buddha. "But you can do it. Forget everything except for your breathing. Counting your breaths. Breathe . . . one, breathe . . . two, breathe . . . three . . . up to ten. Then start again. Eating . . . breathe one, sleeping . . . breathe two, walking . . . breathe three . . . You become breathing until there is no Perle-san, only breathing in the whole universe. Nothing more. You sit in half lotus posture with back and neck straight. Zen is not ecstasy, not intellectual answer to problem, only counting breaths and bravery. Wake-up bell is at five, so you must go to sleep now." The roshi dismissed me with a wave of his hand.

Before leaving for my first sesshin in London I had called a long-time Zen practitioner friend for advice. He'd seemed hesitant, mentioning only that—except for offering a few brief instructions on the physical aspects of *zazen* (sitting meditation), the roshi probably wouldn't tell me much. When I pressed my friend for further details, he said, "Just go to sesshin. Watch what the others do; you'll pick it up on your own." Still, to have come so far and be treated so brusquely was a bit of a shock. As a yoga teacher, I'd been meditating for years. But, as I was to learn, yoga meditation was a far cry from zazen. To begin with, yoga meditation was much more active. It didn't demand that you sit perfectly still for anywhere from twenty-five to fifty minutes doing nothing but silently counting your breaths. And it was more spontaneous and devotional. You could chant out loud or visualize your favorite god or guru, if the spirit moved you; and you could get up and move around when you felt like it. So, like many beginners whose preconceptions about Zen were derived largely from books and other people's stories, it was a letdown to be thrust on my own on that first night of sesshin. Only after years of Zen practice would I come to appreciate the roshi's laconic meditation instructions as his refusal to rob me of my very own individual experience of zazen.

Swaying, my knees shot with needles, I got up from the cushion, picked up my bags, wobbled to the door, and left the room. The slender figure had reappeared on the landing and was motioning me to follow. Nodding briefly at a door marked **Women,** the figure, which I could now make out *was* in fact a man, turned away from me and tiptoed down the stairs. I opened the door and walked into the room. The street light shining into the curtain-less window illuminated an indoor clothesline strung with bras, socks, and panties. An artificial fireplace was built into the far wall. Except for the corner nearest the door where I was standing, every inch of floor space was filled with sleeping women. I put down my bags alongside the only unoccupied rush mat on the floor. Too tired to undress or unroll my sleeping bag, I dropped onto the mat and promptly fell asleep in my clothes.

Did the roshi say sesshin was hard? Cast among thirty silent strangers, eating nothing but tofu, brown rice, and a few paltry greens from tiny wooden bowls at odd hours; struggling to finish every last grain of rice with chopsticks under the ferocious gaze of the tight-lipped roshi; trying not to fidget out of excruciating lotus posture; chanting sutras in Sino-Japanese until my throat was raw, terrified that the roshi, "walking the *kyosaku*" (the long wooden stick used to awaken sleeping or slumping meditators), was nearing my cushion and getting ready to hit me; sleeping fitfully; jumping up with my heart tripping for fear of missing the wake-up bell; sitting in a consti-pated stupor on the toilet of a postage stamp sized WC with people lined up outside, grimly waiting their turn—sesshin wasn't hard, sesshin was hell!

But worst of all was the change in Dokyu Roshi. He'd turned into my father; he was equally obsessed with "Discipline!" and with being on time. No matter how early I arrived for *zazen*, he'd already be sitting on his black meditation cushions looking as stone-faced as the statue of the Buddha on the altar behind him, with the *kyosaku* ominously laid out in front of him and the timing bell alongside it. He even had the same way of shouting like my father, exhorting us to "March on bravely!" every time he walked the *kyosaku*. The mere whisper of his robes as he got up to patrol the room set my teeth on edge—though he usually passed me by. But even then, I was so afraid I would scream out in pain if he were to steal up behind me and whack me between the shoulders that I didn't dare move. Sweat, tears, and snot streamed down my face, but I didn't dare wipe them off. My knees were hurting so much and my body was shaking so hard that I thought the people on the cushions next to me (a skinny young man with a platinum-blond pony tail on my left and a plump, cheerful-looking grandmother on my right) could feel it. Press-ing my fists into my thighs, I marched on bravely.

On the third morning, I was sitting rather well. I had just worked my way into a nice, concentrated breath-counting sequence when I was gripped by stomach pain so sharp that I involuntarily slumped forward on my cushion. Someone lightly touched my shoulder. Lift-ing my head and turning around, I saw the man who'd accompanied me to the roshi's room on the first night. Leaning down, he whispered into my ear, "Interview."

I looked up at him uncomprehendingly.

"Interview with the roshi," he whispered into my ear again, his breath smelling of garlic and cloves. It was the first human contact I'd had in three days.

Dokyu Roshi sat in his third-floor room, as distant as the elusive diamond mountain he'd talked about in Jerusalem.

"I'm having terrible stomach pain," I said. "I'm afraid I might scream."

"So scream," he said, laughing.

"Roshi, my guts are going to come flying out of my mouth if I have to go on sitting like that."

Without so much as blinking, the Roshi picked up the hand-bell near his cushion and rang it. "Next!" he shouted, motioning for me to leave.

Holding on to the walls of the narrow corridor, I made my way downstairs.

I'll go on just to spite you, you son of a bitch.

On the morning of the fourth day, during the eleven-thirty work period, I was dusting the altar and lining up the incense sticks for the afternoon meditation period when Dokyu Roshi himself suddenly appeared alongside me and silently motioned me upstairs. Convinced that he was going to throw me out of sesshin for moving around on my cushion and disturbing my fellow meditators, I followed him upstairs. Without changing his stony expression, he led me to a door across the hall from his room and, opening it, ushered me into a small kitchen with a low table and cushions on a tatami-covered floor. Closing the door behind him, the roshi slipped out of his robes and hung them on a wall hook. He looked so puny standing in front of me in his white cotton T-shirt and pantaloons that I had to resist the urge to reach out and pat his shiny bald head.

"Now, what is wrong with your stomach? You vegetarian?"

"Yes, except for eggs and cheese, and occasionally fish."

"Never mind that. Let me see your belly."

I stuck out my stomach.

"Too big around diaphragm, too much yoga exercise, maybe, and not enough deep belly breathing. Look at me."

I looked down at the roshi's pot belly.

"Ha! Rinzai Zen belly! First time you ever see such a strong belly. Punch!"

I resisted. Antic was one thing, but being asked to punch your teacher in the stomach?

"Punch!"

I rained a few tentative blows on his extended belly.

"Ha! Nothing! You must eat meat. You have constipation? Or sometimes diarrhea, no? Never beautiful golden pagoda, only loose intellectual worm shit. Never make gas? Ah . . . if you make gas like this"—the roshi delivered an enormous fart—"you get instantly enlightened!"

I couldn't believe what was happening. Before I could respond, he spun me around and tapped me on the spine. "Here, this is stomach point. Here . . . can you feel how tight it is?" I felt a shaft of pain coursing through my stomach and pulled away from him.

"Poor Perle-san, your head is in your stomach. Ha! Ha! Ha!" He turned abruptly and went to the stove. Taking up a saucepan and a wooden spoon, he began heaping rice into a bowl. "Here, you eat Japanese white rice and chicken and you feel better. English people's macrobiotic diet very terrible food. You eat chicken and you get well. You will see. I know. I know you from before you were born."

Handing me a pair of chopsticks, the roshi fixed a smaller portion of chicken and rice for himself. Then, bringing a glass pot filled with green tea and two porcelain cups to the table, he sat down opposite me and began eating, making great noisy slurping sounds. Picking up the bowl from the table, I took a few tentative mouthfuls. I'd always been embarrassed by the way people ate in Japanese restaurants, sitting on the floor slurping their food doggy-style. But now it seemed a perfectly natural way to eat, and I was soon happily slurping and smacking my lips along with the Roshi. It was the first meat I'd eaten in ten years. And it was delicious.

Teaching From the Heart

Having just finished reading a sesshin lecture on "Pain as a Teaching," by Blanche Hartman, first woman abbot of the San Francisco Zen Center, I try to imagine what it would have been like if she had introduced me to my first sesshin rather than Dokyu Roshi. As ordained Zen priests, both of them are bald and wear the same black robes. From Hartman's picture, you can't even tell that she's a woman—so, overtly, at least—she and Dokyu Roshi look interchangeably alike. Yet, no two teaching styles could be more different. I'm not making invidious comparisons here, I'm simply pointing out that there are as many ways to teach Zen as there are Zen teachers—and maybe this applies to gender and culture, too.

To begin with, Hartman does something Dokyu Roshi never did—namely, open a sesshin lecture on a very revealing personal note: "I'm having a little bit of trouble with my knee, so I think I'm going to talk about pain today." She confesses to feeling "extremely unstable and uncomfortable" sitting on the elevated cushions she'd arranged in the hope of reducing her knee pain, and mentally chides herself: "Idiot, you should have known better than that, and now you're stuck with [the uncomfortable posture] for fifty minutes." Hartman then depicts her unsuccessful attempts to shift position. You can almost hear her laughing at herself as she says: "Every time I leaned over, I felt like I was going to fall over on my head, so I put the cushion down so I could sit lower, and then I started having sciatic pain, and lots of irritation came up."

Coming from a supposedly imperturbable Zen teacher, Hartman's introductory remarks end with a stunning self-revelation:

"My mind was this big mess, and then the soup wasn't hot and the servers were slow. That was breakfast this morning for me."

Wow! A Zen teacher talking about her own pain and her own irritation and her own messy mind—and during sesshin, no less. Pretty intimate stuff; it makes you wonder how she's going to turn this into a dharma talk. Only a paragraph later, she does just that, segueing into it brilliantly, too. Having posed the problem (pain), she now provides a way of dealing with it. Radically departing from the traditional Zen script by quoting large sections from *A Path with Heart* by American psychologist Jack Kornfeld (a teacher of *vipassana*—"insight"—meditation, not Zen), Hartman invites her students to join her in meditating together on the pain she and they are experiencing at that moment. (Clearly, this Zen teacher has no qualms about using techniques from the rival Theravada Buddhist school of *vipassana* meditation, which I heard Dokyu Roshi contemptuously dismiss on more than one occasion. He was not alone, however; I later heard the same from more "open-minded" Western Zen teachers.)

I am struck by Hartman's use of Kornfeld's title, *A Path with Heart*. I wonder if she's aware that the word "heart" echoes the first part of her surname. Except for the Heart Sutra, (a magnificently condensed Mahayana Buddhist declaration of nonduality that still brings tears to my eyes whenever I chant it), there isn't much "heart talk" in Zen. There's "wisdom"—synonymous with the enlightened mind; and there's "compassion"—represented by the Bodhisattva Vow to "save the many beings," which we recite after zazen. The idea of saving the many beings can be felt very intensely while you're reciting it on your cushion in the zendo, but how you actually put compassion borne of wisdom into everyday practice is another matter. Hartman does this masterfully, continuing to share her own experience as she guides her students in exploring the body/mind nature of pain:

> The first three years I was doing zazen, I didn't sit through a single period for forty minutes without changing my posture. I hated myself every time I did it because there were always macho guys sitting, guys and women, and I felt like a wimp over here that kept changing my posture until I got to the point after three years where I didn't have to change my posture . . .
>
> One attitude in particular that I was carrying when I came to Tassajara was spiritual pride. I had quit my good job and I had come down the mountains to be a monk and save the world. I thought I was doing something special. As long as I was holding the attitude that I was doing something special, I had this particular [back] pain . . . I had a notion that it had to do with pride . . . and then I realized that I had this spiritual pride because I thought I was doing something wonderful for the world by quitting my job and coming to the mountains and sitting zazen . . . When I realized that that was the thought I was holding, this particular point of [back] pain just sort of dissolved. "I got it."[1]

It wasn't until I started reading self-revealing sesshin talks by women teachers like Hartman that I saw the connection between "wisdom"—as *empathy*—and "compassion" in the "heart-to-heart" encounter between teacher and student. But only if both were equally willing to open themselves up completely. This was totally antithetical to Dokyu Roshi's formal Japanese Zen training, and my first response was to reject it as too touchy-feely. Later, when I started teaching Zen myself, I came to appreciate it better. My students at the Princeton Area Zen Group will tell you that I'm a very "open" Zen teacher, but I can't say that I've ever had the "heart" to open myself up during a sesshin talk the way Hartman does. I admire her for it, but it just isn't my style. Her remarks about those "macho guys" sitting in perfect zazen, never moving no matter how dreadful the pain, do resonate with me, however. They're powerful reminders of my own fear of being a wimp.

Looking back at it now, I think the mental pain I endured at my first sesshin in London (and for years afterward in my Zen practice) was even worse than the physical pain. The hardest part was trying to keep a brave face in front of those macho Zen sitters, and not being allowed to make contact with anyone but the roshi. Even after sesshin, when we were allowed to talk, I never really got to know any of the participants. At first I thought it was because they were British, and thus more withheld—but there were at least two Americans among them. Everyone seemed to be so focused on his or her practice, so bent on impressing the roshi with their restraint. I found it all so stiff and unnatural watching a bunch of Westerners trying to act Japanese. Coming from a lively Jewish family in which all we did was talk (and argue), this distant, self-contained, highly regulated Japanese way of interacting with people was totally foreign to me; I missed the warmth. Granted, I loved the Japanese *wabi* (sparseness and simplicity) aspect of Zen—its muted colors, clean lines, and minimalist aesthetic. (I still do.) Even the graceful, silent choreography of sesshin itself appealed to me—the slow, concentrated walking meditation in the garden, the bells announcing the beginning and end of meditation periods, the incense and flowers on the altar, the chanting—all designed to enhance mindfulness. But I just couldn't deal with the Japanese formality reaching beyond the zendo into our social lives.

The Japanese cultural denial of emotionalism remained the norm in most zendos even after Zen had been Westernized. Women (myself included)—who were supposed to be more emotional than men to begin with—were particularly eager to rid themselves of this undesirable trait. Some of us turned ourselves into grim-lipped samurai, shouting, whacking away at people with the *kyosaku* whenever we could get our hands on it just to prove how unemotional we were. This may sound ludicrous, but it never occurred to me until much later in my Zen practice that shouting and beating were expressing emotions of the most blatant kind. And that making war and killing people (the "heroic" samurai ethos) had certainly wreaked more havoc on the world than women's tears.

Zen teacher Linda Ruth Cutts offers a most poignant description of the struggle so many of us women went through: "Along with my own physical feelings and depression, I had incorporated the expectations and ideals of everybody else . . . I had ideals—other people's ideals—that I could never live up to . . . and I was constantly being beaten up and beaten down by this kind of thinking."[2] Cutts suffered such violent emotions while meditating that she would:

> crash from one side of the *zabuton* [the square mat under the zafu] to the other . . . [holding] . . . on tight to the zabuton, because if I didn't, who knew what would happen . . . [As] soon as I went . . . to the zendo, I was a wild woman. I had impulses to pummel the people on either side of me, to hit the divider . . . It was a koan for me for ten years. For ten years I sat with involuntary movement . . . I now understand that it took ten years of zazen for me to thaw out. The involuntary movements were a bodily expression of the feelings I had locked up and shut away. These painful feelings demanded to be heard and thrashed me about until I took notice. Gradually I paid attention and admitted the pain that was alive in me; and the feelings worked their way through me at last, cracking the concrete.[3]

Why do women feel we have to live up to "other people's ideals"? Is it because we're somehow thought of as being passive by nature, and therefore more "spiritual" than men? This question is at the center of an ongoing discussion I've been having with my dear friend Kathy Phillips, a poet and professor of English at the University of Hawai'i. Since I moved from Hawai'i to Australia, we've been continuing our discussion by letter. Here is an extract from Kathy's latest letter, responding to my observation that women tend to dominate in shamanic traditions centered on contact with the spirit world: "I was thinking about your line, 'Women have always been more closely connected to Spirit.' I guess when it is true, the link may come about *because* a particular society has already decreed that 'women are irrational' or 'women are more closely connected to the dead (& hence ancestors) because women give rebirth & should prepare shrouds & keen' or 'women can't talk in their own voice' (but *might* be listened to in a spirit's advice) or 'women are mysterious & inscrutable' (because the speaker hasn't bothered to *ask*) & so on."

Kathy's thoughts on the subject of women and spirituality are important to me, not only because she's my friend but a brilliant feminist scholar. And perhaps even more because in her latest book of poems about Kuan Yin, the Bodhisattva of Compassion, she's introduced me to an entirely new, delightfully irreverent portrait of the "ideal" symbol of Buddhist womanhood. We share a special relationship with Kuan Yin (Kathy uses the Chinese version of her name; I use the Japanese, Kannon). Whenever I'm in Hawai'i, we pay regular visits to the Chinese Northern Sung Dynasty (eleventh-century) polychromed wood manifestation of the Bodhisattva on her pedestal at the Honolulu Art Academy.

Kuan Yin sits cross-legged, her right elbow resting comfortably on her raised knee, her left hand at a right angle, loosely curled fingers turned down toward her lap in her Buddhist "posture of royal ease." The visitor's bench in front of her is always conveniently empty when Kathy and I are there (which is unusual for the academy's most famous occupant.) The Bodhisattva's expression is never the same. Some days she seems to be sitting in meditation with eyes half closed; other days, she seems to be smiling directly at us. We've adjusted to her different moods, either silently meditating along with her or talking to her when she looks like she'd welcome some conversation. On days when we have special requests, such as asking her to intercede for someone who's sick or dying, we sit in front of her with palms together while I whisper the Kanzeon Sutra in Sino-Japanese. I suppose the occasional visitor from Japan or China seeing us sitting there thinks we're worshiping Kuan Yin. But since Kathy isn't a Buddhist, and I'm not what you'd call a worshipful Buddhist, he or she would be getting the wrong impression. We've known all along that, in her beautiful statue form, Kuan Yin is really a manifestation of our own compassionate Bodhisattva selves.

As you might expect, Zen has a totally different view of the feminine Kuan Yin Bodhisattva ideal of compassion I've just described—embodied in the "grandmotherly kindness" of the wildman Zen master. I learned this not only from books but from first-hand experience.

Grandmotherly Kindness

If Zen means having the rug pulled out from under you every time you get comfortable, then Dokyu Roshi was equal to the great

T'ang Dynasty Chinese Zen master Lin-chi (Rinzai, in Japanese) himself. Famous for beating and shouting and tweaking his students' noses when they least expected it, Rinzai, as he's best known in the West, is great fun to read about. It's like watching a Three Stooges movie, in which Curly keeps hitting Moe on the head for no reason at all. But I can assure you that actually living through that kind of conditioning isn't the least bit funny. I wasn't beaten, but I was constantly being shouted at, both privately and in public, and often felt humiliated. I began to feel like Dokyu Roshi's yo-yo, swung this way one minute and that way the next. I'll always be grateful to him for introducing me to Zen practice, but I never did get used to his "grandmotherly kindness" as a compassionate teaching device— Rinzai notwithstanding.

Attributing more benevolent reasons for the roshi's erratic behavior, I told myself he was alternating between playing "good cop" and "bad cop" in order to jolt me into enlightenment. Sometimes, though, he really seemed to enjoy tormenting me. Occasionally the roshi would remind me that by taking me, a Western woman, as his personal student, he was endangering his reputation in Japan, and I would be temporarily mollified. During these "good cop" moments, he even went so far as to admire my sincerity and commitment to the practice. He even told me he thought I'd make a good Zen teacher some day, if I stuck with it.

Westerners would probably call the inconsistent behavior that is so common in Zen training "schizoid," and by Western standards, it probably is. You give someone in your care—a child, a student, an employee—two or more different messages at once and let them try to figure out which one will get you to reward them. When she comes up with the one she thinks you want, you suddenly switch and make it seem she has chosen incorrectly. Then, when she comes up with the alternative choice, you reject that one, too. The same happens if she comes up with nothing. There appears to be no such thing as the right choice, no way to turn. You're blocking every exit, so to speak, giving her no way out. This is the paradox at the heart of Zen, the very essence of the teaching. It is best illustrated by the "fundamental koan" twentieth-century lay Zen teacher Shin'ichi Hisamatsu posed to his students: "Nothing you do will do. Now, what will you do?"

Because we think dualistically, seeing ourselves as separate from everything and everyone else, there appears to be no way of resolving such an "impossible" challenge. We start by analyzing the question. It doesn't make any sense. Next, we examine our options. There are none. Attempting to pry open the question, we hope to find the trick we imagine is hidden inside—to solve it like a riddle. We could go on like this forever. The problem is that we're looking at the self, and the question, and the world as if they've got an inside and an outside. It isn't until this gap is closed, when we realize that we ourselves and the question and Hisamatsu and the entire Pacific Ocean stretching between us and Japan, where he first posed it, are one and the same that the answer reveals itself. But not if we think about it. Only if we *become* it. That was what Dokyu Roshi meant when he told me on the night before my first sesshin: "Zen is not intellectual answer to problem."

The radical way of Zen is to jostle the mind out of its familiar rut, to get it to do an about face and see what we call reality in an entirely new way. Being a creature of habit, the mind resists, grows frustrated, angry—sometimes to the point of going off entirely, which is why Zen "shock treatment" isn't for everyone. It's like the behavioral training of Pavlov's dog: shocks followed by rewards, followed by shocks, followed by rewards, the poor dog never knowing which one is coming next. The frustration can be really awful, and in the wrong hands, such training can turn harmful—as it did during the Zen scandals of the 1980s that revealed the sexual and financial abuse of students by both Asian and Western Zen teachers. (I'll talk more about this later.)

If you take some of the old koans literally rather than as metaphorical teaching devices, even the interactions between the most illustrious ancient Zen masters and their disciples can appear needlessly cruel. For example, in one famous encounter, Nansen, another great T'ang Dynasty Chinese Zen master, comes upon his monks in the kitchen arguing over a cat. He jumps between them, grabs the cat, and says, "If any of you can give me a good Zen phrase right now, I'll spare this cat. If you can't, I'll kill it!" The monks are stunned into silence. And within seconds, Nansen picks up a knife and kills the cat.

Later, his head monk and best student, Joshu, returns from the market, and Nansen tells him what happened.

"What would you have done?" he asks.

Joshu picks up his sandals, puts them on his head, and leaves.

"If you were there, the cat would have been saved!" Nansen shouts after him.

The story doesn't end there because Joshu goes on to become a great Zen master in his own right—many say even greater than Nansen—and considerably less confrontational. Interestingly, Joshu, the hero of the cat koan, is most famous for an encounter involving a dog—perhaps the best-known Zen story of all. It isn't as violent as the one about Nansen's cat, but it's equally confounding, if you try to figure it out logically.

A monk comes to Joshu and asks, "Does a dog have Buddha Nature?"

Joshu replies, "*Mu!*" (Sino-Japanese for "no" or "nothing.")

According to traditional Buddhism, everything has Buddha Nature. So why is the monk asking such a question? Is he baiting Joshu? Or does he really think that a lowly dog couldn't possibly have Buddha Nature? And what about Joshu's answer? He seems to be contradicting one of the most fundamental doctrines of Buddhism. The exchange gets even more complicated when, on a different occasion, another monk asks Joshu the same question and Joshu says "Yes."

If you're looking for consistency, clearly Zen is the wrong place. But so is life, and struggling against life's inconsistencies is what suffering is all about. It's not through thinking that we save the cat (or ourselves), or that we discover whether a dog (or we ourselves) has Buddha Nature or not, but, as Charlotte Joko Beck, another wonderful first-generation Western woman Zen teacher, puts it, through "seeing the truth about who we really are . . . [returning] to that which we have spent a lifetime hiding from, to rest in the bodily experience of the present moment—even if it is a feeling of being humiliated, of failing, of abandonment, of unfairness."[4]

Zen awakening (*kensho*) may come quickly, like a bolt of lightning, or it may flower slowly, like a bud in spring, but the kind of profound awareness Joko Beck is talking about doesn't happen after just one week of sitting—or one lifetime, for that matter. It's no quick fix, no big "Eureka!" ending all your troubles forever, but a process of continuous deepening. You have to commit yourself to it for the long haul, knowing you'll never be perfect. Even the Buddha himself is said to be still practicing.

So why, you might ask, did I expect Dokyu Roshi to be more spiritually advanced than the Buddha? Flaws and all, wasn't he doing his best to guide me toward awareness at every moment? Maybe I couldn't see this because I was new to Zen practice. Or maybe it was because I was too busy protecting myself from feelings of humiliation, failure, abandonment, and unfairness to notice.

2

Greenhouse Person

Zen Cooking

Sesshin ended, and I became the sole student in residence at the London *zendo*. Together, the *roshi* and I developed a routine. On Mondays, after breakfast, we'd go shopping for food in Chinatown. Afternoons, we either went to the movies or to Marks and Spencer's to buy slippers and watches, gifts the roshi intended to give to his favorite monks at the monastery on returning to Japan. We both traveled around London wearing the same navy blue monk's work suits. I bought mine from a tall (that is, tall for a Japanese) novice monk named Gempo who'd spent the past six months in an English-immersion school in Hampstead. Gempo was one of Dokyu Roshi's favorite monks. He'd stopped by to visit him at the London zendo before going back to the monastery in Japan. Considering that despite the immersion school Gempo wasn't exactly fluent in English and that I knew only three words in Japanese, we got on really well—well enough for him to tell me that he and I were both Dokyu Roshi's "favorite monks together." Or maybe I only imagined that was what he was telling me. What I did get from Gempo was that Dokyu Roshi was "very hard Zen master." Gempo went on to add that he would be forever grateful to Dokyu Roshi for this hard training because it had shocked him into enlightenment!

After Gempo left I went crazy and cropped my hair all the way down to the scalp. The roshi didn't even notice. Or if he did, he didn't think it worthy of comment.

On days when we didn't go out, the roshi taught me how to cook traditional Japanese meals. Breakfasts were his specialty: seaweed and crushed soybean stew poured over rice. He said they would cure my stomach problems once and for all. I wasn't convinced. The food was mushy and hard to eat first thing in the morning. But my stomach did get better. And the terrible pains hadn't returned since he'd fed me that first chicken and rice dish during sesshin, so I reluctantly followed his advice and resumed eating meat.

One day, after the roshi's post-lunch nap, we were sitting around the table in his upstairs kitchen talking and drinking green tea. I almost fell off my cushion when I saw him pull an aluminum ashtray and a pack of Kent's from an inside pocket in his robe and light a cigarette.

"I didn't know you smoked," I said.

"Terrible habit," the roshi grinned at me. "I probably die of high blood pressure or cancer one day soon," he said, ending all further discussion of the topic.

But smoking wasn't Dokyu Roshi's worst habit. Chauvinism was. If he hadn't been my Zen teacher, I'd have walked out on him the minute he embarked on one of his anti-Western tirades. Compared to Japanese, Westerners were slovenly, undisciplined, and lacking in traditional manners.

What kind of manners is he showing by slandering Westerners, and therefore, me?

"Then why do you bother teaching us?" I ventured.

"Because today's Japanese monks are even worse!"

I made a face but said nothing. It wasn't a satisfactory answer, but it would have to do.

What else but karma could have drawn me to such a Zen teacher? My first husband probably would have said I was reenacting my unresolved love-hate relationship with my domineering father. Otherwise, why would I tolerate being treated in the same harsh way so long after leaving home? To start with, both Dokyu Roshi and my father were equally obsessed with cleanliness. I've always been a clean person, but I was never clean enough for either of them.

"I show you Zen way of cleaning!" the roshi would shout when, after morning meditation and chanting, we were cleaning every corner of the "dark and poky" little zendo. And, just like my father, he would pull the vacuum cleaner out of my hands and scold me for being too slow or for leaving dust balls in the corners. Dokyu Roshi finally got so disgusted with me that he took over the vacuuming himself and assigned me the childishly simple job of freshening up the water and rice offerings and placing them on the altar before the Buddha.

When, on the rare occasion that I did manage to do something he approved of, Dokyu Roshi's rewards were uncannily the same as my father's—they always revolved around food. Both men were excellent cooks who displayed uncharacteristic patience in teaching me how to fix breakfast. Whereas my father's specialty had been oatmeal, the roshi's was rice. He took great care to show me how to keep the rice from getting lumpy by putting in just enough water, when to place the cover on the pot, and how long to let it boil without stirring. We'd listen to the hourly BBC news bulletins on the radio while the rice was cooking.

Eager to ingratiate myself so the roshi would go on being nice to me, I not only accompanied him daily to his favorite Chinese restaurant and shared his favorite dish of pork spare ribs—but also took up smoking! Fortunately, I never could keep up with his two-pack-a-day cigarette addiction—or his fondness for Johnny Walker Red whiskey, which, when we were invited to social gatherings by London zendo members, I saw the roshi consume with great gusto. Was this Zen, too, I wondered?

And what about all the anal talk—the obsession with farting and shitting? Giving me the same puckish grin each time, the roshi had told me the same story three times, about a monk he'd trained who later became abbot of one of the great Kyoto Zen temples, and how the monk had let down his drawers to shit in a rice field during a bout of dysentery, startled a frog, and was immediately enlightened. Finally, after hearing the story for the third time, I said, "Roshi, do you know what you are? You're what psychiatrists call anally obsessive."

As soon as I'd said it I was sorry. He was my teacher, after all.

To my surprise, instead of launching into an attack, the roshi gave me his puckish grin and said, "Anarl ob-sess-ive. I like that, Perle-san!"

We were in the kitchen, as usual. I was sewing a seam on one of his ceremonial undershirts and he was standing across the room near the stove when he suddenly walked over, pulled the shirt out of my hands, and unleashed a guffaw that shook the walls.

"You sew seam backwards! You just like my teacher Soen Roshi, typical intellectual greenhouse person!"

I shrugged. "I never did learn to sew."

"You exactly like Soen Roshi," he shouted. "He terrible at sewing, planting . . . terrible at everything with his hands. Only talk, talk, talk. One day when a very young monk, Soen was on garden duty. He supposed to plant tree in front of monastery gate. So he dig up a little soil with a spoon and stick tree into the ground. By next day tree was dead, roots outside, leaves all gone. The abbot very angry, and he shout at Soen in front of all the monks. Soen ashamed, so he disappear. He like you, very sensitive, too sincere. He run away to Manchuria for six months and nobody find him. Abbot and Soen's mother sent people, but nobody find. One day Soen come back by himself, standing outside monastery gate with long hair, dressed like a beggar, dirty, like London hippie."

"He came back to the monastery?"

"Yes . . . because, like you, Soen Roshi very pure person, very honest and sincere enlightenment seeker. But too intellectual. Always thinking, thinking, thinking. Not good working with hands. Not like me, a wild human being with no fixed ideas. I don't like intellectual people. I like people who talk direct, concrete, no beautiful words, no dream-talk, like these English greenhouse people. I like wild crab-grass people, like Sochu Roshi, the abbot of my monastery since Soen Roshi retire. Sochu is my best friend. We train together from the time we young monks. Sochu just like me—no mother, no father. But he even worse off. I have grandmother to raise me. But Sochu put in basket when born near a hot spring and brought up by farmer family. Beaten from the time he six years old. When he put into temple at sixteen, he already tough guy, survivor."

The Roshi lit a cigarette and took a long drag. He explained that later, during the war, Sochu lived in an underground tunnel that he dug with his own hands, right on an American army base. He took food every night from the PX and kept himself alive for three years like that. All of his teeth fell out from lack of calcium. At the end of the war, he put up a white handkerchief stolen from the American PX and was liberated, supporting himself by drawing dirty pictures and selling them to American GIs. Sochu was a very good artist. He never married or was intimate with a woman but knew how to make graphic pictures of the female anatomy, which Dokyu went on to describe.

I blushed. Here I was, still getting used to all that "farting" and "shitting" stuff, and now he was talking smut! Was it part of his campaign to change me from a greenhouse person into a crabgrass person? Trying to appear unfazed, I managed to force out a wild, high-pitched laugh—which did not have its desired effect because my blushing gave me away.

The next day we were sitting on a bench in Hyde Park sharing a bucket of Kentucky Fried Chicken when the roshi (perfectly aware of how uncomfortable it made me) resumed his erotic theme.

He told me a story about a "high-class geisha" in Tokyo while he was munching away on a drumstick.

I asked him where he learned about things like that, my phrasing stiff and childishly slow. "You're celibate!"

"I know everything!" he boasted, giving me his don't-be-so-slow-witted look. "I never meet anyone like you before—except maybe Soen Roshi. Completely pure, too pure. I teach you swimming in dirty water. A real fish must swim everywhere. A pure fish die right away."

The roshi grunted, wiped his hands on his napkin, and said, "Your skin too tender, Perle-san. When storm comes, hard times, you scratch and bleed too easy. Your father give you good training, but you still not tough enough."

Later, after the evening meditation had ended and the three zendo regulars who never missed a sitting had finished their tea and gone, I sat at the low table watching the roshi navigate around the tiny kitchen, wondering how long he could keep his cigarette dangling from his lips without losing it. Finally, after stopping at the window to straighten the bamboo blinds and water the philodendron on the shelf above the sink, he turned around, removed the cigarette, and flashed me a puckish grin.

"You have to be born survivor, like Sochu and me, by karma. I come from old Zen family, Japanese temple family . . . born lucky. Karma, that is karma. You have not so good karma . . . born in New York, intellectual greenhouse lady . . . My best Zen student is Israeli paratrooper, army man, like samurai warrior. Not Japanese, but Israeli samurai . . . You not so lucky . . . not Japanese, not man, that unlucky . . . but still, your father train you good."

Turning on the water, the roshi doused his cigarette with a hiss and tossed it into the trash pail behind the curtain under the sink.

"They made me monk at six. My grandmother shave my head and force me to memorize sutras, beating me on bald head with bamboo rod until bleeding. Then mother and father both die, forcing me to survive alone. I learn snake's way, cheating way, to move around in this cheating world. Not like you, only straight way, fixed, sincere, intellectual." He sniffed then strained a cup of tea through the day-old leaves his survivor's instinct compelled him to save in the same cup every night after supper.

"I sell cigarettes to American GIs, and ice cream in the park."

"And then?"

"Become Zen monk!" he roared, grinning, on the verge of a great, belly-shattering laugh.

My lips quivered in anticipation of laughing along with him. But the roshi turned serious suddenly, leaving me with a stupid leer on my face.

"I had temple teacher," he continued, "my father's friend. This old man say I must get enlightenment by five years in monastery or I must come home to work for him in village temple. I did not want to return to that small, poor village temple and be slave for old man who beat me. So I decide to throw out everything, become hard stone head, and, on April 22, 1955, I become enlightenment person!"

I felt my knees buckling at the gravity of the confidence my teacher had just shared with me. "Ah!"

"But I live in the West for too long with greenhouse people like you. Getting spoiled, so Western in my thinking now that when I go home to Japan my older sister say I have 'foreigner mentality.'"

The laughter I'd expected before now broke loose, raucous and wild. And again, just as quickly as it began, it ended. The roshi lit another cigarette. Turning serious, almost grave, he said, "But you are basically enlightened, too. Right now. You must know this. Without theory, without books, you must see that Buddha is right here now. Zen is everyday life. You drink tea; that is Buddha. You walk; that is Buddha walking. You cry, Buddha cries. There is no need for Buddha, for Jesus Christ, for God. Everything is God, without beginning or end—even cockroach. My policy is to tell you these things only three times. If you too stubborn to learn, I not bother with you. There is not enough time. Death cannot be cheated. Pain cannot be avoided. You must start by being humble, accepting pain with bravery mind."

How could I prove my "bravery mind" to him that very minute? Leap from the window and fly over London? Turn a cartwheel? Release a great cloud of enlightenment gas? None of these; I could do none of these. All I could do was stand in front of my teacher like a clod, waiting for him to make me worthy of enlightenment by transforming myself from a puny greenhouse girl into a wild crabgrass samurai *man*. Which was impossible. Because, according to the ancient Buddhist scriptures, I would have to die and be reborn into a man's body for that to happen.[1]

"Do you remember landing at London airport?" the roshi asked, gentler now, almost conversational. "It is like that. Flying above the weather it is always sunny, clear. Then when airplane begins to land, clouds appear—many, many clouds full of rain. But you know that sun is always shining above those clouds, like your essential nature, always shining, always clear."

"Why can't I see it?" I exploded with a wrenching cry.

"Because, Perle-san, you always window shopping for truth. Because you Ph.D., always speculating." The roshi rotated his finger near his temple. "Always thinking and talking, talking and thinking . . . You want to see Buddha Nature like it is movie inside your brain. You make pictures, then when outside world is different from your pictures, you disappointed. Like you tell me your marriage disappoint you."

"Maybe it's because I'm still hoping for the perfect partnership."

"Typical American mentality. Why do you need perfect partner? This I do not understand. A man from California once came to me in

Jerusalem zendo and say he going to India to surrender to his guru.
What is all this talk about surrendering to a guru, or a relationship, or
even to a Zen teacher? You yourself already perfect as you are! Don't
need anybody—" the roshi stopped as if to recall himself. Then pointing his finger at me, he said, "Ah, but you are not yet clear. When you
clear, you see this."

"Will you help me, Roshi?"

"You must help yourself, train and discipline yourself. Dogen
Zen Master say we all enlightened but we must train our own bodies
and minds until not even one trace of dust remains. Remember,
Perle-san, I will not come and pat you on back or tell you I am so
sorry it hurts. If you need psychologist, you go get treatment. I no
psychologist. That remind me . . ." Pulling a letter from the sleeve of
his robe and handing it to me, he said, "I forget to give you this,
Perle-san. It letter from New York, from husband. Maybe you think I
stone-hearted. But like I tell you before, Zen monk have no time for
relationship problems."

More Cultural Baggage

Though he was probably unaware of it, Dokyu Roshi's ambivalence
about working so closely with a deeply committed woman Zen student
has a long history, going all the way back to the ancient Indian Mahayana Buddhist scriptures. They are all relentlessly sexist, with one or
two exceptions like the Lotus Sutra or the Vimalakirti Sutra. Given the
roshi's apparent dislike of everything "intellectual," I wondered
whether he had read either of them. I can't say I would have blamed
him if he hadn't. The ancient sutras can be pretty tedious. I read the
Lotus Sutra only because feminist religion scholar Diana Paul says it's
among the most liberal of all Mahayana Buddhist sutras in its attitude
toward women. That may be true, but it's still not exactly what I would
call feminist in its basic assumption of our second-class status.

Although the Lotus Sutra refers to sincere women Buddhist practitioners as "good daughters" and "spiritual friends," it clearly states
that we can become enlightened only under the guidance of "good
sons," not independently. Those of us who are especially gifted can become teachers, and, after many lifetimes of training, bodhisattvas

(compassionate beings, like Kuan Yin, who postpone their own final enlightenment to remain in the world and enlighten others). Still, no matter how you look at it, women are only peripheral to the Lotus Sutra, which is really a story about the making of a male Bodhisattva. The hero is Sadaprarudita, a young prince who, early in his practice, is guided by a significantly unnamed merchant's daughter, a "spiritual friend" who, initially, is further along the path than he. This situation is only temporary, for their roles are reversed as soon as Sadaprarudita attains the supreme, perfect enlightenment unavailable to the merchant's daughter who—no matter how spiritually developed—is still an ancient Indian Buddhist woman with too many "relationship problems" to get enlightened on her own. It is only after Sadaprarudita becomes her teacher that the unnamed merchant's daughter attains supreme, perfect enlightenment too. And she and the prince live happily—and separately—ever after.[2]

Not being a scholar of Buddhism, and having no knowledge of Sanskrit, Pali, Tibetan, Chinese, or Japanese, I don't presume to offer an opinion on the matter of whether the Buddha really meant it when he said that *all* people could get enlightened *on their own* regardless of gender, color, caste, or any other distinction invented by human beings. I'll leave that to feminist Buddhist scholar/practitioners who've been wrestling with the problem longer than I have. What interests me even more than what the Buddha taught (or didn't teach) is what was going on in the mind of that unnamed Indian merchant's daughter. What it would be like to *be* her, a woman far enough along on the path to be called a "spiritual friend"—with a good head start on that spoiled royal boy Sadaprarudita. Giving him all that time and energy while she was busy managing a large Indian household. Caring for husband and kids, doing all the shopping, cooking, and cleaning, bathing her mother-in-law's feet every night after dinner. After all his whining and complaining, did she resent having Sadaprarudita turn the tables on her by becoming *her* teacher?

Wait a minute. That's not how the story goes. The merchant's daughter isn't married. She lives in a tower on her very rich father's estate, attended by a retinue of five hundred ladies and musicians. She's looking out the window of her tower one day when she happens to see Sadaprarudita wanting so badly to impress his teacher, the Bodhisattva Dharmodgata, with his desire to "attain the Perfection of

Wisdom" (that is, get enlightened) that he's cutting up his own body. He's just about to slice his chest in half when the merchant's daughter, followed by all five hundred ladies and musicians, rushes down from her tower and asks him why he's mutilating himself. Sadaprarudita tells her that he's doing this as an act of reverence to his teacher, Dharmodgata. The merchant's daughter cleverly diverts him from finishing himself off by engaging him in a conversation about his teacher. Once she's gotten his attention, she gently persuades this would-be bodhisattva to stop mutilating himself, using flattery, and even a little bribery to bring him back to his senses.

"Good son, if what you say is true, then you have no equal on heaven or earth. You should not injure yourself in this way. I will give you gold, silver, and many precious jewels. I will follow you with my five hundred women attendants. I also would like to pay reverence to the Bodhisattva Dharmodgata and would like to hear the [Perfection of Wisdom] sutra."

Immediately after the merchant's daughter has spoken, Sakra, the king of heaven, intervenes, makes Sadaprarudita's mutilated body "the same as it was," and leaves the restored young man in her care before returning home to heaven.

Still uncertain about her charge's mental state, the merchant's daughter invites him to accompany her home so she can give him the gold and silver and precious jewels she promised him. She assures him that she and her five hundred ladies and musicians will follow him after they've "reported" to her mother and father.

Like any normal parents, her mother and father are a bit taken aback when their daughter returns and explains to them what has happened. But being worthy Buddhists, they agree to her plan, even going so far as to say that they too would have made the journey to hear Dharmodgata preach the Sutra of the Perfection of Wisdom if they weren't so old.

This young woman is obviously the apple of her father's eye, for he offers her anything she wants before she leaves. Without hesitating, the daughter asks for the gold and silver and precious jewels, and the pilgrims take off in five hundred treasure-filled carriages to a series of marvelous adventures that eventually culminate in Sadaprarudita's supreme enlightenment and the merchant daughter's submission to the newly minted bodhisattva.[3]

I don't know enough about ancient Indian Buddhist women to tell you what the merchant's daughter was feeling as she was going through all of this. What lengths she went to, what psychological sacrifices she had to make to accompany her male teacher Sadaprarudita on her inferior "woman's journey" to enlightenment. Whether her sacrifices were excessive or normal for a wealthy Indian Buddhist woman longing for the perfection of wisdom. I wasn't that dutiful a daughter, and my parents weren't rich, and I certainly didn't grow up with five hundred serving ladies. We didn't even have a house cleaner. I can only imagine what the merchant's daughter felt by remembering how I felt when I was following Dokyu Roshi around in search of my own supreme enlightenment. The fact that the merchant's daughter has no name doesn't make it any easier to identify with her, either. So I'll call her "Brigid," which is the name of one of my closest dharma sisters. That would be a good first step in helping me get to know her better. Next, I'd start exchanging daily e-mails with her—like I do with my New Zealand-based friend Brigid Lowry. Brigid's a writer and long-time Zen practitioner, too. And though she isn't rich and doesn't live in a tower, Brigid has been the student of at least two male teachers, and, like the Indian merchant's daughter, she certainly sacrificed a lot to travel the Zen highway. Here, with a few minor alterations, is what one of our cyberspace "dharma conversations" would look like:

> Perle: Hi, Brigid. Here's a question for you. What is it like for you, as a woman searching for enlightenment, to study with a male teacher?
>
> Brigid: They say it is the questions that are important, not the answers. They say it is the journey, not the destination, that matters. Zen is my journey. A lifetime of breathing in and breathing out. Years of attempting to hold it all in wide loving arms, as [my teacher] Ross Bolleter Roshi advised. Failing miserably. Trying to hold that in wide loving arms.
>
> Perle: Can you tell me more about those "important questions" you mentioned—especially the personal ones?
>
> Brigid: Yeah, like:
>
> > How can I be Avalokiteshvara [the male version of the bodhisattva of compassion, Kuan Yin] and hold the

whole world of suffering in my arms when I can't be at ease with the vicissitudes of my ageing body? When sometimes all I care about is whether my haircut is any good.

How come I took a precept about not using drugs yet on certain nights a glass of wine is the only medicine that works?

How come I get very angry with my teachers sometimes? How can I love the part of them and the part of myself that is so very hard to love?

How much is enough? (Food, sex, time with others, time by myself.)

Greed, hatred, and ignorance rise endlessly. How can I possibly abandon them? How can I live with a clear conscience if I don't give it my best shot?

Perle: (Sigh.) You sure do have a way of hitting those major buttons, girlfriend. What is it, do you think, that makes us women so guilty about not measuring up? Ever. Not to the Buddhist Precepts. Not to our teachers. And most of all, not to ourselves.

Brigid: Speaking for myself . . . I was born into a tribe of creative people who have a tendency toward addiction and mental illness. I've blundered through this life, burdened with anxiety and depression. Meditation, long walks, self-help books, therapy, recreational drugs, antidepressants—I've tried them all, with varying amounts of success. I've been thin and fat, aborted and pregnant, fast and slow, up and down. And now I'm muddling through the menopause, a complex time when the mysteries of my own body are a foreign land. How do I make my way, when sometimes even getting through the day with dignity seems impossible?

Perle: I was wondering—why do you think our male Zen counterparts never write about "blundering" through life? Or "muddling" through their own middle-aged male versions of menopause—like leaving wives and kids behind and taking off with a string of younger women Zen students? Or buying a Porsche instead of paying the mortgage? Is it that the men are too socially conditioned against revealing even the slightest crack in their armor for fear of losing the respect of their Zen teachers? Or if they *are* Zen teachers themselves, their Zen students?

Brigid: This deserves a phone conversation. What do you say I call you tomorrow at noon your time.

Perle: You're right. Till tomorrow at noon, then . . . xoxo.[4]

I still can't get that ancient Indian Buddhist "good daughter" out of my mind, so I go back to one of my favorite books, Susan Murcott's excellent translation and commentary on *The Therigatha*, a collection of enlightenment poems by women of the sixth century B.C.E.: "Under the Buddhist system, a woman, regardless of her role, was considered to belong to an intermediate plane between animals and men. To be born into a woman's body was considered a cause for special suffering on account of menstruation, childbirth, and menopause. Although a woman could achieve the highest goal of *nirvana*, still, it was considered the greatest merit for a woman to be reborn as a man."[5]

What is an American woman teaching Zen in the twenty-first century supposed to make of this? Ignore it. I tried, but it doesn't work. I have to grapple with this infuriating Buddhist koan every time a woman challenges me for being too "male identified." Until now, I've been able to chalk it up to my years of samurai Zen training. Blame it on Dokyu Roshi.

3

Expect Nothing

Now You See Him, Now You Don't

It was my last week at the London *zendo* and I couldn't seem to do anything right. The *roshi* fluctuated between ignoring me and yelling into my face until I cried. I kept telling myself that Zen masters were supposed to be like this: "antic," "unpredictable."

"I am formless," he said one day, after I had accused him of being inconsistent. "Stop looking for your fixed picture of me. I never same person because I change with every situation, new every second, not like you with stuck cassette tape in your head."

I consoled myself with his intermittent displays of picaresque charm, when he exchanged his robes for ordinary street wear (a striped blue and white polo shirt, a pair of old chinos, and a New York Yankees baseball cap were his favorite civilian clothes), and when his growls turned into belly laughs. But the roshi seemed determined to elude me. When we were out shopping together, he would slip away from me and disappear into the crowd. I'd have to run to keep up with him, could never manage to finish a sentence within his earshot. Not that it mattered; the roshi was so bored by what I had to say that he would yawn in my face as soon as I'd caught up with him.

For two days in a row he didn't ask me to come up to the kitchen for breakfast after morning *zazen*. On those days I went out to the pub on the corner and had a stale scone and a disgusting cup of white coffee. I sat in a booth picking the rock-hard raisins out of the scone, wondering what I had done to make Dokyu Roshi so mad at me. I came up with a whole list of reasons, not the least of which was that he'd suffered unspeakably at the hands of the Americans. His mother's family lived in Hiroshima, and though he never said what happened to them after it was bombed, he did tell me that he'd been sleeping in his hammock below deck on a navy ship fifteen miles away from Hiroshima when it was erased from the map. He claimed to have been such a sound sleeper that he "snored right through the blast of a thousand suns," waking up only when the explosion tilted his ship upright in the water. Maybe just hearing me talk reminded him of the GIs who bought ice cream from him, calling, "Hey, Shorty," or "Over here, Nip!"

I was convinced that shutting me out of the kitchen for two days in a row at breakfast time was Dokyu Roshi's first step in getting rid of me. Then, inexplicably, he not only welcomed me back into the kitchen for breakfast on the third day, but invited me to a pork spare-rib lunch at his favorite Chinese restaurant. It was a silent lunch. I knew better than to stretch my luck. Then the bill came, and I picked it up, forgetting that he always got testy when I offered to pay. I thought it would be a good idea to treat him for once. I was totally unprepared for his response.

"What you think, I cannot pay my own bill?" he screamed, his face turning purple as he pulled the check from my hands.

The Chinese woman behind the cash register motioned me over and gave me a handful of cellophane-wrapped fortune cookies free of charge, she felt so sorry for me. Her gesture must have shamed him. At least he stopped yelling. Then he paid the woman, without his usual, "You have a nice day, missus," and ran out of the restaurant. I ran down the street after him apologizing. Finally, when I caught up with him, the roshi said, "You make me nervous. I getting headache from your neurotic, your overcaring . . ." His English lapsing, he started walking away from me. I caught up with him again. "Please don't be mad, Roshi." He lit a cigarette. "Okay, okay. Everything okay." Frowning, he threw the newly lit cigarette on the pavement and stamped it out.

What if he gets cancer? What'll I do without him?

"I promise I'll stop overcaring," I said, amazed at myself for whining. This wasn't me. Not the fourteen-year-old girl who told her father to go to hell and ran away from home for three days so the police had to come after her.

Just then an old woman with a huge carbuncle on her nose stepped into my path and dropped her shopping bag down in front of my feet as if deliberately trying to trip me.

"You should be ashamed of yourself, girlie," she said, causing three women standing in front of a fruit stall to turn around and stare at me.

The Bodhisattva Kuan Yin herself, come to remind me not to be such a doormat.

We were approaching Piccadilly Square. The roshi stopped and looking directly into my face, said, "I never worry. If I cannot get what I want, I cannot get it. That's all. Otherwise getting big headache."

I caught my breath. Adopting the most normal tone of voice I could manage under the circumstances, I said, "So does that mean you never have plans? None whatsoever?" It didn't help, I still sounded whiney.

"In the situation."

"Immediate?"

"Yes, in the immediate situation. So, if I cooking monk in monastery, I never plan menu. I go to market and look at what they sell that day. Fresh vegetables, bean curd, eggs. I cook what I find."

"No advance planning menu?" I persisted.

"No. If advance planning, I lose chance to find something new, unexpected—like avocados, maybe."

I knew I had to tread lightly, keep him on the topic of the monastery. (Through much trial and error, I'd learned that talking about the monastery usually got the roshi into a better mood.)

"If I go to market with list and cannot find what I want, I become disappointed, like you, no? Better to expect nothing. Zen person expects nothing. Accepts everything."

We traveled back to the zendo on the Underground without saying a word to each other. The roshi tilted his head and read the advertisements posted above the windows. For a maddeningly long time, he sat there feigning interest in a business school that promised potential students a higher salary and a more rewarding job.

When we reached the zendo and he'd unlocked the front door, he turned to me wearily. "Please, Perle-san, today no tea. I tired. Must lie down and take nap, then bath before sitting. Very sorry, no tea."

Ready to burst into tears, I raced upstairs past him and into my room, slamming the door behind me.

The next day the roshi acted as if nothing at all unpleasant had happened between us, and I obliged him by doing the same. We spent the afternoon eating strawberry ice cream sundaes and reading newspapers in a Shaftsbury Avenue tea shop across the street from the movie theater where we'd bought tickets for the four o'clock showing of *The Seven Samurai*. It was opening day, and the ticket line was curled around for blocks. The roshi said it was the fifth time he'd seen the film, and he slept through most of it. When the lights came up, he turned to me and said, "Best Zen student is like samurai, best fighting partner—like you and me, Perle-san."

Not wanting to provoke him into changing his mind, I hid my pleasure at being complimented and said nothing.

This time as we rode the Underground back to the zendo, he was very talkative and never once looked at the advertisements. We were sitting opposite each other. At one point he leaned over and said, "Roshi like samurai general. Monks like samurai sergeants."

"Do you think I can ever become a samurai sergeant?"

"You? Greenhouse person! Maybe you have nervous breakdown if I treat you hard." He said he toughened up his students by having them chop wood every day. Then he would take them to the movies and buy them nice pork cutlets for supper.

Well, at least you've taken me to the movies.

"Maybe one day . . . maybe you become samurai sergeant, too," the roshi mused, scratching his chin.

My heart was pounding against my ribcage so hard that I was afraid he might hear it.

Now's the moment when you invite me to come back to the monastery and train with you.

We reached our station. As we were walking toward the staircase leading to the street, the roshi said, "But it is very hard to do Zen practice in married life. Monastery life impossible for married lady like you, Perle-san."

"I've been traveling on my own for so long now that it's almost like not being married," I mumbled.

"Not good. Married lady must take care of husband."

"That's not the kind of marriage I'm in. Besides, the last thing my husband wants right now is a wife who takes care of him. He needs to be off on his own. And so do I."

"You get divorce?"

"No. We just need some time away from each other."

We were nearing the pub on the corner, and I was getting ready for the usual race back to the zendo when, to my utter amazement, Dokyu Roshi stopped, looked me straight in the eye, and said, "Okay, Perle-san. You come with me to Japan. I take you to monastery."

Leaving No Traces

Dokyu Roshi was right—traditional monastic Zen is impossible for married women—and for married men, too, I might add. The Japanese word for monk is *unsui*, one who travels through life like a cloud over water leaving no traces. A homeless wanderer with no attachments—especially not the householder kind. What do you expect when the Buddha himself abandoned a wife and newborn son and a palace full of retainers to wander around India in search of enlightenment? Or when Bodhidharma, the legendary founder of Zen (also not a family man) paddled his way across the Indian Ocean on a leaf all the way to China from Central Asia to spread the Dharma? The whole history of Buddhism is antithetical to householders.

But that hasn't kept American Zen Buddhists from trying to change things. Starting in the eighties, several teachers began experimenting with a practice they felt would be more compatible with life in the West. Fusing monastery and marketplace, they created a hybrid: the ordained "lay-monk"—shaved head, robes, regalia and all—men and women living at home and working at regular jobs outside the monastery or Zen center, married, partnered, or single, with children or without, gay or straight, celibate or not. It used to be that most of these American pioneers were men, but over the years women have become increasingly active in forging a still more inclusive, family-friendly version of Zen practice.

Having trained with traditional Japanese Zen teachers, first-generation American women teachers like Blanche Hartman, Charlotte

Joko Beck, Joan Halifax, and Yvonne Rand have retained some of the rituals and ceremonies, such as those revolving around transmission and lineage, while incorporating Western psychology, *vipassana* meditation, shamanism, and Tibetan meditative techniques. Others have eliminated every vestige of monasticism. The most prominent of these is Toni Packer, one-time successor of Philip Kapleau Roshi at the Rochester Zen Center, who left to establish her own meditation center and doesn't even use the word "Zen" to describe her teaching. Marian Mountain, a former student of Suzuki Roshi (author of *Zen Mind Beginner's Mind*) and resident of Tassajara Zen Monastery, went even further. Refusing ordination by two illustrious Japanese masters and returning to the traditional Zen notion of "homelessness," she left the monastery and became a wandering hermit, substituting Nature for her teacher and *sangha*.

Husband-and-wife teams are the most recent, and historically speaking, perhaps the most interesting phenomenon in the feminization of Zen. In Oregon, for example, Western husband-and-wife Zen teachers like Kyogen and Gyokuko Carlson and Jan Chozen and Laren Hogen Bays have ingeniously fused the functions of the traditional Japanese temple priest with the monastery abbot, distributing and sharing both roles between them in equal partnership.

Surprisingly, the radical idea of a couple sharing temple responsibilities has its roots in Japan. Since the late nineteenth century, Japanese Buddhist temple priests have been permitted—indeed, expected—to marry. A typical Japanese Zen monk is ordained as a priest at a young age. After training at a monastery for a year, he returns to his home temple with his new wife and takes it over from his father. The priest's retired parents remain in their home, and the young couple now fills their place, the husband ministering to the congregation's religious needs by performing all ritual and ceremonial functions, and the wife assuming his mother's responsibility for the temple's practical and social business. Very few Zen Buddhist priests teach meditation. It's the great monasteries, led by celibate abbots, where serious candidates train as monks and become roshis, who, in turn, become abbots, and so on. But the monasteries are struggling. The situation is a little like that of the Catholic church, with its declining number of priests. For a variety of reasons, mostly having to do with celibacy and the lack of candidates with a "true calling," there's a shortage of committed Japanese young men enter-ing monasteries. The situation is even worse for nuns, whose num-bers are shrinking alarmingly despite the valiant efforts of Japanese women Zen masters like Aoyama Roshi, abbess of a flourishing nun-nery in Nagoya.[1]

These days, people aren't flocking to join Zen monasteries in the West, either. Enthusiasm flagged after the Zen boom of the eighties, partially because a new generation of Americans eager for the latest quick fix discovered that Zen was more fun to read about than to prac-tice. As Dokyu Roshi's teacher Soen Roshi wryly put it: "Zen is very boring, very painful." Despite all the interesting variations on the practice I just mentioned, the fact is that Zen is deeply rooted in Bud-dhist monasticism. And traditions die hard—even in America, so prac-ticing Zen still isn't easy for lay people, especially those with children. (I say this as a lay Zen teacher working with lay students for almost fif-teen years.) I have long since given up wanting to join a monastery or practice like a monk, but I do feel that anyone wanting to seriously devote herself or himself fully to the practice, as I did, has to take a year or two out of lay life, leaving work, school, and family behind to join a residential Zen center—though not necessarily in Japan.

This is as much the case for women today as in ancient times. As we saw in the story of the merchant's daughter, the only way an an-cient Indian woman could freely follow the Buddhist path was by leaving her family and becoming a nun or a homeless wanderer. Here's Susan Murcott again: "Whether living in solitude or with the company of others, the ideal common to all [early Buddhist women] wanderers was the renunciation of the home-life for the sake of a higher spiritual life."[2] Twenty-first-century Western women may be freer than our Asian Buddhist foremothers to choose what we do with our lives, but it's still hard, even for women today, to escape our tradi-tional female roles as wives, mothers, and caregivers to engage in seri-ous Zen training. It takes nothing less than becoming a "homeless wanderer." Or, as it did in my case, a would-be monk.

4

A Monk at Last!

All Roshis Different

The arrivals lounge at Narita Airport was as organized and clean and spare as a *zendo*. And so was everyone in it: the "head monks"—policemen in starched uniforms and spotless white gloves shouting *"Mushi mushi!"* into walkie-talkies while directing pedestrian traffic; the "Zen students"—diminutive company men, all wearing exactly the same off-the-rack blue suits, all carrying identical gift boxes of XO Napoleon brandy and bowing in unison to the *"roshi,"* a straight-backed elderly gentleman with an authoritative air whose custom-tailored Italian blue suit clearly distinguished him from the men bowing to him. I knew that the Japanese prized conformity and condemned individuality, but I was startled at seeing how truly alike they were.

Dokyu Roshi was annoyed with his Tokyo hosts, the Hanakawas (I've changed their names). They were late, which he claimed was disrespectful to him as a Zen Buddhist priest—and to me as his foreign guest. When Mr. Hanakawa and his son finally did appear, the roshi didn't greet them but scowled and pointed at his watch. The two men responded with a peremptory bow and, as far as I could make out, some excuse about the traffic. But I could tell from the way he looked past them that Dokyu Roshi wasn't mollified. The younger man, Omu, who spoke a bit of English, introduced himself, and then his father. Omu was slightly taller than his taciturn father, who greeted me with a grudging nod and didn't bother shaking my extended hand.

Both were wearing the same blue blazer, gray slacks, white shirt, red tie, and Gucci loafers. I guessed Omu to be about thirty, his father about sixty-five.

Seeing how rudely the roshi's indifferent hosts were treating him unnerved me. Even worse was the fact that, despite his beautiful brown traveling priest's robes and matching cap, no one at the airport had bothered taking notice of him. The customs officer had spoken to him gruffly, opening his bags and scattering his underwear in search of hidden gifts from London. And when the roshi had shouted for help with his luggage after being humiliated by the customs officer, the porters in the arrivals lounge ignored him. What unnerved me most, however, was that, under the fluorescent airport lights, Dokyu Roshi's skin was no longer golden but the color of Dijon mustard.

On our way to the car, Omu explained to me in halting English that the House of Hanakawa had supported Ryutakuji Monastery for six generations, and that his grandparents had favored the old abbot, Soen Roshi, while his parents were partial to Dokyu Roshi. Omu shyly admitted that his family had never entertained a Westerner before, but he assured me that, as a student of their beloved roshi, I was most welcome. I had trouble adjusting to his habit of punctuating every sentence with a bow, and found myself dropping my head to my chest whenever he did.

From the moment the Hanakawas appeared, Dokyu Roshi ignored me entirely. As soon as he started speaking Japanese, it was as if I didn't exist. Having relegated me into the back seat of the Hanakawas' black Rover sedan along with Omu and the luggage, he launched into a boisterous conversation with his chain-smoking companions that pointedly excluded me.

I looked out at the bleak industrial landscape, the skeletal bridges leading to enormous heaps of landfill, the endless railroad tracks and rickety shanties bordering the graffiti-sprayed freight cars . . . it was all so ugly. The sky, however, was luminous, stunningly mauve and orange with pollutants and punctuated by a resplendent setting sun. Stopped in traffic on a clogged one-lane freeway, the men ignored me and went on talking and smoking. Feeling carsick, I pressed the electric button that rolled down the window and stuck out my head for air.

I will not vomit on the back seat of this car. I will not embarrass Dokyu Roshi on my first day in Japan.

Groggily alternating between nausea and landscape gazing, I watched the immense orange ball of sun play hide-and-seek with the endless smoke stacks lining the fields on either side of the freeway until the car started moving again.

※

I was still wet, hardly out of the Lilliputian shower in my dollhouse-sized hotel room, when the telephone rang. Omu, who had not been exaggerating when he'd said that my room would be small, was waiting for me in the lobby, right on time. Despite the shower, I was exhausted and longed to sleep. I dreaded meeting the rest of the Hanakawas and talking pidgin English to Omu. I chastised myself for never having taken a conversation course in Japanese. Straightening up, I put on fresh clothes, threw a red- and-black shawl over my shoulders, slipped into my sandals, and went downstairs.

Of course Omu was smoking. Everybody in the lobby was smoking.

"You like raw fish?"

"Yes. Yes." Omu was walking too fast for me to keep up with him. Looking at the back of his head, I admired his stylish haircut.

"You eat everything?"

"Yes."

"Okay. Good."

We speed-walked through the wide, clean streets of an elegant residential neighborhood. Then Omu made an abrupt turn and entered an underpass that turned out to lead not to a subway station, as I thought it would, but to a subterranean mall lined with shops and restaurants. Ushering me into an open sushi bar, he removed his shoes and set them on a platform into a row of perfectly aligned footgear of all shapes and sizes. I did likewise.

"Best Japanese restaurant in Tokyo!" Omu announced.

I followed him into a tatami-floored side room and was immediately confronted by the other Hanakawas, who, like the shoes outside, were also lined up and silent. Mama and Papa sat on cushions at the head of the low table; Tomoe, Omu's pretty wife, was seated to their right; and Dokyu Roshi was seated with his back to a scroll painting in a tiny alcove, the traditional place for honored guests. He had changed into a soft, flowing beige robe and a matching tri-cornered brocade cap and looked positively elegant. A cushion had been left empty for me between the younger Hanakawas. I lowered my eyes as I walked past the roshi to my seat. Perching uncomfortably on my knees, I looked across the table and caught Mama Hanakawa giving me the once-over. Evidently satisfied with what she saw, Mama Hanakawa smiled and handed me her business card, which was printed in Japanese script on one side and said "Managing Director," in English, on the other, along with the company name and address.

Mama Hanakawa had a round, playful face and a gold tooth that flashed when she smiled, but I soon discovered that her jolly appearance was deceptive. She snapped orders at the kimono-clad waitress, made rude faces at her taciturn husband, and bullied Dokyu Roshi. Before long, using Omu as her translator and gesturing with her plump, square-tipped fingers, Mama Hanakawa turned her attention to me.

"She say you go to Nikko, Nara, Kyoto, Kamakura—see great Buddhist shrines and temples. She say, 'Why you bother going to monastery? Monastery boring place. Monks not good monks. Much more interesting sights in Japan.'"

Omu's pretty wife sat mutely at his side.

"Thank you for your suggestion. I'll try to see them all," I said, waiting for Omu's translation.

Leaping from her cushion with a great snort, Mama Hanakawa responded angrily. Omu almost couldn't keep up with her, she was talking so fast. The roshi and Papa Hanakawa were too busily engaged in their raucous conversation to pay attention to her outburst.

"She ask why you waste time with a monk like Dokyu?" Omu's face turned red as he translated his mother's response. Then he added a comment of his own: "I thought roshi bring someone fat."

Thinking I'd misunderstood, I looked at Omu's lips and asked him to please repeat what he'd said.

"Fat." Omu motioned with his hands in front of his chest, simulating big breasts.

The kimono-clad waitress poured sake all around. Omu drank and grew more voluble. No longer interested in me, Mama Hanakawa berated the head waitress for a breach of service. At the head of the table, Dokyu Roshi and Papa Hanakawa were drinking sake and laughing. The sushi arrived, superbly displayed on an edible doily of pink radish flowerets and octopus-stuffed seashells. An exquisite miso-dipped tofu and shredded turnip salad dish came next. Then a white custard dish appeared, and the roshi interrupted his raucous conversation with Papa Hanakawa to call to me from across the table, "Wall! You don't have to eat it."

"What?"

"Wall!"

"He mean whale," Omu intervened.

The roshi nodded and resumed his conversation with Papa Hanakawa.

"I can't eat that," I said in a loud voice, shocking even Mama Hanakawa into speechlessness. "I'm against killing whales."

Omu, whose business specialty was food processing, said politely, "Yes, but you Americans kill cows, so many cows for hamburger. Japan fishmen must kill whales, must use every product."

I turned to Omu's pretty wife. "Very beautiful food."

"Yes, traditional Japanese," she answered in perfect, British-accented English.

"You speak English!"

Omu's wife put her hand to her mouth and giggled. "You do Zen," she said pettishly, then sat back on her cushions, mute and lovely as before.

Omu said, "Zen, well, I do not sit . . . Zen is not for young people in Japan. It is like church in America. Most people my generation don't care religion, don't go." Resuming the hangdog expression he'd worn when translating for his mother, Omu settled down to the serious business of eating whale.

Trays heaped with food kept coming out of the kitchen: eel in black lacquered boxes, fried tofu, clear soup, pickles, rice, and an oily sliver of salmon on a ruffled lettuce leaf.

"March on bravely!" the roshi shouted at me in English, causing Papa Hanakawa to laugh so hard that he almost choked.

At the end of the dinner, filled to bursting with food, sake, and beer, I put on my shoes and staggered back to the hotel, accompanied by Omu and his pretty wife. The roshi and the elder Hanakawas had gotten into the family sedan and driven off into the night without as much as a farewell.

"Do you know Sochu Roshi, the abbot of Ryutakuji monastery?" Tomoe asked testily. With her in-laws gone, she'd grown bold.

"No, but I'm looking forward—"

"He is a very funny man."

I wanted to ask Tomoe what she meant by "funny." Strange? Eccentric? But Omu wouldn't let me get the words out.

"All roshis different. Sochu Roshi is . . . ah . . . funny. And old Soen Roshi is crazy." Omu placed his finger on his temple, and his wife slapped it away, laughing. But not before remembering to cover her mouth with the other hand.

Dokyu Roshi and I took a taxi to Ryutakuji monastery the next day. Leaving me to make out the driver's attempts to point out the sights in unintelligible English on my own, the roshi slept for the entire duration of the three-and-a-half-hour trip, which, because of an endless succession of construction detours, took almost two hours longer than it should have. Jet-lagged and still hung over from the night before, I could barely keep my head up. By the time we finally pulled up to the monastery gate, I was totally disoriented. The place was nothing at all like I'd expected. Perched on a mountaintop surrounded by modern suburban sprawl, Ryutakuji looked more like a theme park than a venerable Zen monastery. Subdivisions leading to and away from it were being gashed out of every neighboring hill and hummock. The citizens of Hara, the surrounding hamlet, were frantically building carports the size of airplane hangars, annexing them to their matchbox houses. Adding to the din, the air was abuzz with the incessant jack-hammering, sawing, and droning of an ambitious highway construction project designed to span the one-hundred-plus-mile distance between Mishima Prefecture, Mount Fuji, and the Sea of Japan. For a split second, I was tempted to ask the taxi driver to turn around and take me back to the airport.

The roshi, silent and glum, was now awake and smoking up a storm. He got out of the taxi and started pulling my bags out of the trunk. The driver didn't move a muscle to help him.

Okay. Now's the time to tell him you changed your mind, that you want to go back home.

Too late. The roshi was waving at a tall, Caucasian, black-robed monk who'd come out of the main hall and was approaching us.

I took a deep breath, and got out of the taxi. Leaving the bags in charge of the tall monk, Dokyu Roshi walked up the porch steps of the main hall and, without so much as giving me a backward glance, disappeared inside. The monk slammed down the trunk, and the taxi sped off in a shower of gravel.

"The zendo is closed, so you won't be sitting in meditation very much. I'm to show you to your *daishi*—women's quarters." The tall, black-robed, Caucasian "monk," as it turned out, was a British *woman* with a shaven head and a crazed look in her eyes. She picked up the bags and, swinging them over her back like a teamster, led me down a cinder path away from the main hall.

"The monk in charge of the zendo hates meditation, so he just locks up the place," she said sourly as we passed a bamboo grove surrounding a lotus pond. Beyond the bamboo grove there was a huge wooden building fronted by a raised platform. "The kitchen," snapped the woman. I looked into the open doorway. A roaring fire in an open grate cast a sinister glow across the smoke-stained walls of a cavernous room. Two simmering vats hanging over a cast-iron hearth resembled a pair of medieval witch's cauldrons. No one tended the fire. The kitchen was eerily empty.

We reached a small cottage in a bowl-shaped clearing bordered by cedar and pine trees. Before entering, I stopped to inhale the tree-scented air. It was fresh and lovely. But the picture-book prettiness of the tree-lined clearing could not dispel the overall despondency of the place, or of my guide's mood, and I soon found myself enveloped by a form of claustrophobic depression I'd never experienced before. I felt my life was over. I'd entered a prison and would never again be able to return to the world a free woman.

Inside, the cottage was hotter than a boiler room.

"You'd better get used to it . . . Japan in July. People are known to drop on the streets like flies. There's no air-conditioning in the monastery. And no heating in winter. You either boil or freeze to death—nothing in between. Part of the training entails overcoming your vulnerability to the elements."

"I'm Perle Besserman," I said, extending my hand.

"Priscilla Devon." (Not her real name.) She turned away and left me standing there with my hand outstretched. Opening a door and revealing a tiny wooden toilet, she said, "Here's the WC and bath. It's a complicated affair that takes the better part of an hour to heat—that is, if you can't do without warm water. And you're not to waste water or leave the gas on and asphyxiate yourself during the night."

I wished Priscilla would leave so I could pee and then make myself a cup of tea in the kitchenette I'd spied on entering the cottage.

"Morning service is at 5:00 A.M. in the main hall. I'll fetch you, but you are responsible for waking up on time yourself. I do hope you've brought an alarm clock. The last American woman who came thought she'd be awakened by the monks' bell. But we're too far from the monks' quarters to hear it, so we women must make do on our own."

I was now desperate for Priscilla to leave; I had to pee so badly. To my relief, she moved toward the screen door. Then she suddenly stopped in her tracks and glared down at the sandals I had left on the porch. "You aren't supposed to wear your own sandals. There's a pair of regulation straw sandals in the wardrobe. You'll wear those at all times."

I nodded.

"And I strongly advise you to remove your lipstick; no perfumed soap or cologne, either. You're not to stimulate the monks." Pushing aside the screen door, Priscilla abruptly walked away, and I made a dash for the toilet.

Changes

With Dokyu Roshi nowhere to be seen and only Priscilla for company, I had to improvise a whole new version of the practice routine the roshi and I had established when we were living at the London zendo. I posted my new schedule (fleshed out a bit here) on the inside of a kitchen cupboard:

- *Wake up at precisely four-fifteen instead of six every morning*
- *Roll out of my futon—in less than three minutes rather than linger for five*
- *Wash my face—with cold water because I don't have time to light the fire in the gas stove*
- *Brush my teeth—also with cold water—hurriedly—even if it means sometimes skipping toothpaste in order to quickly get into my blue monk's suit (I'll have to buy another one soon)*

- *Open the door to the porch and fetch my straw sandals*
- *Lace up my straw sandals while standing on one foot—a complicated affair when compared to slipping into my Birkenstocks, so leave a little extra time for it*
- *Step out into the darkness (better get accustomed to this, because in London, DR didn't leave the zendo until after breakfast, when it was light)*
- *Follow behind Priscilla on the cinder path with eyes fixed on her bare, straw-sandaled feet*
- *Be careful not to trip on stones and/or fallen branches while padding along in the glow of her "torch"—British for "flashlight" (though "torch" more aptly suits my senior dharma sister's Inquisitorial persona)*

Priscilla and I would arrive at the zendo even before the monks were awake. Once there, we'd sit down on a bench near the open toilet (I, secretly nibbling on a green tea biscuit I'd hidden in my pocket while Priscilla meditated) and wait for the newly awakened, hacking, spitting, peeing monks to prepare for the meditation period preceding the early morning chanting service in the main hall.

At the sound of the bell, Priscilla would jump up from the bench and swish past me in her black robes like Torquemada passing before a condemned heretic on the morning of her execution. Pointing to the raised women's meditation platform behind a screen separating us from the monks, she would enter the zendo and I would follow. The lantern-jawed zendo monk would push aside the *shoji* screens leading to the porch, and the lonely sound of the morning bell would announce the first period of zazen. *Ting! Ting! Ting!* We'd sit for thirty minutes, after which the sullen zendo monk would signal us to our feet and hurry us out onto the wooden walkway leading to the main hall for the morning service. Awkward in my straw sandals, I would make flapping noises as I ran along, last in line. Priscilla would turn to scowl at me, and I would be very pleased.

The Ryutakuji monks loved their abbot for his leniency. But what I think endeared Sochu Roshi to them most was his fondness for upscale consumer goods—washing machines, computers, portable telephones, vacuum cleaners—anything that made their lives easier. As for Sochu Roshi, I think cars were his favorite mark of status. There were three Toyota sedans and one snappy red Toyota pickup truck at his and his head monk's disposal at all hours of the day and night. Ryutakuji's abbot had a reputation in Japan for being up-to-date. But that was only on the surface. You had to live there to know that the monastery was a hybrid of the latest in modern convenience and medieval squalor. A case in point: the twenty modern self-flushing Toto toilets for guests, back-to-back with the twenty matching lime pits servicing those of us in residence. As Ryutakuji's newest recruit, I was in charge of cleaning them all. Not that I minded: the toilets were far away from Priscilla, who spent the work periods proving she was as strong and tough as the monks by pruning branches in the orange grove and lugging cordwood to the kitchen from what was left of the forest bordering the monastery. Still, no matter how hard I tried to keep out of her way, Priscilla always managed to catch up with me on the path leading to the toilets as I was leaving the refectory after breakfast to go to work. She was furious with me for getting Sochu Roshi's permission to take off after I'd finished cleaning the toilets.

I remember one particular morning.

"You know he's only cutting you so much slack because you're a *guest* and not an actual novice-in-training," Priscilla said, sneering as she spat out the word "guest." Then, blocking my path, she immediately launched into the first of what I came to call her "Jane Eyre Routines." For example, did I know that old Soen Roshi was confined to a hut above the main hall? That he'd sometimes go out on nights when there was a full moon and howl like a dog? "Surely," she promised with a perversely gleeful smile, "you'll be treated to one of his visits soon, especially as his beloved mother died in your cottage and is believed to haunt it still."

I put down my rags and water bucket. For a minute I was tempted to ask Priscilla why she'd chosen to remain at Ryutakuji if she hated it so much, but two things stopped me. The first was that Priscilla was almost six feet tall; she towered over me, and frankly I was a little afraid of her. The second was that I didn't want to give her the satisfaction of a reply. So I picked up my rags and water bucket and headed for the toilets.

"Don't forget what I told you! You're to clean out the pits by hand," she yelled after me. "No sponge-on-a-stick here!"

"Up yours," I muttered under my breath, briskly walking away from her.

So much for Zen sisterhood.

Zen Professionals (Male)

The majority of the monks at Ryutakuji were from temple families, men in their early twenties who considered themselves unlucky for being eldest sons forced to become priests so they could inherit the family business. These "temple monks" were for the most part lazy and disgruntled. Some of them already had their fiancées picked out for them by their parents. They were the ones who rushed through services and slept during *zazen* in order to make the time pass quickly. They couldn't wait until the day they left the monastery and returned home, where they'd be able to sleep late while their wives cooked, cleaned, made babies, and kept their parishioners at bay. Needless to say, these soon-to-be temple priests had no interest in enlightenment. In the old days, they used to remain in the monastery for at least eighteen months. To accommodate the demands of modern life, the training for Zen temple priests had to be cut down to one year, and I recently heard that it's been further "streamlined" to six months.

The second most common variety of monk I met at Ryutakuji was a young man, usually born into a struggling rural farm family that hoped to climb up in the world by producing a priest. The zendo monk was one of those: a barely literate farmer, but tough and shrewd, with a taste for hard work and equally hard drinking—but not for meditating.

The third kind of monk was the rarest: as far as I could tell, there was only one at Ryutakuji when I was in residence. This was most often a man in his early thirties with a university education and a promising career who had turned his back on the world to search for the answer to life and death. Most of them came from well-to-do families, sometimes (like the Buddha) leaving them behind. Yo-san, the head monk, was one of these.

He appeared at my side one morning as I was standing in the yard behind the kitchen at the post-breakfast bonfire, watching the garbage burn during a five minute break before going to clean the toilets. He was small, delicate, and bespectacled.

"I was a political leftist before I became a monk," he said. Just like that, with no introductions, not even telling me his name or asking mine.

"So was I," I said.

"I am Yo-san." Reaching into the sleeve of his robe, he produced an orange and handed it to me.

I nodded my thanks and began unpeeling the orange.

"I attended a lecture by Soen Roshi at my university. I was educated by Catholic Brothers all my life, in English . . . I even think in English . . . Western religion, philosophy, later, Marxist politics. I wanted to change the world. I thought Japan was backward."

Here, in the unlikeliest of places, in a body that least resembled mine, I had met the mirror image of myself. What a droll piece of karma.

"Then what?"

"I came to challenge the roshi, to heckle him. I called out and interrupted him while he was talking, asked him how Zen proposed to change the world, make it more bearable for the suffering masses. The audience was stunned at my rudeness. One of the monitors was about to throw me out. But Soen held up his hand, signaling that I was to be permitted to stay. He looked at me quietly for a few seconds. Then he said very gently, 'Who is it that wants to change the world? Find me this man first and then talk to me of change.' That confrontation resulted in my becoming his monk."

"Yes, that sounds like Soen Roshi. I never met him myself, but I knew one of his first students in Israel. She said she knew she'd found her Zen teacher after meeting him for the first time at a tea ceremony in Jerusalem. She said all it took was seeing him whip up the green tea in a bowl." I threw the orange peel into the fire, watching it curl and blacken.

"And now, do you still consider Soen Roshi to be your teacher even though he's retired?"

"No, Sochu Roshi is my teacher since Soen Roshi became sick," Yo-san murmured, looking away from me.

I was about to ask Yo-san about the mysterious "sickness" that kept Soen Roshi in his hermitage behind the main hall but was interrupted by the surly zendo monk who'd just emerged from the kitchen. Wedging himself between us, he started tossing garbage into the fire, spreading sparks everywhere.

"You go working. Clean shitting place!" he jabbered at me.

Yo-san tried calming him down, but the zendo monk turned on him and the two of them got into an elaborate Japanese argument, so I left.

Zen Professionals (Female)

It took me five years to stop believing that you couldn't be a genuine Zen "master" (I've long since given up using that word, exchanging it for the more democratic sounding "teacher") unless you were Japanese, male, and a monk—what Dokyu Roshi called a "Zen professional." It took me almost ten years to admit that you could be a woman "Zen professional," although I must confess to harboring a vague notion of somehow fitting that category myself one day—if I trained long and hard enough at a "real" Zen monastery in Japan. Which is ironic, because—except for one or two scurrilous remarks about baldheaded, oversexed nuns—I never heard a word about Japanese women Zen practitioners the entire time I was at Ryutakuji. The monastery had a good library of books in English, and I spent my time off reading them, but found hardly any mention of women in the old Zen stories I loved so much. Yes, there might be an occasional reference in one or two koans to a nun passing through town and visiting some great Chinese Zen luminary, but nothing indicating that women actively participated in making Zen history. Now, thanks to the Internet, I have learned that women existed not only as foils to the great masters, but that they were important enough to be named alongside the Patriarchs in the illustrious Zen lineage charts, with stories of their own.[1] It was humbling to find out that I wasn't training to be the first woman Zen professional, and that I wouldn't be the last, either.

5

"How Can a Woman Ever Do What a Man Does?"

Karma Matters

I still get this strange feeling in my stomach every time I see a Western woman Zen teacher with a shaved head dressed in full monk's regalia—probably because a secret part of me understands why she'd want to do it. What I don't understand is why this remnant of what I jokingly call "baldy Zen" still clings to me. Could it be that somewhere deep inside I still want to be a Zen professional? The question hit me full force the other day when I was reading Jiyu Kennett Roshi's memoir describing the emotional and physical hardships she suffered as a British woman in a Japanese Zen monastery. Surprisingly, instead of hoping she'd pack her bags and get out, I found myself rooting for her not to leave but to stay on until she'd met her goal of becoming the first Western female *roshi* in Japan. I guess it was because I also experienced hardships— though on a smaller scale. (I didn't last as long as Kennett did, and unlike her, I never became a roshi.) I think I saw myself in her cheeky refusal to be broken by the blatant sexism of her teachers. I couldn't keep from cheering out loud when, in her first encounter

with the monastery's sexist vice-abbot, she demanded to be allowed
into the meditation hall with the monks instead of being forced to
sit alone on a bench outside.

> "When shall I be admitted to the meditation hall properly?"
> He glared at me. "It is up to Zenji Sama [abbot of the
> monastery, the roshi Kennett practiced with in England who'd in-
> vited her to Japan] . . . If he wishes to break the rules here presum-
> ably he can whenever he wishes. In Japan women are slow; you must
> understand this. You are in Japan now."
> "Maybe Japanese women are slow," I countered, "but whether I
> am in Japan or not, and although my head is shaved as yours is, the
> skull, and the brain inside it, are still British and are going to behave
> like it."
> "How can a woman ever do what a man does?"
> "According to *Shusogi* even a little girl of seven can be the cele-
> brant at morning service if she is sincere in what she is doing.
> Dogen Zenji [thirteenth-century founder of the Soto Zen Sect] says
> so and he meant it. He also says that there is complete equality of
> the sexes in Zen."
> "How dare you to teach me the Scriptures?"
> "No, simply to remind you of them."
> He paused. "Can you *really* put up with what these young men
> do here?" he asked. [Kennett was in her forties when she left Eng-
> land to practice Zen in Japan.]
> "I can put up with anything that anyone can put up with any-
> where . . . whether it be man, woman or animal . . ."
> "We will see," he said and left me.[1]

Thinking about Kennett's ordeal makes me wonder what it is
about monastic Zen that still attracts me. Why, for example, am I still
drawn to stories of women like her and the Indian merchant's daughter? Stories that go as far back as the Buddha—like the one about
Mahapajapati, the Buddha's aunt and foster mother, who nursed and
raised him after his mother died in childbirth. How she and her entourage of women, abandoning their aristocratic life and becoming
homeless beggars in their desperation to join his religious community as nuns, were rejected by the Buddha himself. What kind of
Buddhism is this—a religion touted for its egalitarian message that

all beings can be enlightened regardless of class, race, or sex! Am I supposed to take comfort in the fact that Ananda, the Buddha's nephew and favorite disciple, somehow managed to successfully intercede on the women's behalf? Or to be grateful that the Buddha reluctantly accepted them—but only after establishing a set of sexist regulations designed to keep nuns under the heels of the monks and women Zen practitioners like me forever subordinate to male teachers? Am I supposed to identify with Asian nuns famous for sacrificing themselves in order to be allowed to practice Zen—desperate women like the seventeenth-century Japanese Ryonen Gesho, who "entered a Rinzai training monastery (Hokyo-ji) but was denied ordination by two masters because her beauty would distract the monks. She burned her face with a poker and was then ordained by Haku-o. He certified her enlightenment and she became abbot of Renjo-in and a respected poet."[2] Why should a woman have to scar her face in order to be ordained? Or have her enlightenment "certified" by a man? Or need permission to teach from a male roshi after getting enlightened? No matter how deeply I search, I can't find the answer to these questions. Maybe there is no answer. Maybe it's hidden in the deep, mysterious net of karmic affinities still hanging on from past lives. That's how Dokyu Roshi once explained life to me. According to him, we only control 25 percent of our lives; the other 75 percent is controlled by karma.

Before practicing Zen, I had studied and taught yoga for almost twenty years, so I thought I knew what karma was—at least, what the Hindus meant by karma. Though I have to say, the idea that you were reincarnated and had to pay for whatever you did in a past life struck me as pretty fatalistic. Traveling throughout India and seeing all those people lying around waiting to die and be reborn into better karmic circumstances didn't help me understand it any better. It wasn't until I began reading about Buddhism that I saw karma in a whole new light.

The Buddha, interestingly enough, didn't talk much about theological matters. In fact, according to him there is no god—which is why some scholars say that, technically, Buddhism is more of a philosophical system than a religion, but that's only if you define religion as having to do with a god (as in monotheism) or gods (as in polytheism).

Most Asian, and many Western, Buddhists would strongly disagree. All you have to do is go into a Buddhist temple, and you'll find the same sorts of religious services and ritual paraphernalia you'd find in any church. Though I am myself a Buddhist and enjoy some of the rituals, I must admit that the "religious" aspect of Buddhism never appealed to me much. Fortunately, the form of Zen "Buddhism" most often found in the West tends to emphasize meditation above all else, so I've had the luxury of picking and choosing what I wanted from the practice.

What interests psychologically oriented Americans in particular is the Buddha's focus on exploring the mind in the here and now, and realizing that nothing is permanent—not even the self that is doing the exploring. Until we experience the impermanent nature of the self and of everything else in this world and awaken to this very passing moment manifesting as Buddha Mind, we remain bound to the ceaselessly revolving wheel of suffering produced by our karma. In this sense, karma is simply nature's law of cause and effect. Whatever we implement—either physically or mentally—has a result. If we throw a ball into the air, it's got to land somewhere at some point, so it's helpful to know if we're throwing it up in the air and are ready to catch it, or if we're aiming it directly at our neighbor's window. Likewise, if we think of love, we are embodying love at that moment, and if we feel hatred, we are embodying hatred at that moment. Since "everything passes quickly away," no particular value judgments are assigned to the laws of cause and effect. Granted, this wide-open interpretation of what we do and think and feel (or don't do, think, or feel) can have dire results.

Sad to say, even the greatest Zen masters haven't been exempt from the notion that being enlightened means they're somehow beyond the laws of cause and effect. Hakuun Yasutani Roshi, for example, was one of the most illustrious and beloved twentieth-century teachers to bring Zen from Japan to America. Yet, even as late as the 1970s, he was still spouting militaristic fascist slogans justifying Japan's role in World War II just before he died. Unfortunately, he wasn't the only one. Most of the great twentieth-century Japanese Zen masters were militarists who were not ashamed to publicly express their feelings. My own teacher, Dokyu Roshi, used to brag of his "samurai lineage" and clearly preferred the Israeli soldiers in his *sangha* to the peaceniks. "Samurai Zen" is a very old tradition in Japan. No doubt there were those who weren't as chauvinistic, but you don't hear much about them. There is one exception, however: a young Soto Zen master named Gudo Uchiyama, whose picture my husband and Zen teaching partner, Manfred Steger, found in a second-hand bookstore in Honolulu. After cutting the picture out of the book, we framed it and placed it on the wall above our home altar. The text accompanying the picture informed us that Gudo Uchiyama was an antimilitarist socialist activist who dared to speak out against the Japanese government during World War II and was publicly executed for it. Though Manfred and I know nothing more about him, Uchiyama Roshi is our Zen hero.[3]

The Teacher in the Mirror

Speaking of Zen teachers thinking they're beyond the laws of cause and effect brings me back to a subject I must confess I've been avoiding: sex between male Zen teachers and their female students. Zen writer Natalie Goldberg is much braver than I am. Counterpointing her relationship to her sexually inappropriate father and her response to the sexual misconduct of her teacher Dainin Katagiri Roshi, she personally explores this issue in her latest book. By Dokyu Roshi's standards, Natalie is definitely a "greenhouse person"—too sensitive, too intellectual, too interested in relationships, and definitely too "overcaring." Finding out after his death that her adored teacher had sex with some of his female students almost destroys her practice. Fortunately, Natalie is mature enough in Zen to work through her disillusionment, concluding that: "we are drawn to teachers who unconsciously mirror our own psychology. None of us are clean. We all make mistakes. It's the repetition of those mistakes and the refusal to look at them that compound the suffering and assure their continuation."[4]

Natalie's book evoked a whole series of questions about the unequal distribution of power in Zen instruction. It was a very painful story for me to read, because I saw so much of my hypercritical, judgmental self in it. Clearly, Natalie's done a better job of exorcising her demons than I have. But then again, I don't think she ever buried her disappointment as deep as I did. Natalie was mad and hurt, but she wasn't crushed into selective forgetting, like I was. Thank you, Natalie, for writing *The Great Failure* and giving me the courage to come to terms with what I, too, felt were my serious misgivings about authority and gender in Zen.

The discussion rages on among feminists over issues like whether or not pornography constitutes violence against women; whether affairs between professors and students, bosses and employees, and spiritual teachers and disciples is less about sex than about power.[5] Not even the monastery had prepared me for this ongoing concern among feminists worldwide. Though looking back now, I realize that it should have.

Messy Female Notions About Love

Except for a glimpse of him on the morning of a patron's banquet, when he changed direction to avoid meeting me, I hadn't seen or talked to Dokyu Roshi since the day we'd arrived at Ryutakuji three weeks before. When I returned to my cottage one day and pushed aside the screen door, I found that he'd left me a box of strawberries, a packet of Emmenthaler cheese, and a tin of my favorite green tea biscuits. Recalling how determined the roshi was to avoid greeting me as he hurried past on the cinder path, with a cigarette dangling from his lips, looking like a clown in his beige stocking cap and wooden clogs, I was puzzled to find his gifts. *Why is he giving me the silent treatment?* I had wondered.

I thought of asking Yo-san about it, but decided it wasn't appropriate. I was a novice in a Japanese monastery and had no right to special treatment from my teacher. He'd left me food to let me know he hadn't forgotten me. I would have to content myself with that.

A week later, shortly after the morning sutra-chanting service, the *zendo* monk knocked on the door of my cottage to announce that the abbot was leaving for Europe and wished to interview me, informally, in the kitchen.

On the raised platform that served as the monastery dining area, Sochu Roshi stood among his three attendants directing the packing of his dozen trunks and cartons with a soft, fleshy index finger. A small, conical-shaped volcano with glutinous skin, slashes for eyes, and two thick lines for a mouth, he bellowed at the scurrying monks in a deep bass voice, his imperious finger pointing belied by his jovial delivery. It was the first time I'd seen him close up. At morning services, when I was sitting too far back to get a good look, Sochu Roshi would enter the main hall, poised on the balls of his feet, with the portly grace of a performing walrus. With one deft fling, he would cast his red silk bowing mat to the floor, bow three times in front of the Buddha, gather himself up, and scurry out of the main hall before the monks had finished the last line of the Great Vows.

Sochu Roshi's outfits were lavish, produced with an eye toward elevating his height and social status. He wore his colorful reputation like a badge. Monks and monastery supporters alike boasted about his wartime career as a thief of American PX goods and a sketcher of dirty pictures. Everyone but Priscilla seemed impressed by the abbot's artistic talent and humble origins. Driven by British snobbery, she never ceased to dwell on Sochu Roshi's "appalling bad taste." Seeing Priscilla rattled whenever the subject of Ryutakuji's abbot came up only increased my interest in him. I took to watching him more closely during morning services; turning my attention away from the sutra book, I'd follow his every move. Before long I found myself eagerly looking forward to his ceremonial displays of sartorial splendor: the sunflower-gold robes and saffron surplices, the purple brocade vests worn inside out with the label showing. I marveled at the abbot's theatrical sense of timing, his graceful gestures, and the confidence with which he had forged such a unique and magnificent persona. I thrilled to see him prance into the main hall on tiny, *tabi*-clad feet and, depending on his mood, boom or stage whisper the sutras while fingering his amber rosary beads with his eyes closed, his features disappearing into their soft mask of flesh as if they were being stretched taut under a nylon stocking.

Now here I was, standing face to face with the remarkable Sochu Roshi himself, holding my interview gift—a bottle of Jamaican rum— in my outstretched hand. For three weeks I had kept it hidden in my suitcase, waiting for the occasion to present it, never imagining that my first interview with the abbot of Ryutakuji monastery would not only take place in the kitchen, but that it would also be my last (for he was to die of a myocardial infarct not long after—as rumor had it, while enjoying a ride in a Venetian gondola).

"Firewater," the abbot said, laughing. "Stomach on fire, you drink that." He pointed his soft plump finger at his navel.

"Caribbean firewater," I said.

"Make crazy," the abbot replied with the sweet cunning of a child.

We both laughed, and the interview was over. Sochu Roshi clapped his hands once, and, loading themselves up like mules, his three attendants carried his baggage outside.

Priscilla crept up behind me as I was standing in the circular driveway watching the abbot's best Toyota sedan, a late-model, fully equipped Camry, careen down the mountain.

"He's a wonderful Zen teacher, but he hates women because his mother abandoned him at birth. He calls us *akema*, evil spirits."

"Then why do you study with him?"

"Because he is the only enlightened Zen master in Japan who will let me study with him." Priscilla turned sharply and walked away, her straw sandals crunching noisily against the driveway gravel.

It was the first time I had heard anyone at Ryutakuji use the word "enlightened," and it worked on me like a subtle poison. Priscilla had called Sochu Roshi the *only* enlightened Zen master in Japan. What did that make Dokyu Roshi, then? Plagued by doubts, I wondered if he was really enlightened or if he'd faked it and was hiding the lie under his quirky Zen master façade. For days afterward, instead of counting my breaths on my meditation cushions, I tormented myself with questions. Could monks who broke the Buddhist precepts— sadists, seducers, liars, cigarette smokers, meat eaters, and alcohol drinkers—be enlightened? I pictured Sochu Roshi, that brilliant shifting bundle of amorphous flesh, sketching hairy vulvas and frying pork chops in his private kitchen, the fragrant smoke purling from the chimney making my mouth water as I was on my knees cleaning the lime pits. Sochu Roshi didn't look or act like an enlightened person. But, then, what did an enlightened person look or act like? Soen Roshi? But he was up in his mountain hut, rumored to have transformed himself into a demon with hair down to his ankles and nails like tiger claws.

I started comparing Dokyu Roshi and Sochu Roshi, the two most likely "enlightened" occupants of Ryutakuji. Sochu was soft and easy going; Dokyu was hard and testy. Both had been scoured raw by their Zen training; neither was emotionally "needy." They were the opposite of needy, in fact. What happened to you once the bottom dropped out of your ego? Did you never again need a friend or a partner? Was it like Jamaican firewater that made you "crazy"? Turned you into a *funny* roshi? Could that have been what Omu's wife Tomoe meant when she told me that Sochu Roshi was "funny," laughing and hiding her teeth behind her hand?

Poor Priscilla. For the first time I began to feel sorry for her. I wondered whether she sometimes felt a little "crazy"—not from firewater, but as a result of Sochu Roshi's notions about women. Imagine working with a Zen teacher who called you an evil spirit! Even if he was joking, it must have been awful. I was glad the abbot had gone off to Europe, leaving Dokyu Roshi in charge. My teacher was a drill sergeant, but at least he didn't think of me as an evil spirit—a greenhouse person, yes, but as far as he was concerned, all Westerners, including men, were in that category.

I longed to hear more from Priscilla. I desperately missed speaking intimately to a Westerner, a woman, but Priscilla never gave me an opening. She was too intent on killing her ego to make common cause with me, too busy chewing the poison capsule of her womanhood down to a fine powder of time-released rage.

I spent my free time rolled up in my futon drifting in and out of sleep. I had a recurring dream that I was dancing at a wedding in a sun-drenched meadow. That I was wearing a black velvet dress and star-shaped diamond earrings. I lost my appetite and frequently skipped meals. I wondered if Ryutakuji weren't driving me a little crazy, too.

My Real Zen Role Model

This would be a good place, I think, to talk about the "craziness" of women trying to adapt to the rampant sexism of our male Zen teachers. Certainly, no amount of reading about the hostility we would encounter could have prepared those of us who cut ourselves off from our Western roots by going to Japan and immersing ourselves fully in monastic Zen. But you didn't have to go to Japan to feel the brunt of it. I can think of several first-generation women Zen teachers, all students of traditional Japanese male teachers in the United States, who did not practice in Japanese monasteries but eventually broke with their teachers over their mistreatment of women. One woman in particular stands out for me in this context—Soen Roshi's only female dharma heir, the late Maurine Stuart. I met her in person only twice, and talked with her only briefly about her experiences as Soen Roshi's student and successor, so I can't offer an extensive biographical account of her life in Zen.[6] But I did have a year of fairly regular telephone contact and correspondence with Maurine Stuart between 1982 and 1983, when she generously assisted Dokyu Roshi and me in establishing the Soho Zendo in New York.

Though she never went to Japan to train at Ryutakuji, Maurine was a true product of Soen Roshi's strict Rinzai Zen School. Born on the prairie in Saskatchewan, Canada, and disciplined from childhood by years of piano practice in preparation for a concert career, she slipped easily into the practice of dedicated *zazen*. Lenore Friedman quotes Maurine referring to herself as a "warrior woman," but anyone who met her—even once—would know immediately that Maurine was no samurai. Hers was what I would consider the truest form of "grandmotherly kindness" Zen had to offer. Her students, in fact, called her "ma-roshi." A wife, mother, professional musician, cook, friend, healer, and advisor, Maurine had no interest in imitating the life and style of a Japanese Zen master, not even that of her beloved teacher Soen Roshi, who, like Maurine, was an artist, and deeply devoted to music. (Soen was famous among his Western students for ending *sesshin* with Beethoven's Ninth Symphony.) Maurine was too authentic and original to imitate *anybody*, whether in Zen or in music or in her relationships with her students. She embodied each and every moment with unmatchable intensity and expressed her profound spiritual understanding in every personal encounter. There was no "one size fits all" where Maurine Stuart Roshi was concerned. She respected people too much for that. This was evident to anyone fortunate enough to come into contact with her in the relatively short span of her life as a Zen teacher.

Maurine had studied with both Soen Roshi during his protracted visits to the Zen Studies Society in New York, and with Eido Roshi, Soen's principal successor in the West. By the time we met, Maurine had already broken with Eido Roshi over issues involving his attitudes toward women, and she'd only just been unofficially made roshi in Soen Roshi's typically unconventional fashion. "He stopped me on the staircase as I was coming down and said, 'Tell everyone I made you roshi,'" Maurine explained to me. This obviously didn't sit well with Soen Roshi's Japanese male successors, who, as I heard it discussed both in New York and Japan, regarded Maurine's unwitnessed, informal dharma transmission as another one of Soen Roshi's "jokes."

Our first meeting took place in New York; our second took place in Boston, when Maurine invited me to be her guest at her Zen center in Cambridge, seven years before she died of cancer.

Maurine had flown down to New York to confer with Dokyu Roshi and me about opening a new Ryutakuji-affiliated zendo in New York. Primed by my experience at Ryutakuji with Priscilla, I had expected a dour, muscular martial arts type to come walking through the door and wasn't ready for the strikingly handsome woman with a shock of thick white hair, wearing a stylish hat, high heels, a fashionable dress, and makeup, who entered and greeted both Dokyu Roshi and me with a warm, perfumed hug.

Eido Roshi and his Japanese constituents weren't too happy to hear of our plans to establish another of Soen Roshi's successors in New York. He and Dokyu Roshi had visited each other and exchanged polite Japanese gifts of expensive cognac and fine green tea, but the tension between them was still pretty high by the time Maurine entered the picture on Dokyu Roshi's behalf. The Zen establishment had ramped up their assault against the legitimacy of Maurine's roshi's credentials, and even Dokyu indirectly questioned her credibility as Soen Roshi's true successor. He liked Maurine and respected her Zen insight, but that did not belie the fact that she was a woman, and a Westerner, and a typical greenhouse person unworthy of Ryutakuji monastery's vaunted Kyoto Myoshinji temple Rinzai lineage. Like his fellow Japanese "Zen professionals," Dokyu Roshi seemed to have conveniently forgotten that the great sixth Chinese ancestor of Zen, Hui-neng, a layman, had also been given secret transmission (in the kitchen) by his teacher in order to protect him from being murdered by the jealous monks at the monastery where the illiterate peasant who was to be among the greatest of the Zen patriarchs had been hired as a lay kitchen helper (an appropriately "feminine," and therefore "lowly," position in the monastery hierarchy).

Her rejection by the Zen establishment did not seem to faze Maurine. Steady and self-confident in her insight, she was as dignified a Zen master in her high heels and makeup as Sochu Roshi was in his purple robes and saffron surplices. As soon as she walked through the door, I knew I'd met my first real Zen role model. I think that was when I actually resumed wearing makeup and stopped wearing my monk's blue work suit and began sitting zazen in "civilian" black T-shirt and black drawstring pants. I can even remember wishing I could move up to Cambridge and become Maurine's student. But I had come too far to abandon our plans for the Soho Zendo; I was on the verge of giving up my marriage, my academic career, and my savings, in the hope of establishing Dokyu Roshi in New York.

Our conversation centered mainly on the nuts and bolts of setting up a new Zen center. Maurine had plenty of experience by then. A few years before, she'd been compelled by her husband's job to leave New York and move her family to Boston. Distraught about not having anywhere to practice, she'd turned to Soen Roshi, who had assured her that she'd find help and so sent her to meet one of his patrons, Elsie Mitchell, the woman who was to become Maurine's close friend and foremost supporter. (Elsie eventually bought and donated the house in Cambridge where Maurine taught Zen until she died.)

I think of Elsie and Maurine in connection with all the ancient women patrons of the great Japanese temples without whom there would be no Zen practice. And I am angered by the ingratitude of the roshis throughout the ages who took money from their female supporters while excluding them from their monasteries—not to speak of ridiculing those few courageous women who, like Maurine, refused to be defeated by their slander.

Here's what she had to say in a sesshin dharma talk on the subject of transmission: "Much harm has come from being overly concerned with transmission. These symbols and certifications have become hindrances. What sort of proof are they anyway? We don't need a paper certifying our awakened state. True awakening fills the whole universe. Acknowledgment in Zen is different from receiving a diploma from a university. People often ask me, 'What koans have you passed? Did you do all 1700 koans?' This matter of acknowledgment in Zen is very precious, very intimate, and is not something to discuss."[7]

The fact that Maurine never got the official paraphernalia of a bona fide Japanese roshi didn't stop hundreds of people from becoming her Zen students. Nor did it stop Maurine from putting her own unique, creative stamp on the American practice of Zen. She was an innovator in so many ways: without referring to herself as a feminist, she was probably the first Zen teacher to hold a sesshin for women; a brilliant improviser, she adjusted the rhythm and time of practice to the needs of her busy lay students, cooked sesshin meals for them herself, and patiently worked with deeply disturbed people any other Zen teacher would have thrown out the day they arrived.

Everyone remembers Maurine as gentle but strong—strong and sure enough in her own Zen insight not to have to complain about her exclusion from the traditional fraternity of male roshis. That strength comes through in another one of her talks as she reflects on her position as a woman Zen teacher, comparing her rejection to that of her ancient Japanese predecessor, Shido, the nun:

> There was a nun in the Rinzai School who was given . . . transmission from her teacher and allowed to teach—and some of the monks were a little hesitant about this. Was it all right for that lady to give a discourse on the *Rinzai Roku?* Is it all right for this piano player from Saskatchewan, Canada, to be up here giving a talk on the *Rinzai Roku?*
>
> Well, that nun, Shido, who was the founder of Tōkei-ji, was confronted by the head monk, who did not at all approve of her having been given [transmission]. He decided to question her. Aha, I will trap her and show how stupid this lady is he thought . . . So he said to her, "In our line, one who receives [transmission] gives a discourse on the *Rinzai Roku.* Can this nun really brandish the staff of the Dharma in the Dharma seat?"
>
> Shido faced him. She drew out her ten-inch knife, which was carried by all women of her warrior class, and she held it up. She said, "Certainly a Zen teacher of the line of the patriarchs should go up on the high seat and speak of this book. But I am a woman of the warrior line, and I should declare our teaching face-to-face with a drawn sword. What book should I need?"[8]

In my opinion, Maurine's gentleness was an even more powerful expression of the way she brandished her Zen "warrior woman's knife." She was famous for applying her own healing hands on her students' backs and shoulders in place of the stick during sesshin—massaging, rather than beating them into enlightenment. "When I see that you need a little massage, a spinal pickup, I come and do that for you," she wrote. "But the rest is up to you. This is our practice. Zen is not some cold, austere, held-back kind of practice. It is full of warmth, full of a loving nature, full of giving to the whole universe."[9]

"I don't continually come around with the stick and hit you; I don't say, 'Kensho [enlightenment], kensho, kensho.' I have experienced that approach myself and I have found it singularly unhelpful."[10]

I'd intuited as early as 1982 that what American Zen needed was more of Maurine Stuart's brand of "grandmotherly kindness," and that hers was certainly the sanest way for a woman to practice. But the time wasn't right. I still had more craziness to live through before I could truly appreciate Maurine's legacy enough to make it my own.

6

Zen Is for Funerals

Zen Women Don't Cry

It was funeral season at Ryutakuji and we were servicing a steady stream of guests, which meant I found myself almost continuously scouring toilets. Instead of tiring me out, the increased physical activity left me manic. I went on a cleaning binge. Returning after work to my cottage, I would dust every corner of every room, polish the floors, wash the windows, do the laundry, and hang it out to dry. I was determined to be very "Zen" about it all. Just going along with each moment, taking it as it came. Dust, breathe one . . . polish, breathe two . . . wash, breathe three . . . and so on . . . up to ten and back . . . until there was no Perle-san—only cleaning—in the whole universe. I didn't let myself think about what would happen the moment I finally, and inevitably, crashed.

Priscilla came by one day to say she was taking a week off, staying with friends in Kyoto. What friends? Who would have Priscilla as a friend? Of course I didn't ask her. We stood in my cottage doorway staring each other down for a while. When Priscilla saw that I wasn't going to invite her in, she cleared her throat and said, "I don't suppose you could do me a favor?"

I gave her a suspicious look. "What is it?"

"I've left enough cat and dog food . . . well, you see, um, there's a small army of stray animals who've collected themselves around me, um, particularly a dog—my number one problem—Soen Roshi's abandoned pet."

Amazed that Priscilla could actually care for anything besides her own precious enlightenment, I relented and invited her in. Refusing the invitation, but still standing in my doorway, she said, "I'm surprised you never spotted him. He's quite bedraggled, really. Looks like a ghost running through the bamboo grove."

"No, I never have," I said.

Priscilla looked down at her chapped red feet and said, "Well, I've been feeding him since Soen Roshi abandoned him, and several wild cats who can take better care of themselves than poor Sherau . . . that's the dog's name. It means 'white.'"

"What about the monks? Why don't they look after him?"

Priscilla looked up at me with disdain. "Haven't you learnt about them yet? I've seen them kick Sherau in the ribs . . . They're brutes. Besides, Sochu Roshi has imbued them with his own superstitious hatred of animals—particularly cats, which, he says, embody evil female spirits."

Not wanting to hear more, I promised Priscilla I would care for the animals and wished her a pleasant trip.

We were beset by rainstorms that entire week. The bamboo grove surrounding my cottage came alive and moaned. The pine trees shivered and tossed their branches over the roof, and the wind shook the fragile windowpanes so hard that they cracked. One morning after breakfast, I found a note from Dokyu Roshi on the bulletin board instructing me to "Clean toilets twice today. Big funeral ceremony. Make sparkle for monastery patrons."

Later that morning, as I was hurrying from my cottage to an early lunch, I heard the telephone ring in Yo-san's office behind the kitchen. There was some garbled shouting, and then Yo-san himself ran out into the rain, crying, "It's for you! A man's voice from America!" His arms were flailing like millwheels. I'd never seen him so excited.

I ran toward the office and picked up the telephone just as the monks started chanting the meal sutra. I knew they wouldn't wait for me, that if I wanted to eat I would have to talk fast. I wished the monks would slow down the chanting, the way they did when they wanted to drag out services to delay going to work, but they seemed to be hurrying it along even faster than usual. They were no longer following Sochu Roshi's lenient schedule, and Dokyu Roshi's strict rules against lingering over meals wouldn't spare them the time. Except for emergencies, monks and guests in residence didn't get telephone calls during training periods at Ryutakuji, so I was somewhat apprehensive as I picked up the receiver.

"You sound sad," my husband shouted in response to my hello. "And a little detached."

I laughed. "Zen women don't cry," I said, relieved that this wasn't an emergency call.

He laughed, too, a shivery sound that rattled and echoed across the storm-tossed telephone lines.

"What about you? Any new patients?"

"No, I'm not taking anybody new because I'll be traveling."

"Where to?"

"To a holistic health seminar in California."

"Oh. How long will you be gone?"

"About a month. The seminar is being held at the Beverly Hills Hotel. You can always reach me there, in an emergency. I'll try to call you. I can't tell you exactly what day, but I'll keep you informed of my whereabouts."

The conversation was on its way to being over. I would have to speak fast. "Sure . . . let's both keep each other informed of our whereabouts," I said wanly.

There was a pause; then, in an unfamiliar gravelly voice, he said, "I love you."

"Uh huh . . ." I waited for him to beg me to leave the monastery and join him in California, but he didn't.

Then the roof shook and the line went dead.

I replaced the receiver back in its cradle and stood staring down at Yo-san's open account ledger with its unintelligible Japanese squiggles. Then I looked up at the wall at Soen Roshi's framed calligraphic drawing of the Zen circle symbolizing emptiness, and below that, at the stained teapot on its hotplate. My nose was running, but I wasn't crying. Wiping my nose on my sleeve, I tiptoed back to my cushion on the tatami mat at the long narrow bench that served as a dining table, and sat down in *seiza* posture among the monks. In a few minutes my knees would be numb, my ankles prickling. I would have to eat twice as fast as everyone else to catch up.

Fumbling with my bowl and chopsticks, I struggled not to think of home, of family, of love. I remembered Dokyu Roshi telling me once that he didn't love anyone, not even his mother or his sister. There was no room in Zen training, he said, for messy female notions about love. Monks didn't fall in love. Love, to a real Zen monk, meant sacrifice, hardship, loyalty to his master, all of which earned him *toku*—merit—on his journey to enlightenment. I repeated the roshi's words in my head, keying them to the pace of my chewing. But it was no use; I'd been infected by the telephone call from the world of "messy" emotions outside the monastery. I had even begun imagining that the monks surrounding me had been infected, too; that, like me, they were brooding, tired of the rain, tired of the endless round of chanting and meditating and cleaning; sick of their diet of rice and pickles, curious about the telephone call from far away, and hungry for a bit of messy female love themselves.

Yo-san sat at the head of the table munching on a salted plum. The telephone call coming in the middle of lunch seemed to have unsettled him, too. He flitted, made an awkward charade of avoiding me; chanting shrilly, he snapped his fingers to show he was angry with the cook for passing the food around too slowly.

Dokyu Roshi arrived as we were reciting the last meal sutra, his face red and pinched. He joined the chanting in a high, cracked voice that grated against my spine, making me want to stick my fingers in my ears and shut it out. I could feel the food turning in my stomach— a bolus of pickles, radish, salted plums, seaweed soup, turnips, rice, and cold chard. Two days ago we'd been served fresh tomatoes, and I'd lunged at them greedily. I thought about the new packet of Emmenthaler cheese the roshi had left on my doorstep the night before, and my mouth watered. Sherau had been standing next to me on the porch, sniffing at the cheese as I picked it up, but when I tried coaxing him inside, he'd turned away and disappeared into the bamboo grove. Soen Roshi's dog had continued to pay me occasional visits since Priscilla's departure, but I could never get him to come into my cottage. I wondered where Sherau spent the night during all that rain.

Dokyu Roshi announced a free hour after lunch while he and the senior monks prepared for the funeral ceremony. As I was standing in front of the kitchen door lacing up my sandals, he came up to me and tapped me on the shoulder.

"Okay you sit in back of main hall with ladies," he said tersely. "Good opportunity to see typical Zen-style funeral."

The mourners started arriving at two o'clock in the afternoon. The main hall was banked with flowers and baskets of fruit; clouds of pungent incense swirled around the altar, where, according to Buddhist custom, an oversized portrait of the deceased stood draped in a laurel wreath. The dead man had been a local schoolteacher with many friends and relatives and students from abroad. The photograph featured an elderly man with pouches under his eyes and a kind, sad smile.

The women mourners were dressed in black designer suits and veiled hats; around their necks and in their ears they wore pearls the size of pennies. They immediately took their places at the rear around the widow without looking at me. The deceased's wife was a stylish woman in a black crepe dress. Instead of pearls, she was wearing tiny jet earrings. None of the women was crying.

Gathered opposite were the men: they were all wearing the same black three-piece suits, white shirts, and gray silk ties. It was hot, and the men wiped their faces with expensive monogrammed white handkerchiefs.

Judging from the affluence of the guests, I was sure the monks would dine in style that night.

A sudden rustle in the doorway announced Dokyu Roshi and his entourage. I caught my breath.

The Zen master's traditional high seat had been brought out of storage and placed directly in front of the altar, where a huge golden statue of the Buddha sat in perpetual bliss. Dokyu Roshi wore a gold brocade robe and carried a red lacquer flywhisk under his arm. His immaculate white *tabi* barely touching the floor, he approached the high seat. His movements were stiff, staged, and deliberate, like a performer in a Noh drama. The monks chanted a steady accompaniment to the clamor of cymbals, drums, and bells. I recognized the familiar sutras, but in this setting they sounded strange, slow and warped and otherworldly. The roshi sat stone-faced above the congregation, never once looking down.

A man in a black cutaway slipped out of the crowd and stepped up to a microphone I hadn't noticed before that had been placed on the dais in front of the altar. The monks stopped chanting, and the man in the cutaway began reading condolence telegrams in a shrill, singsong voice. When the last telegram had been read, the man sat down and Dokyu Roshi got up and walked slowly to the altar. Holding a stick of incense in the air, he traced a circle of smoke around the photograph of the deceased. Stopping in midair, he made a sharp, unexpected gesture with his flywhisk and returned to the high seat.

Again the man in the cutaway approached the microphone, this time calling on members of the congregation to speak. Several friends and relatives got up and made little speeches. A heavyset man with beautifully manicured fingernails came up and talked to the photograph as if the dead man could hear him. (Yo-san later told me that according to Japanese Shinto and Buddhist beliefs, a departed person's spirit remained in this world for forty-nine days after death.)

I stifled a yawn. It was four o'clock and the ceremony showed no signs of ending. I folded and unfolded my legs under my long black skirt. The guests stopped coming to the microphone. The monks chanted. Dokyu Roshi recited a poem in the high-pitched nasal voice of a priest in a Noh drama. I was just about to fall asleep when I suddenly heard him let out a ferocious yell: "KAAAAAAATZ!" It was the traditional Rinzai Zen shout of enlightenment. The roshi was forever talking about the famous Zen master Rinzai's shout but had never actually demonstrated it for me. And now he was crying it out for all to hear! At a funeral, no less! I craned my neck, eager to see what the roshi would do next, when he just as suddenly turned and abruptly left the main hall with his entourage of monks following behind. Now the man in the black cutaway was coming back to the microphone to resume listing condolence messages, and I would be left sitting there for as long as it took him to finish reading—which, judging from the bulky sheaf of papers in his hands—would take at least an hour. What a letdown.

Does a Singing Dog Have Buddha Nature?

It was five-thirty when I finally got out of the main hall. The rain had not stopped all that day. The ground was glutinous and muddy; noisy streams of water gushed from the gutter pipes in the eaves of every building. I took a meager supper along with the three novice monks who hadn't participated in the funeral ceremony. Together we sat wordlessly slurping our soup. The main dish was cold, unseasoned chopped chard. I reached for a salted pickle and mixed it in with the chard. I needed protein badly. In the mirror above the sink in my cottage bathroom, I'd been watching daily as my skin grew dried and patchy from lack of fatty oils.

I was washing the supper dishes when Yo-san—now changed out of his ceremonial finery back into his monk's work suit—came out of his office behind the kitchen.

"You look miserable," he said. Then putting his finger to his lips, he whispered, "Meet me outside when you're done. I have something for you. It's a standing fan from Sochu Roshi's secret storehouse. Keep it in your room. Don't tell anyone. It will be paradise."

The fan was huge and clumsy, but I wouldn't think of not taking it. As I was dragging it through the mud to my cottage, a burly monk with a "reputation," jumped out of the bathhouse and blocked my path. He had a towel wrapped around his head, was bare-chested, and wore black cotton pantaloons. He held a white shopping bag in his right hand. Afraid he was planning to pull the fan away from me, I took a step back. Then, to my surprise, instead of trying to take the fan, the monk handed me the shopping bag.

"For you," he said.

"Me?" I hadn't exchanged one word with the monk. I had stayed out of his way because Priscilla had informed me that he had a black belt in karate and could become very unfriendly when he had something to drink.

"Fruits." He pointed at the shopping bag. "Fruits."

I looked into the bag and saw three bananas, three perfect Sunkist oranges, and a small green pineapple.

"Thank you. Thank you very much." With my hands full, I could only bob my head up and down to show him how grateful I was. The two of us stood there awkwardly looking at each other with nothing else to say. At last I took a step forward and the burly monk stepped aside, and we each went our separate ways. Halfway to the cottage, when I was sure I was out of earshot, I called out to the trees in the bamboo grove, "Thank you for the fruits you filched from the funeral! And thank *you* Yo-san, for the fan you filched from Sochu Roshi's storeroom! Thank you both!" Answered by the sound of my own voice echoing through the valley, I hurried along, dragging the fan behind me in one hand and carrying the fruit-filled shopping bag in the other.

At the cottage door I was met by Sherau, the wettest dog in creation, an overjoyed mass of dirt and glistening fur. The dog eyed me unblinkingly. Then following me to the porch, he ran over to eat from the bowl of soggy kibble I'd put out for him early that morning. When he'd licked the bowl clean, he hopped onto the porch ledge under the eaves. It was all the frightened dog would do to escape the rain. He seemed to be limping. But no matter how much I pleaded with him, Sherau would not come into the cottage. Too exhausted to coax him further, I went inside. Another funeral service was scheduled for the next day. Dokyu Roshi had left me a second note on the kitchen board letting me know, in his inimitable English, that he expected me to be there. I'd had enough of funerals. I'd come with him to Ryutakuji to practice Zen, not to attend church ceremonies or entertain wealthy supporters. My enthusiasm for monastery life was waning fast; now I was tired and all I wanted to do was sleep.

Looking out the window I saw Sherau prick up his ears. Someone in the valley below was playing a melancholy tune on a flute. The dog began to howl. Keeping perfect time, waiting always for the last notes of the flute to die away, Sherau lifted his muzzle to the sky and howled his dog version of the music. I didn't dare move for fear of startling him. He stopped howling only when the flutist stopped playing. I was desperate enough to believe it was old Soen Roshi singing to me through his dog. Again I tried coaxing Sherau inside. At first he ignored me, then, edging a little closer to the screen door, he eyed me with a look of mistrust.

"I don't blame you," I said. "The way you've been treated around here, why should you trust me?"

Knowing that pain was the price of too much human contact, both dog and master had become hermits. Soen Roshi was in his mountaintop hut; his dog had taken refuge on the porch of my cottage. They would both be okay. Neither of them needed me. Anyway, I was only a guest at the monastery, not a real monk. Once I'd gone, both dog and master would again be at the mercy of their karma and the waywardness of the monks with whom they shared the mountain.

The rain fell interminably. I switched on the fan and aimed it at my futon. Then I stripped down to my panties, slipped into a T-shirt, and lay down. Peeling one of the monk's oranges I received earlier and eating it slowly, I reflected on the strange dream that had become my life. In the course of a single day, Dokyu Roshi had delivered his thundering enlightenment KAAAAAAATZ, Yo-san had given me a fan, the burly monk had handed me a shopping bag full of fruit, and I'd been serenaded by Soen Roshi's singing dog. What was next?

Food, of Course

When I woke up it was dark and my alarm clock read one o'clock. Too early to roll out of the futon and prepare for meditation. A cow down in the valley had interrupted my sleep with its mournful lowing. I buried myself deeper into the futon. When I next awoke, sunlight was pouring through the window; the alarm clock read eight-thirty, and Dokyu Roshi was calling me from the doorway.

"Perle-san! What happen? You miss morning service. You sick?"

"No, I'm just tired."

"Ah . . . you thinking, thinking, thinking. Nothing come out," he said amiably.

"You wouldn't understand," I mumbled into the pillow.

"What you say?"

"I'm tired."

"Tomorrow you come with me and Yo-san to French restaurant. You feel better. Okay?"

Food, of course. I was sick and tired of feeling ignored and humiliated, then lured like a child by the promise of food. The game had grown stale and I no longer wanted to play.

"You meet these people I introduce through friends. One is a medical doctor, like your husband. The other man owns French restaurant, like in Paris."

I longed to tell Dokyu Roshi to shut up and go away, to quit stuffing me with food and start treating me like an adult, like Yo-san, or like any of the other monks, even Kyu-san, the cook, who was only nineteen. I longed to stop the Zen game of being treated like shit and then stroked. I couldn't take it anymore.

The roshi pushed aside the screen door and came inside. It was the first time he had ever entered my cottage. Men were not permitted in the women's quarters, not even abbots. Here I was in bed, to the bargain, in my T-shirt and panties, with what was left of my cropped hair sticking up in clumps and my eyes red from having cried myself back to sleep.

"You look terrible," said Dokyu Roshi, sitting down across from me on the *tatami*-covered floor with his legs crossed.

"You don't look so good yourself."

He laughed.

I noticed he was again wearing his clown outfit—beige weskit, white pantaloons, and brown woolen stocking hat.

The roshi pointed his finger at me. "Husband-san call you and make you lonely for home, no?"

"Yes."

He moved close enough for me to reach out and touch the index finger he was pointing at me. I suddenly remembered that the forbidden fan was standing in full view, noisily blasting air at us, the perfect emblem of my greenhouse frailty.

"Yo-san gave it to me," I said apologetically, pointing at the fan in the hope of deflecting his gaze away from me. We'd spent lots of time alone together in the London Zendo, but there was something unsettling about sitting with Dokyu Roshi in the monastery cottage in Japan, he looking at me in bed in my T-shirt and panties, probably with the same appraising gaze he'd reserved for the giraffes at the London Zoo.

"I know. I tell him to," the roshi said softly.

"You did?"

He nodded.

The cow moaned in the valley.

"She kept me up all night," I said.

"You sleep today. Tomorrow we go to French restaurant. Big supporter treat us in style." Dokyu Roshi stood up and walked to the door. Stopping in front of it, he lit a cigarette. Then, without looking back at me, he opened the door and stepped out on the porch.

I got up and walked over to the window and watched him walk down the cinder path toward town. I did not return to my futon until his beige weskit and white pantaloons and brown woolen stocking hat were no longer visible among the trees.

Matriarchal Encounters

It didn't take more than two weeks of monastery life to show me that in my desperate attempt to become a Zen professional I'd lost my "self." Not in a good way; not like Zen Master Dogen's "losing the self to gain the Self," but suspended between my old ideas about who and what I was, hovering like a ghost in the astral ether over some imagined notion of what I would have to do to be reincarnated in this very life as a monk. (Women were, and still are, so marginalized in Japan's Zen hierarchy that it never occurred to me to think of becoming a nun.) I hung suspended between genders, sexually neutralized but still dangerous for occupying a woman's body. As my father would say, I was "neither fish nor foul nor good red herring."

The ancient sutra stories about women on the verge of bod-hisattva-hood being lifted out of their miserable female bodies and being turned into men might have inspired the first Indian women Buddhists, but they were clearly of no use to me in a monastery in twentieth-century Japan. No Buddhas or bodhisattvas were around to magically help my transformation. We may have chanted the sutras every morning at Ryutakuji, but we spent no time at all studying them. The practical, down-to-earth Chinese Ch'an version of Bud-dhism that eventually became Japanese Zen was as far away from magical, metaphysical India as you could get. Zen was beyond all words and scriptures, anyway. Too much thinking, thinking, thinking about anything—especially Buddhism—was discouraged. The great old Zen masters had, in fact, urged us to "kill the Buddha" if we met him. Only hard sitting and paying full attention to cleaning toilets counted for anything. Dokyu Roshi used to laugh whenever I talked about my experience as a yoga teacher. He equated yoga with getting into weird postures in order to induce trances, and would scold me for "dream-talking." Once, as a joke, I think, though I'll never be sure, he assigned me the Indian mantra "Om" instead of the first Zen koan "Mu" to meditate on.

Lately, in searching for a precedent to my bleak situation as an aspiring Zen professional, I have discovered the names of some of the first Ch'an/Zen women, and learned a little bit of their history.[1] There still isn't too much available in English about the Zen matriarchs—certainly not nearly as much as what we know about the patriarchs—but it's comforting to know that they existed at all. There are clues, beginning with the sixth-century legend of Bodhidharma, the founder of Zen in China, and in the eleventh-century lineage enlightenment stories gathered under the title *The Transmission of the Lamp*. Since there was already a well-established Buddhist monastic tradition in China before Bodhidharma got there, most of the women who came to Ch'an were nuns. The first was Tsung-chih, daughter of an Emperor of the Liang dynasty, said to be the only woman among Bodhidharma's four disciples. The *Ching-te chuan-teng lu* (Record of Bodhidharma) doesn't mention how Tsung-chih got to the Shaolin mountain cave where Bodhidharma sat facing the wall alone until his first disciple, Hui-ko, was taken in after cutting off his arm to show the master how serious he was about the teaching. We do know that after nine years or so Bodhidharma acknowledged Hui-ko as his primary dharma successor, telling him, "You have attained my marrow."

Less is known about Tao-fu, the next person to appear at Bodhidharma's cave. But we are told that he was sufficiently enlightened for the master to assert: "You have attained my skin." And to Tao-yu, his third disciple, Bodhidharma declared, "You have attained my bone."

True or not, that Ch'an lineage founding story, and a number of others surrounding Bodhidharma's adventures in China, all involve men. Though the Chinese record keepers seem not to have thought it remarkable for a woman to be one of the original quartet of Bodhidharma's Ch'an disciples, the nun Tsung-chih only figures in the story when the master is about to return to his home in Central Asia. Other than the fact that she passes Bodhidharma's final koan test and is told, "You have attained my flesh" during the dramatic transmission ceremony, we hear nothing more of the first Ch'an woman Tsung-chih.

It wouldn't have been unusual for three monks to make their way to study with the founder of Ch'an, for, having been interviewed by the Emperor of China himself, Bodhidharma was already pretty famous by then. We know, for example, that Hui-ko, Bodhidharma's main successor, the man who was to become the "second patriarch of Zen," was desperate to have his mind pacified, so much so that he stood freezing out in the snow for three days and had to cut off his arm before Bodhidharma would even come out and look at him. Some scholars speculate that Hui-ko may have been a one-armed man to begin with, and that the story was fabricated around his disability to show the depth of his yearning. This reminds me of Sadaprarudita, another enlightenment seeker who cuts himself up to get his teacher's attention; and of Ryonen Gesho, the "too-beautiful" woman who scars her face to convince her teacher of her sincerity. (One hopes these are merely metaphors and not literal accounts.) But I wonder what burning desire could have driven Tsung-chih to first give up her luxurious life as a princess to become a nun, and then leave the safe confines of her nunnery, traveling alone on bandit-infested roads, risking rape and possibly even murder, in order to climb all the way up a mountain to sit facing the wall with a "red-bearded, blue-eyed barbarian" in his cave. Once she got there, what did she have to do to prove herself worthy of Bodhidharma's acceptance? Did she, too, mutilate herself? And afterward, how long and hard did Tsung-chih have to sit before the master confirmed her enlightenment, saying, "You have attained my flesh"?

What was it like being the only woman up on that tight-knit little mountaintop *sangha*, I wonder? Did Tsung-chih have her own section of the cave especially set apart from the men? Was she attracted to any of them? Were any of the men attracted to her? Was she old, young, big, small, gregarious, or quiet? We'll never know.

Given that Tsung-chih's seventeenth-century Japanese dharma sister, the beautiful Ryonen Gesho, would later be considered too tempting for the monks to be allowed into Hokyo-ji monastery, it would seem that things got worse for women after Ch'an left China and became *Zen* in Japan. The eighth-century story of Mo-shan Liao-Jan, the first woman dharma heir in Chinese Ch'an Buddhism, corroborates this assumption. Also known as Summit Mountain, Mo-shan Liao-Jan was a disciple of Lin-chi (Rinzai School) Ch'an master Kao-an-Ta-Yu. Miriam Levering, who translated the "Records of 'Summit Mountain,'" writes that Mo-shan "was the first nun to be portrayed in Ch'an texts as doing what male teachers do—being an abbess, welcoming and challenging students in that role."[2] A chapter in the Chinese book of enlightenment stories, *The Transmission of the Lamp*, describes how Mo-shan became the first woman Zen teacher of a male student. It happened this way.

Chinese monk Kuan-chih-hsien was traveling in search of a teacher when he came upon Mo-shan's temple. After a typical Ch'an exchange ("where are you coming from?" and so on), Chih-hsien recognized Mo-shan's profound spiritual attainment and immediately became her disciple. Five centuries later, Dogen (who studied in China and returned to Japan to found the Soto Zen sect) praised Chih-hsien for his willingness to be taught by a woman. Dogen was known early in his career for his liberal attitudes toward women, but pressure from the monastic establishment later caused him to harden his views. By first breaking the Buddhist rule prohibiting a monk from bowing before a nun—and then compounding his defiance by becoming her student—Chih-hsien turns out to be more of a "feminist" than Dogen.

Though not a nun, another eighth-century Chinese powerhouse is Lingzhao, daughter of the most famous nonmonastic Ch'an master, "Layman P'ang."[3] Forced by famine and the emperor's persecution of Buddhism to leave their farm and family behind, Lingzhao and her father took to the road as traveling peddlers. Because she earned her living by selling house wares, Lingzhao became the prototype of "Fish-basket Kuan Yin," one of the thirty-three forms of the female bodhisattva of compassion. In order to keep up their Ch'an practice, she and her father took up residence in a cave, eventually gathering a dedicated core of students that included the provincial governor himself. Lingzhao was known as a formidable Ch'an woman, but perhaps her most fearless act was to illustrate her realization of "no-self" by sitting down next to her dying father in *zazen* and dying along with him.

Then there are what I call the "challenger nuns," women with enough self-confidence in their spiritual attainment to call any monk's bluff. Liu Tiemo (Iron Grinder Liu) is at the top of my list. Known for "grinding up" the delusions of anyone courageous enough to face her, this ninth-century Ch'an woman lived in a hut ten miles away from a famous male Ch'an master named Kuei-shan Lin-yu. We find her sparring with him in the eleventh-century *The Blue Cliff Record*, a famous Chinese koan collection that is still used by Zen teachers

today. Liu's teaching style was known to be "awesome and dangerous," so her exchanges always got the sparks flying. Needless to say,
Iron Grinder Liu's "dharma combats" with the great male Ch'an masters of the day always ended in a draw.

Skipping over the centuries, let's turn to the story of a nun who
spent forty turbulent years wandering in search of enlightenment.
Born in 1896 on Japan's northern island of Hokkaido, Satomi Myodo
was the daughter of poor farmers.[4] A typical Japanese country girl
programmed from the time she was a child to want nothing more than
to marry and have sons, Satomi seems like the least likely woman to
dream of becoming a Zen nun. Nonetheless, even at an early age,
there's something different about her.

Contrary to her parents' expectations, Satomi becomes pregnant
in her teens. Although she doesn't love her child's father, she marries
him for her family's sake. The turning point in what would seem to be
this ordinary village girl's life comes when Satomi spontaneously
comes up with the koan that will drive her "passionate journey" to
Zen. Developing a virtual obsession with the meaning of "sincerity,"
she eventually becomes so desperate that she almost gets up the
courage to leave her husband in search of the answer to her spontaneous koan, but the thought of abandoning her child stops her. Finally, it's her husband who abandons her and their child, leaving
Satomi with no choice but to return to live with her parents. Here,
the strain between her spiritual longing and her family obligations
causes her to suffer a nervous breakdown. Finding no one in her little
village capable of understanding her condition, and still actively hallu-
cinating, she steals away and heads for Tokyo with her baby daughter
in her arms.

After an unsuccessful attempt to find the answer to her "sincerity
koan" by studying Buddhism as a part-time student at Tokyo University, Satomi descends into psychosis. Her husband reappears in her
life at this point—not to rescue her, but to take away their daughter,
leaving Satomi to struggle through her illness on her own. In the tradition of her Zen foremother Ryonen Gesho, Satomi remains determined to pursue her spiritual search despite (or maybe because of) her
"madness." Moving to Nagoya, she becomes an actress, takes up with
a younger man, and finds a Shinto teacher. The couple split up, and
Satomi embarks on the shamanic path, her first genuine spiritual

practice, by seriously immersing herself in Shinto ascetic rituals and meditation. Returning to her home village, she spends the next years as a successful *miko* (Shinto medium) but still feels that there is something missing in her spiritual life.

One day, at the start of World War II, she is drawn to enter the gates of a Zen temple and is welcomed to sit *sesshin* with the visiting roshi. Immediately, Satomi realizes that she's found what she's been looking for. Determined to become enlightened, she moves into a hut behind the village's Kannon shrine she's helped to build, and intersperses practicing zazen and working in the fields. Intuitively determining that she's ready for the next phase of her practice, Satomi moves to Sapporo to study Buddhism with a new teacher, who ordains her as a mendicant nun and grave keeper. Now truly a homeless Zen wanderer, she comes and goes, until she meets another Zen master, who directs her to the Mitaka convent in Tokyo. You'd think at this point in the story that she's finally found her true dharma home—but Satomi's karma still has a few more twists and turns, and she never makes it into the convent. Unlike her first Zen encounter, she's told at the gate that the abbess is in sesshin and can't be disturbed; this time, instead of being invited to join the sesshin, Satomi is turned away. She has one more step to go.

Directed to Taiheiji, another Tokyo temple, she finally meets the man who will become her true Zen teacher, Yasutani Roshi. Satomi's forty years of wandering are rewarded at an autumn sesshin, when she experiences awakening to the koan "Mu." At last at peace with her karma, she shaves her head and renews her nun's vows with Yasutani Roshi. Reflecting on her life's travails after her enlightenment experience, Satomi says, "I can see now that things which seemed redundant or insignificant at the time were all necessary conditions to be followed."[5]

Though Satomi Myodo completed her koan practice and could have become a Zen teacher in her own right, she chose not to. Instead, she spent the rest of her life as Yasutani Roshi's attendant, serving him until she died at the ripe old age of eighty-two. Zen had tamed her. A good Japanese woman to the end, all those who came in contact with Satomi remember her as "always calm, quiet and self-effacing, with a broad, beaming smile and infectious laughter."[6]

Satomi's autobiography opened all my old wounds; I cried most of my way through it. So much suffering. Too much to bear. All because a question pops out of nowhere into a young girl's head: "What is sincerity?" The question won't go away. It stalks her day and night, invades her dreams, and makes her do "bad" things. Alienates the girl from those who love her. Drives her from home. Takes away her mind.

My question came when I was five. I was standing in my parents' bedroom in front of my mother's triptych of mirrors, looking at the infinite reflections of a girl with a red ribbon in her hair. "Which one of those girls is me?" *Who am I?* That was how my "passionate journey" started.

Anyone who has seriously practiced Zen will tell you that the path is never straight, that it's filled with sacrifice and suffering. But if you are a deeply committed, truly sincere seeker like Satomi Myodo, you go on, no matter what the cost. You can't do otherwise. I'm beginning to think that's the *real* meaning behind all those self-mutilation metaphors that keep cropping up in the sutras. Easy enough said. But, putting your unconditional trust in a Zen teacher, regardless of what he says or does to you, isn't easy at all. At least for me, it wasn't. Maybe it was because I got too close to my teacher too soon, that I got so caught up in judging instead of learning from him. Things might have been different if I hadn't let our cultural differences get in the way. I don't know. But that's all hindsight. What I *do* know is that a Japanese-style "monks' night out" was a major confrontation that would eventually contribute to my break with Dokyu Roshi—and with Japanese Zen.

7

That Extra Jaw Muscle

Not-So-Spiritual Hunger

Mr. Yamato, the owner of the French restaurant Dokyu Roshi had invited me to, came in his custom-designed Toyota to pick us up himself. I was the only woman in the car, and of course the conversation was entirely in Japanese. Dokyu Roshi sat up front with Mr. Yamato, wearing the same princely priest's outfit he'd worn the night we dined with the Hanakawas in Tokyo. Let me see. That was on the night of our arrival in Japan . . . How many eons ago? Yo-san sat between me and the restaurant owner's nephew in the back seat, pretending I didn't exist. Without the *roshi* ordering him to, he didn't dare translate as much as a word for my benefit. So I spent most of the forty-five-minute drive to the restaurant making up my own version of the men's conversation, imagining sexist jokes at my expense, stock market quotations, monastery gossip, and every anti-American cliché I could conjure up. I got bored after a while and decided to talk to the nephew, who, the roshi told me as we were getting into the car, had trained as a chef in Paris for two years.

Turning to face him, I asked the nephew in French what he thought of the five-star Tour D'Argent in Paris but he didn't even bother to look at me, no less answer my question. Through Yo-san, whom he addressed from the rear-view mirror, the uncle let me know that his nephew had never learned French, that despite the two years they'd spent training as chefs in Paris neither of them had learned any words in that language but the names of food and wine. I found this hilarious and burst out laughing—too long and too loud, as it turned out, for Dokyu Roshi swiveled around and glared at me angrily. Women, I remembered too late, do not speak in Japan unless they are spoken to; decent women do not laugh out loud with their mouths open—and I had guffawed. Fortunately, we pulled up to the restaurant then.

We walked down a steep flight of carpeted stairs and through a vestibule smelling of overcooked egg, and were ushered into the restaurant proper and seated at a table elaborately set with gold-rimmed dinner plates and sculpted crystal goblets. We were the only diners, as Mr. Yamato had closed the restaurant to the public for the evening. A second monastery patron joined us a few minutes later and was introduced as "The Doctor." Something about the man— maybe it was his handsome face and silver hair, or his British tweeds and Sulka tie, or his refined manners, I don't know which—encouraged me to say a few words to him in English. To my delight, "The Doctor" gave me a polite English reply. He also shook my hand Western-style instead of bowing, which made me almost giddy with gratitude. Unfortunately, "The Doctor's" English was limited to polite greetings only, and he had a penchant for launching into long Japanese monologues. But I'll say this for him: he did try to include me in the conversation by making eye contact and waiting for Yo-san to translate his remarks into English for my benefit. That is, until Dokyu Roshi grew annoyed at the interruptions and ordered Yo-san to stop.

The meal opened with a traditional Japanese tea ceremony, with Yo-san doing the officiating. That took almost an hour. By the time we finished I had a splitting hunger headache. The waiter passed around a basket of hot towels and then a tray of Japanese hors d'oeuvres accompanied by several bottles of wine. First there was sherry, then cold sake, then an awful resinous Japanese Blanc de Blanc, and then an excellent French Chablis, then a passable German Moselle . . . an entire United Nations of wine. On and on it went. I made so many trips to the toilet that the Roshi suggested in a loud voice, in English, that I change seats with Yo-san, hinting that I might have an accident. Feeling my face go red, I looked around the table to see if anyone but Yo-san had understood the Roshi's insult, but the other men were too busy talking and drinking to take note of my embarrassment.

"You like?" the restaurant owner pleaded with me after every sip of wine. (As the only Westerner at the table, I had been appointed chief wine taster.)

"Ah . . . very . . . ah, crisp," I said, trying not to wrinkle my nose as the Japanese Blanc de Blanc burned its way into my gut. After drinking six and a half glasses of assorted wines, it was becoming impossible to distinguish a glass of port from a margarita. Besides, I was having enough trouble keeping my trips to the toilet to a minimum so as not to ruffle Dokyu Roshi's feathers.

Seated to my right, Yo-san, his nose red from drinking, wasn't eating a thing. Not that there was anything much to eat: not one piece of bread, not so much as a pat of butter had been placed on the table since the wine had arrived. We weren't even served water, the crystal goblets having been appropriated for the endless flow of wine. At last the waiter appeared with a tiny fish pate, which I tried eating slowly and with as much appreciation as I could muster, since the pleading eyes of the restaurant owner were trained directly on my mouth. The sauce in which the pate swam, a sugary Japanese plum wine concoction, made it virtually inedible. I looked up at Mr. Yamato after every bite, enthusiastically nodding my approval.

A creamed green tea soup followed next, then a tepid rolled fish filet in another version of the Japanese plum wine sauce, each course accompanied by yet another bottle of wine. I was beginning to feel less like a Buddhist monk than a guest at a Roman orgy getting ready to retire to the *vomitorium* before resuming the next round of eating and drinking.

Through the wine cloud that floated over the table, I heard the names "Dogen" and "Hakuin" and realized that "The Doctor" was haranguing Dokyu Roshi with "philosophical Zen talking," one of his least favorite dinner topics. "When eating, just eat. When sitting *zazen*, just sit *zazen*. No need philosophical Zen talking," he'd

admonish me whenever I had tried to engage him in serious conversation in the London *zendo* kitchen. The roshi had a sour look
on his face, but since "The Doctor" was a big Ryutakuji supporter,
he couldn't tell him to shut up the way he might have if I were haranguing him with "Zen talking" while we were eating. The roshi
wasn't eating much, and he only sniffed at the wine as it came his
way. I, on the other hand, had already finished almost seven glasses
of wine by then, and our Francophile host was standing over me
with yet another refill. I pretended to take a sip then pushed away
the glass as he left to fetch the next bottle.

An abbreviated slab of tissue-thin beef soaked in watery mayonnaise and green onion relish was served next, propped against a slice
of whole wheat toast on one side and a thick heel of rye bread on the
other. I was surreptitiously reaching under my blouse and opening the
top button of my skirt when the waiter came out of the kitchen with a
salad—four strips of shredded cabbage and two carrot slivers soaked
in the same watery mayonnaise as before, only this time accompanied
by chicken bits.

When, as all good things must, the meal finally ended, I allowed
myself a final visit to the toilet. On my way I could not help remembering the monks back at Ryutakuji eating their rice and pickles while
the abbot, his head monk, and I, who was not a novice-in-training but
an American "guest," were dining in an ersatz French restaurant and
getting drunk. Poor Yo-san looked ready to fall off his chair, yet he
kept right on bowing and smiling. "Is there no limit to Japanese formality?" I thought. "Or is it all those years of Zen training?" It was
getting awfully hard to tell where one began and the other ended.

In the middle of one of "The Doctor's" monologues, Dokyu
Roshi suddenly sprang up from his seat.

"We go, Yo-san," he announced in English.

Undeterred, "The Doctor" went on to make a final point about
Dogen's great Zen classic, *Shobogenzo*. But the Roshi was already
headed toward the exit.

"How you like?" Demanding a final verdict, Mr. Yamato stood in
the vestibule smiling at me.

"*Magnifique*," I said, tottering away from him drunkenly. To Yo-
san, I said, "Tell him I especially liked the second Japanese wine, the

Chateau Brilliant 1977, the one he said Queen Elizabeth liked so much on her visit to Japan. It was as good as the French."

Beaming with pride, Mr. Yamato presented me with gifts from behind the cloakroom counter. I felt like an ingrate as I accepted the medallion embossed with the restaurant's fleur-de-lis logo and a dozen long-stemmed, fuchsia-tinted white roses.

"*Arigato! Arigato!* It was wonderful, just wonderful!" I called over my shoulder as the door closed behind me.

The first thing I saw when I stepped outside was Dokyu Roshi crossing the street, heading toward a kiosk in search of cigarettes, cutting a weird monkish figure in his robes as he pushed his way through a group of leather-jacketed bikers lounging against their parked Harleys. I saw from his expression when he returned that he was ready to explode, and that his anger was directed at me.

"People should not talk philosophy when they eat!" he screamed into my face. "Eating time is no time to spoil the taste of food with philosophical talking. Make sick. I don't like intellectuals!" Hunching his shoulders, the roshi stalked away from me, got into the back seat of the car, and slammed the door shut before I could get in. I opened the door and climbed in over him. Tucking myself into the opposite corner of the back seat, I focused every bit of my attention on not vomiting all over the roshi's elegant robes or Mr. Yamato's Givenchy-designed upholstery. Yo-san was already sitting up front. Mr. Yamato had remained behind to close the restaurant, and his wife, making her first appearance of the evening, was introduced as our designated driver.

Mrs. Yamato had pink curlers in her hair, talked with a cigarette dangling from one side of her mouth, and drove like a maniac. Evidently, the roshi was enjoying her droll patter, for he'd quickly dropped his bad mood. Throwing back his head and slapping his knee, he roared with laughter at every nonphilosophical word coming out of Mrs. Yamato's mouth. The more he laughed, the more furious I got; at one point I had to resist the temptation to lean over, open the door, and push him out of the speeding car. Was I jealous, or what?

Leaving my gifts behind on the seat, I was the first to jump out of the car when Mrs. Yamato pulled up to the main hall with brakes screeching. As soon as the roshi got out, I walked up to him and told him in no uncertain terms that he had no business insulting me in public, that I wasn't so dumb that I couldn't tell the difference between a "Zen teaching" and plain old rudeness—Japanese or American.

In the middle of trying to light a cigarette that refused to be lit with a damp match, the roshi was caught off guard.

Silenced by my outburst, Mrs. Yamato stuck her head out of the driver's window and waited to see what would happen next.

"Perle-san, why you angry? You tell me. I walk you home." The roshi took hold of my arm.

"No! Let go of me!" I pulled away from him and ran down the cinder path toward my cottage.

Dokyu Roshi exchanged a few words with Mrs. Yamato; then she started the car and drove off.

Pushing and Pulling

I stopped running only when I had reached the lotus pond and was too far away for the roshi to catch up with me. Something compelled me to stop exactly at that spot and look up. It was amazing. I'd never seen anything like it. There were so many stars overhead that they appeared to be crowding each other out of the midnight sky. They reminded me of the passengers in the Tokyo subway stations crammed into the trains by the white-gloved "pushers" stationed at every door. I couldn't believe how alike they were, those masses of silent, impassive stars, and those Japanese subway riders—equally silent and impassive in the middle of all that pushing. No one complained. No fights broke out. No one seemed to resent being crammed into the trains, and the pushers themselves weren't particularly hostile or aggressive. On the contrary, they were extremely courteous. It was exactly the opposite of the New York subway, where the smallest thing could set off a fight at any moment, and where, at the time I left, homicidal maniacs were pushing riders onto the subway tracks in front of oncoming trains on an average of once a month. How, I wondered, did the Japanese manage to be so brutal and so civilized at the same time? Was this what Zen "discipline" was about? And where did I belong in all of this?

It wasn't exactly a moment of great spiritual awakening, but standing at the lotus pond looking up at the stars did spark an insight into my troubled relationship with traditional Japanese Zen. I was a subway rider and Dokyu Roshi was a "pusher." Japanese etiquette demanded he be courteous—to an extent. But it was his job to push me into the train, even if it meant he had to push me hard, or else I might miss the train. An experienced pusher, he knew I wouldn't complain because I really wanted to get on that train, that I was determined to make that journey no matter what happened. On the other hand, I'd shown him that I wasn't a *Japanese* subway rider but an American walking around in monk's clothing, only pretending to be Japanese. Of course, being American, I'd bucked up against being pushed. From the roshi's Japanese vantage point, I had acted inappropriately, pulling away to protect myself like a "typical greenhouse person" (his favorite euphemism for tender-skinned Westerners). Worse yet, I was a woman! Hadn't he told me often enough that I was his bad karma from a past life come back to haunt him? If he really believed that (and I was beginning to think he did), why *shouldn't* the roshi resent me? He certainly wasn't shy about letting me know when I was getting out of line.

I was sure he'd deliberately staged the little scene in front of the restaurant to push me back into my place on the enlightenment train, to let me know I wasn't, like Yo-san, *real* potential roshi material, and—unless my emotions got out of the way—never would be. True, the roshi had been furious with "The Doctor" for spoiling his meal and ruining his evening with "Zen talking," but his outburst clearly had been aimed at me. Who better embodied everything he hated about Westerners?

A case in point: After the string of funerals at the monastery, we'd taken a weekend off and traveled together to Kyoto. As we were sitting in a soba shop eating udon soup, the roshi suddenly looked up from his bowl and said, "No matter how long you live in Japan, you never learn to eat noodles like real Japanese person."

Having just finished slurping a mouthful of noodles with what I believed was the requisite amount of gusto, I asked, "Why not?"

The roshi pointed to his jaw and said, "Because Japanese person have extra chewing muscle right here."

I laughed so hard I sprayed a mouthful of soup and noodle bits in his direction.

"Sorry," I said, covering my mouth with my napkin as soon as I could catch my breath and stop laughing. "You don't really believe that, do you, Roshi?"

"I serious. Japanese scientist write this in newspaper I read long time ago."

I hadn't noticed until then that behind him, perched like a Buddha on a raised altar, the gargantuan Sony television set had been turned on. Every diner in the soba shop was fixated on the screen, watching a televangelist Buddhist priest deliver a raise-the-roof sermon, and they were all slurping their noodles in unison with that extra Japanese jaw muscle!

"Like everything else in Japan, eating noodles is tradition," the roshi said.

He had also used the word "tradition" in describing the contents of every Kyoto shrine, temple, and tacky souvenir shop we visited that weekend. Yet, when I pressed him to look around, pointing to the punk teenagers with their pink and purple Mohawk hairdos hanging around the train station, even the roshi had to admit that the core of Japanese tradition had long been lost. Even he hadn't been able to hide his disgust at the empty formality passing for Zen in the great temples whose evangelical abbots were being chauffeured around Kyoto in their Mercedes limousines and dispensing TV dharma to the masses.

Hoping for a closer look at one of those Zen abbots, I turned on the television set in my hotel room on my last night in Kyoto, but it must have been too late for sermons. All I got was a videotaped tea ceremony repeated every hour on the hour on the same cable station offering "pornographic dreams" in English. Well, wasn't that what Dokyu Roshi would call a true Zen experience? After all, if Bodhidharma, the founder of Zen himself, said there was nothing holy, then did it really matter whether you delivered a televised sermon or performed a tea ceremony or had pornographic dreams?

I thought of old Soen Roshi sitting in his little hut on the mountaintop. Was it too much purity and too little sex that had driven him out of circulation? Yo-san had once told me that the sexual misadventures of one of Soen's students had broken his heart, and that Soen had withdrawn to his hermitage when he had received calls pleading for him to intercede. Soen Roshi had been celibate all his life and apparently was unable to deal with sexual transgressions.

Could sexual deprivation be the reason so many monks were alcoholics, I wondered. At the monastery, after the lights-out bell had been rung, I used to hear the monks laughing in the bamboo grove behind my cottage as they passed around a smuggled bottle of sake. Once, someone even brought a radio and I heard them dancing to disco music. Listening to their muffled laughter, I recalled stories that Mama Hanakawa had told me about the monks. I was shocked then, but not anymore. On arriving in Japan I had naively expected Zen monks to be bodhisattavas, like the serenely smiling statues with gentle faces I'd seen in Western museums. But I learned soon enough that monks weren't statues. They were living, breathing, flawed human beings. It wasn't the monks that were the problem. It was me.

The Irish American Kannon

I may not have been cut out to be a monk, but Maura O'Halloran, an Irish American woman who preceded me by five years, certainly seemed better suited to Japanese monastic life. Given the dharma name "Soshin" by Go Roshi, her teacher, Maura came to Japan in 1979 to study with him at Toshoji, his small suburban Tokyo temple. Stunning not only her teacher with her quick and profound enlightenment experience, but her fellow monks and temple patrons (as well as everyone else in Japan who came in contact with her), Maura appeared to be born to the Zen life. One of those spiritual prodigies every Zen practitioner dreams of being, Maura seemed to be picking up her past life as a monk from the day she landed in Japan. The speed with which she came to her first awakening and then sprinted through several hundred koans in a matter of months is legendary not only at Toshoji, her home temple, but throughout Japan. Maura was not merely ordained as a priest but was given transmission and declared a Zen teacher after only three years of training! Considering that she was only twenty-six at the time of her certification, it seemed her course was clear: Maura would become head monk, then temple priest, and finally, roshi. This would have been quite a feat—since Go Roshi seemed determined from the very first that Maura "Soshin" O'Halloran, a Western woman, would be one of his principal successors—in Japan. Tragically, Maura's Zen career was cut short when she was killed in a bus accident while visiting Thailand.

A testament to her brilliant but all-too-brief Zen life, memorials and eulogies poured in from all over the world in the wake of Maura's death. At Kannonji, Toshoji's affiliate temple, a Kannon statue was dedicated in her honor. The Japanese inscription, translated by Shiro Tachibana, is worth quoting as an example of the Soto Zen community's love and admiration for their Irish American Kannon.

> **"*Maura Kannon (A Brief History)*"**
> *Miss Maura O'Halloran from Ireland.*
>   *On the 10th of October . . . [1979], at Toshoji Temple she became a nun and completed 1,000 days of continuous Zen practice at Toshoji and Kannonji Temples. Her daily practice included three hours of sleeping in the zazen position and twenty hours of devotion to her studies in order to attain salvation not only for herself but also for all people. . . .*
>   *She is given the posthumous name of "Great Enlightened Lady, of the same heart and mind as the Great Teacher Buddha." Miss Maura has been a real incarnation of Kannon Bosatsu to be loved and respected forever. . . .*
>   *Nirvana Day [February 15th] . . . [1983], by Tetsu-gyu So-in, founder of Kannonji Temple.*[1]

Nothing I've ever come across, from either the Japanese Soto or Rinzai Zen community, matches this iconic tribute to a Western woman's spiritual accomplishment. Clearly, Maura O'Halloran was a major exception to the Japanese monastic rule. Personally, though, I value the posthumous record Maura left behind in her collected letters and journal entries more highly than the formal recognition of the Zen establishment. The intimate picture of her struggle as a Western woman trying to be a "Zen monk" in Japan is, to me, even more touching than her public persona. As a woman who tried but failed to follow the same path, I can especially identify with the emotional swings she experienced, the highs and lows, moments of assurance quickly followed by seemingly endless days and nights of deflation and self-doubt—an up-and-down roller coaster ride of emotions: loving monastic Zen practice one day, and hating it so much the next that she was ready to pack up and leave without notifying even her beloved roshi.

Maura describes the struggle in her own words in the following sampling of letters and journal entries collected by Ruth O'Halloran after her daughter's death.[2]

December, 1979: On first arriving at Toshoji, Maura writes an effusive letter to her mother telling her, *"The place is totally non-sexist . . . I saw wood and move furniture with the rest of them . . . I'm totally 'one of the lads,' except I'm not bald."*

But her spirits are quickly dampened only a short while later, after her *dokusan* (interview) with Go Roshi. Certain that she's experienced her first *kensho* (enlightenment), instead of being confirmed, Maura is abashed when the *roshi* curtly orders her to "continue" meditating before ringing her out of the room. In her journal, she writes despairingly: "I felt crushed. He didn't know. Didn't he know? How could he know? But I knew. Damn . . . I was cold and sick of [cleaning] . . . so from guilt I was working more. Hating the guilt. Thinking of home and family and how long I'd be stuck doing stupid, menial cleaning and with no enlightenment . . . I decide monastery life is not for me. I love life too much to lock myself away. Maybe six months, a good chance to work on myself . . . Zen is very important to me. I think I'll leave by summer but continue to study Zen when I get to Paris."

Maura's decision to give it all up is immediately followed by a change of heart after Go Roshi and the monks arrange back-to-back, Western-style Christmas and New Year's Eve parties especially for her. She notes in her journal: "These men are wonderful. They show me such genuine warmth and love that I'm thriving . . . At first . . . I felt I was going mad . . . Now I'm not so extreme, but maybe it's necessary to go a little crazy to break the ego. Or maybe that's 'Zen sickness.' . . . Little by little I'm gaining understanding, though my meditations have been very shallow." Then ending her New Year's Day reflections on an ecstatic high note, she adds: "I want to be a Zen master."

Maura's commitment to becoming a Zen master grows stronger as she progresses in her practice, yet she still longs to return to her life in the West. Realizing that she can't have it both ways, she writes in her journal: "I do want to continue with my outside life at some stage and finish the koans. So maybe I should find a suitable temple and get on with it, as I'll have to break from here sooner or later. I love, respect, and trust Roshi completely, yet I should not be attached even to him."

After three months, the harsh realities of monastery life take over as the novelty wears off and the monks grow less friendly. Irked by Go Roshi's open preference for his *gaijin* (foreign) woman disciple, they no longer ply their now shaven-headed, black-robed dharma sister with gifts and parties and kind words. Writing in her journal that the monks now "bark" at her instead of talking to her, Maura attempts to cope with their hostility by attributing it to changing "causes and conditions" and partly blames herself for not always being "gentle and kind."

At last, during a sesshin at Kannonji, Go Roshi's affiliate temple, her enlightenment is publicly confirmed. And then, to everyone's astonishment, the roshi announces his plans to turn Kannonji Temple into an international Zen center and make Maura the head priest. No less astonished than Go Roshi's other monks (all of them Japanese, and some her seniors), Maura is even more torn than before between her commitment to the priesthood and her desire to return to the West as a lay Zen teacher. Even more daunting at this stage is her discovery that "Women are really repressed here, forced into the mold of a giggling innocent. At first I rather enjoyed the surprise and admiration with which I was treated. Now I feel its oppressiveness, for it's only because I'm female."

Gradually, it begins to dawn on Maura that she is in fact being regarded as some sort of exotic pet. To confuse her further, Go Roshi announces at a short *sesshin* in the spring of 1980 that she could become "the greatest woman priest in Japan." As Maura wryly comments in her journal, "the competition is not exactly overwhelming."

When a television crew appears to interview her, Maura now suspects that she is being exploited. With media persistency amounting to almost daily harassment, she fears her reputation as the *gaijin* Zen "wonder woman" is being turned into a publicity stunt. Could she be a pawn in a political maneuver engineered to fill the thinning ranks of Japanese monks by bringing more Westerners to Soto Zen?

What happens in March of 1981 proves that Maura is indeed being groomed—if not exploited—for something big. In a letter to her mother, she writes of being *"floored"* when Go Roshi tells her that for refusing to marry the man of his choice, he has stripped his daughter of her dowry and plans to give the temple to Maura as a *"wedding present with which to build an international Zen dojo"*—provided she marries *"a good Zen man."* Though alarmed (and flattered) by the roshi's offer, Maura has the presence of mind to refuse him. In her journal, she muses: "I've been socialized, I don't know how or who did it . . . but now I jump up, get the tea, fetch like a servant or a dog or a Japanese wife. It is a real socialization because I wasn't even aware of it and don't really mind. But thank God I wasn't born here and will never marry a Japanese man."

When Go Roshi persists in his attempt to make Maura head priest of Kannonji temple by marrying her off to the one remaining monk she hasn't rejected, she "finally [clicks] on the reason for all the marriage bit: My purpose is to make kids."

Again Maura refuses the offer. But Go Roshi is determined to impose his plans for her future and won't be thwarted. Insisting that she marry a Japanese man, he begins "pushing" her to "stay in Japan and become his successor." (Note that she, too, uses the word "pushing" to describe the way her teacher treats her.) Responding to the pressure, a "disoriented" Maura confesses in her journal: "All my previous principles, goals, opinions, seem totally changed. Whether I'm here or in Ireland, married or not, none of it seems a big deal. It seems I should assent and truly throw my life away for training . . . In the real world, Roshi's and my ideas are so different. But it seems I have no criteria left by which to make a decision. Anything is okay. It's a strange feeling, not a problem, but definitely disorienting."

Though often typical of monks at her advanced stage of training, Maura's total surrender of identity is a form of "Zen sickness," what the ancient teachers called "sitting on top of a one-hundred-foot pole." It happens when you feel so freed of your "self," so emptied, that you're ready for a total makeover by your teacher. Fortunately in most cases, this is only a stage, and you come out of it as your practice matures and you begin to stand on your own two feet. Maura is already on her way to taking the next step off the hundred-foot pole when she is assisted by a little "push" from one of the senior monks who complains of Go Roshi's "exaggerations of [her] worth and his condemnation of the Japanese." Lamenting in her journal that she "[wishes] he wouldn't do it," Maura is finally ready to assert herself. However painful her parting from Go Roshi will be, she knows she must leave Japan and carve out her own Zen path in the West. Tragically, she never makes it back home.

In her afterward to *Pure Heart, Enlightened Mind,* Patricia Daien Bennage extols Maura "Soshin" O'Halloran for paving the way for the second wave of Western women who, like herself, have chosen to practice monastic Zen in Japan. An advocate of hard training, Patricia refers to the freezing, sleeplessness, and malnutrition Maura endured as "polishing." I wonder . . . Has she been reading the same journal and letters—or is she talking about someone else, a different Maura O'Halloran from the one I'm talking about, a woman filtered through Patricia's own monastically inclined lens? Then again, as I said at the outset of this story, I never succeeded in becoming a monk, in Japan or anywhere. Apparently Patricia did a better job of it. Maybe that's why she ignores the fact that in the end Maura "Soshin" O'Halloran abandoned the life of a Japanese Zen professional for that of a Western lay woman and was on her way home when she died.

Could it be that after everything was said and done, Maura had had enough of "pushing"? Enough of the kind of asceticism that borders on martyrdom? Enough of seeking after sainthood? When you come down to it, how much "pushing" is too much, especially when, unlike the Japanese, you don't have that extra jaw muscle to rely on?

Tolerance levels vary. Though not in Maura's or Patricia's league, mine was pretty high—or so I thought.

The Final Push

We'd finished morning zazen and I'd remained behind to talk to the roshi after the regular sitters had left. He was standing with his back to me, shouting into a cordless telephone in Japanese. He was wearing a white tank top and sky blue monk's workpants with a rope for a belt.

He had tied an oversized handkerchief around his head and was smoking. His glasses lay on the counter. He had made tea. Moving so as not to disturb him, I sidled past him and poured myself a mug of tea. The roshi turned around and, seeing me standing there, shook his head. Seeing he wanted privacy, I took the mug back into the zendo, opened a folding chair, sat down, and turning my back on him, drank my tea.

Hollering "*mushi mushi*" into the receiver, the roshi snapped the cordless telephone back into its cradle and came out of the kitchen.

"What happen, Perle-san? You too much drinking last night? Is that why you sleeping through morning zazen?" he laughed, pointing at me with the cigarette nesting between his middle and index fingers.

I got up from the folding chair and turned around to face him, the mug shaking in my hands. I set it down on the island counter dividing the kitchen from the zendo.

"No, it's not a hangover, Roshi."

"What, you have fight with husband? I tell you many times it better you not fight with husband and make him angry."

"He's not angry. He's doing quite well, in fact."

Motioning for me to sit down, the roshi pulled up another folding chair for himself, opened it, and sat down opposite me.

"You all white in face, no look good."

"Roshi, can you please put out the cigarette? The smoke is bothering me."

Tossing the cigarette across the counter into the sink, the roshi turned to me and said, "You want more tea?"

"No thanks."

The two of us sat silently looking at each other. That was the day I left Dokyu Roshi for good. As a woman, and a feminist, it would no longer be possible for me to go on training in a Zen tradition dominated by misogyny. Even the Buddha himself was highly conflicted when it came to his feelings about women: "[Will] I now desire your daughter, that container with its nine orifices filled with feces and urine? Quite apart from taking your daughter by the hand and kissing her I would be disgusted even to wipe my feet on her as I would on a door mat."[3]

That tirade makes you wonder whether the Buddha wasn't a little bit tempted, doesn't it? Which—if you will indulge me in a little foray into cultural anthropology—brings us to the subject of Western guilt vs. Japanese shame.

The debate started just after World War II, when American anthropologist Ruth Benedict published her controversial book *The Chrysanthemum and the Sword: Patterns of Japanese Culture.*[4] Much was being written in those early postwar years about Japanese and Western cultural differences because the American occupiers were intent on "democratizing" a fascist Japan. (Turn on your television set or your computer and you're bound to find a similar debate on Iraqi versus American culture today.) Benedict argued that because the Japanese did not worship one god but were animists and had no word for "sin," they did not suffer guilt. Instead, they had constructed an elaborate system based on loyalty to the "tribe" that excluded all others. So tightly knit was this exclusive ("superior") society, that even the slightest tear in the fabric was punished by ostracism—a shame so great as to leave only suicide as an honorable way of rectifying it. Hence, the Japanese obsession with saving face, and the hyped-up samurai ethos of *seppuku* (ritual suicide by self-disembowelment). How, one might ask, is this Buddhist? It's not. Japanese Buddhism is really a combination of indigenous Shinto (shamanist) religion, and Buddhism, Taoism, and Confucianism—all imported from China. Infused with a heavy dose of militarism, Zen became the samurai version of Buddhism.

Imbued by the Judeo-Christian notion of sin, Westerners find the notion of shame too ambiguous and seek something akin to guilt as a rationale for "moral" behavior. Since the Japanese have no word for "sin," this can frustrate Westerners who value confessing guilt (and accepting punishment) for "immoral" behavior over saving face. But, as Robert C. Christopher, a journalist who spent many years in Japan, points out: "[T]he Japanese as a people distrust and shun straightforward verbal communication . . . As [they] see it, plain speaking . . . tends to commit the speaker to a hard-and-fast position, and thus can easily provoke direct confrontation—which all Japanese dread."[5] Christopher goes on to say that those Japanese who have contact with Western people or have lived in the West often "try to accommodate to this strange foreign taste [for confrontation] without much success."[6] He added that sex in Japan "is not a moral issue," that "male philandering, whether with occasional partners or with a regular mistress, has always been taken as a matter of course,"[7] and that Japanese men feel superior to women simply because they are men. This may account in part for why—despite their own and their teachers' efforts to accommodate each other's contradictory attitudes toward guilt and shame—Western women like Jiyu Kennett and Maura O'Halloran also decided to leave Japan and practice Zen in the West.

In her memoir *Diary of a Zen Nun*, Nancy (Nan shin) Amphoux, an American expatriate living in Europe, describes a Japanese Zen master who blew the whole theory of guilt versus shame by dispensing with them both. Like Nancy, Taisen Deshimaru Roshi (who preferred to be called *sensei*, "teacher," rather than "roshi") was also an expatriate living in Europe. After leaving Japan and establishing La Gendronniere, a Soto Zen monastery in Alsace, he went on to create Zen centers throughout Europe that are still flourishing two decades after his death. A married priest, Deshimaru was among the most successful Japanese Zen masters in the West. Famous among his students for his worldly sophistication, he was so good at adapting to French culture, for example, that he had a bar built on monastery grounds where "on certain evenings" students were allowed to dance and drink beer, sake, liquor, and wine. Nancy writes approvingly:

> Sensei's best idea was the bar . . . [he] called it the Bonno Bar (*bonno* meaning illusions, delusion, passions, attachments) and insisted, despite much criticism and perplexity . . . that it be allowed to remain; partly because Zen does not exclude anything and tolerance is good for us all—especially, perhaps, the saintly; . . . partly because it is better for us to wash our dirty linen among ourselves than to . . . gain an unsavory reputation for ourselves; and partly because we bring our illusions with us and are seldom if ever separate from them so it is inaccurate . . . to pretend one is "retreating" into spirituality. Better that illusions should be seen and heard, he thought, and forgotten . . . But do not try to leave none at all or create no karma . . . Hence, the bar.[8]

Deshimaru's tolerance of his own, and his students' illusions, however, did not extend to shame, guilt, or remorse—none of which, he felt, had a place in a community where openness prevailed: "The past is over. Only the right action, now, counts; right for the whole group. And as circumstances are never the same twice, this minute's right action will not be right tomorrow. This is a community, so there are rules; but no rule."⁹

At first, it looks like Deshimaru has solved the problem of applying Japanese monastic discipline to lay life in the West. But when Nancy goes on to describe how this guiltless approach to Zen actually played out in daily life at La Gendronniere, the psychological expectations, and hang-ups, of Western Zen students, things get more complicated. Deshimaru inevitably becomes an omnipotent father figure, and the sibling rivalry resulting from his training produces a whole array of problems. Responding to their sensei's "intimidation," the "weak egos . . . would feel envious [of those he'd flattered] and see their envy and be stimulated," while those who had been flattered feared losing his approval.¹⁰ Even a smile could become "a slap in the face." The students' responses are mostly "childish." But some are really serious; Nancy alludes to addiction, alcoholism, and at least one "spectacular suicide." The tension must have been unbearable.

There's an inherent conflict between the self-realization at the heart of Zen practice and the unhealthy division of power between teacher and student, not just in Japan, but anywhere Zen is practiced. It's a pattern I've seen over and over again—the roshi (which in traditional Japanese Zen is often translated as "the old man" or "the old boss") becomes the father whose love and affirmation are the be-all and end-all of your existence, the ultimate authority on all aspects of your life. And you must woo him, just like you do a father. Some do it by seduction, some, like Jiyu and Maura and Nancy and me, by a combination of emulation and strong-willed obedience. The roshi may not be manipulating you; after all, his intention is to help you get rid of your "illusions," but that isn't the way it happens—especially not if you're a Westerner, and a woman.

Nancy's observations are right on target when she writes about the ideal relationship between Zen teacher and student: "A master may scold and rant and lash out, may resort to trickery and knavery in teaching your tricky and knavish ego, but a master is not trying to seduce you or possess you or do anything to you. Except, when you start pecking at the shell, help you out of it."¹¹ Though there's something slightly unnerving about her use of the term "master," she's honest about her teacher's flaws, describing him as sometimes drunk and still trying to please his dead father. Deshimaru's human weaknesses notwithstanding, Nancy goes on to praise his "heroic undertaking for a Japanese steeped in discipline and carefulness, however liberated from them he may have become by his practice, to find himself at the head of a gang of clumsy and unruly adolescents of every age in the guise of disciples, having to be scoutmaster and parent and zookeeper to all these people who were forever trying to trip him up and forever relying on him for everything."[12]

I believe Nancy Amphoux was willing to cut her sensei so much slack because she was writing from the perspective of a mature Zen practitioner looking back on her growing pains—but not as a *woman Zen practitioner*. Lumping together Zen students of both genders as "clumsy and unruly adolescents," she never singled out her own or other women's problems for discussion. And as we know, male and female "adolescents" have very different problems relating to their fathers. I think Maura O'Halloran better expressed what most Western women Zen practitioners go through when she complained of becoming "socialized" into female servility in her efforts to please Go Roshi—almost to the point where she let herself be pushed into marrying a Japanese man of her teacher's choosing! You could say that, until she took her Zen practice—and her decisions about her life—into her own hands, Maura's obedience was motivated by guilt. (She'd been a Catholic before becoming a Buddhist.) In the case of Nancy, a free thinker, Deshimaru's rejection of guilt as an obstruction to Zen practice was equally important in fostering her independence. Otherwise, I don't think she could have been as detached in assessing her teacher's spiritual gifts *and* his flaws. Although they came to it from opposite sides of the fence, Western "guilt" seems to have been instrumental for both women in sustaining their Japanese "shame-based" Zen practice.

In the end, however, I wouldn't put too much importance on the shame versus guilt debate. Accounting even for significant cultural differences between Japanese and Westerners, it would seem that neither guilt nor shame, but sexism, is the universal phenomenon that trumps them both. This became evident when Zen moved from "misogynist Asia" to the "sexually liberated" West. Over centuries, Zen had changed and adapted to suit every country it traveled to, from India to China, Korea, Japan, and Vietnam. So why, when it came to the West, wasn't it adapted to suit our more egalitarian societies? It certainly didn't take long for Western male Zen masters to exploit female students or deny them a place in the teaching hierarchy. Unfortunately, a good number of them went even further than their more traditionally sexist Asian Zen masters—until Western women themselves finally forced the issue. So maybe the problem isn't only about culture. Maybe it's about gender.

With this thought in mind, let's turn to the story of "How WomanZen Won the West."

Part Two

8

"American Layman Zen"

Zen in Hawai'i

My experience in Japan had pretty much cured me of the notion that Zen in the West was somehow less authentic. Nevertheless, it took a year for me to sufficiently recover from my break with Dokyu Roshi before seeking out another Zen teacher. Though still somewhat skeptical about what he'd sneeringly called "American layman Zen," I decided to take up the invitation of a woman I'd met in Jerusalem to come to Hawai'i and experience Zen lay practice for myself with her teacher, Robert Aitken. Referred to as the "dean of American roshis," Aitken had trained with both Soen and Yasutani Roshis in Japan before becoming the student of lay Zen teacher Yamada Roshi, Yasutani's successor. A conscientious objector and peace activist, Aitken's wartime experiences as a prisoner in Japan had strongly influenced the direction he would later take as Yamada Roshi's successor. A married householder, poet, schoolteacher, and well-known author of books outlining a more appropriately democratic form of Zen practice, Aitken's antimilitarist stance had brought many disaffected Western and Asian American Zen students to his Hawai'i Diamond Sangha. Impressed by the gentle, ethical tone of Aitken Roshi's *Taking the Path of Zen* and eager to meet him in person, I flew to Hawai'i.

Landing at Honolulu airport in late autumn of 1986, I was a little disappointed to see that it was not Diane, the friendly Zen student I'd met in Jerusalem, who came to pick me up, but a sour-faced woman with straw-colored hair. (I'll call her "Linda.") Unprepared for the heat, and rubber-kneed from the twelve-hour flight from New York, I made my way through the perfumed air—"Plumeria," Linda informed me, "from the leis they bring the tour groups." At the baggage carousel, I looked around for help with my suitcases, but Linda didn't offer any. Standing off to one side, still holding her "Koko An Zendo" sign, she didn't so much as look in my direction.

I dragged my luggage outside and piled it into the backseat of the car, a faded yellow two-door Toyota that was too rusty on the passenger side to open and had a string holding together the handle of the door on the driver's side. Following Linda's instructions, I entered first, squeezing past the steering wheel and climbing over the automatic gear shift into the passenger seat.

"You won't need half of what you've got there," Linda said, pointing to my luggage piled high in the backseat.

"Yeah, well . . ." I mumbled, wondering what it was about her that made me feel like apologizing for everything. Was this going to be another "Priscilla Devon" experience?

The car's air-conditioner wasn't working, so I rolled the window a quarter of the way down, which was as far as it would go. Linda didn't appear to be interested in pursuing further conversation and drove on in what I construed to be meditative silence. Not feeling particularly meditative myself, I looked out the window. It was caked with dust, casting a brown patina over the passing scenery. As far as I could tell, we were driving on a nondescript American freeway bordered by pink and ochre sandstone apartment buildings that reminded me of Miami. The difference here, though, was the light. It was magical—like no other light I'd seen in anywhere else in the world.

Leaving the freeway, Linda pulled the reluctant yellow heap uphill, then downhill into a lush green residential neighborhood in a valley, stopping on a paved incline in a narrow lane bordered by a mixed grove of mango and avocado trees that all but hid a big weathered white clapboard house with an enormous lava stone chimney. After getting out of the car and watching me again squirm my way over the automatic gear shift and past the steering wheel, Linda, still offering no assistance, suggested I leave the luggage where it was in the back. I must have looked doubtfully at the rope-fastened door, because she smiled at me for the first time then and said, "Don't worry, nobody will steal it."

I followed her down four steep stone steps onto a stone path dividing a vegetable patch from a miniature Japanese rock garden with a baby Jizo Buddha statue bordered by a tiny goldfish pond. Depositing our shoes in a wooden cupboard filled with an assortment of sneakers, zoris (sandals), and mud-caked Wellingtons, we entered the house through a screen door, into a forlorn-looking kitchen which, except for the excited chirping of birds invading the open louvered windows, was devoid of any sound. From the foyer leading to what I presumed was the *zendo*, came the fragrant whiff of sandalwood incense.

"Are they meditating?" I whispered.

"No, everyone's at the beach." Linda motioned toward the refrigerator. "Want some apple juice?"

"Just water, thank you." I shook my head. "The beach?"

Linda smiled, "When we're not doing *sesshin*, we sit twice a day, at six in the morning and at seven at night. We eat breakfast together in silence after chanting meal sutras, do two hours of *samu*—work practice (you'll most likely be assigned to tending the compost heap out back)—and then we're off on our own till five, when we eat supper together out on the porch." She handed me a glass of water and poured some apple juice for herself. We'd just finished drinking when, hearing someone moving around in the next room, Linda motioned for me to follow her.

"Oh, lucky for you. Manfred's here. He'll be able to help you upstairs with your luggage."

Originally Robert and Anne Aitken's private residence, the house had been converted into a Zen center. The zendo (meditation hall) was on the first floor, in what had been the living and dining room areas. Midway, a screen door led out onto a large wood-floor porch at the center of which stood a long wooden table. The bronze bell and clapper used for announcing *dokusan* (interviews with the roshi), set in a wood frame, was standing in a corner. Above it hung the *han*, the thick wooden board used for striking the meditation and meal time hours. A cottage containing a library that doubled as the roshi's interview room and the small, self-contained apartment he and his wife occupied during sesshin stood in the back yard a few feet away from the main house.

Inside the zendo, opposite the screen door leading to the porch, was a staircase leading to the residents' sleeping quarters: two bedrooms for men on the right at the head of the stairs, one large bedroom on the left for women, and a bathroom between them. At the zendo's far wall, set against a lava rock fireplace, stood a mahogany altar, at the center of which an impressive red and gold painted statue of Bodhidharma, the legendary founder of Zen, surrounded by an incense pot, flowers, and two offering bowls of rice and water, gazed over two long rows of black meditation cushions lining the walls.

A very tall man in black monk's robes had just gotten up from the cushion closest to the altar and was heading for the porch when Linda blocked his path to the door. "Gotcha!" The man, who looked to be in his early thirties, had a strong, square face and was wearing old fashioned, wire-rimmed glasses. Immediately, I saw that this was no traditional monk, for, despite the black robes, he was not bald and clean shaven but had a head of thick brown hair and a matching brown beard.

"Manfred, meet Perle. She's just arrived from New York and has hundreds of bags and with my bad back I can't help her lift them, so will you help her bring them upstairs? Please, pretty please?"

I watched in awe as, chirping and battering her eyelashes, Linda transformed herself from the sour-faced woman who had greeted me at the airport into a seductive flirt.

Manfred removed his glasses and, moving closer, peered into my eyes. "You look very familiar. Have you ever sat sesshin in Europe?"

"I sat in London. And you?"

"I'm from Austria. I sat with Sasaki Roshi and his successor in Vienna."

"Were you a monk?"

"Not officially. But I trained in hope of going to Japan and becoming one someday."

"How did you end up here in Hawai'i?"

"I read Aitken Roshi's *Taking the Path of Zen* and decided I'd had enough of monastic training."

"Me too—"

"Well, you two seem to be hitting it off perfectly," Linda interrupted. "I'll be leaving. I have to go shopping; we're running low on brown rice. Bye." Forgetting that my bags were still in the car, she dashed out the screen door to the porch, slipped into a pair of zoris, and drove off before I could stop her.

Manfred laughed. Putting his glasses back on, he said, "Never mind the bags for now. Let's you and I go to the library. I have a feeling we have a lot to talk about."

We'd met less than five minutes ago, but as I followed Manfred to the cottage I felt as if I'd known him all my life. The feeling was strengthened by our two-hour conversation in the library, and again, later that night, when I dreamt Manfred and I were Japanese monks on autumn *takuhatsu* (alms-begging) together. Dressed in traditional traveling robes and sloping straw hats, our conversation consisting of bits and pieces of our earlier exchange in the library, we were talking as we made our way through heaps of red and yellow leaves. Manfred was describing his five years of hard training with Rinzai Zen teacher Sasaki Roshi.

"I learned a lot from Sasaki, but I'm glad I left and came to Hawai'i. Five years of killing yourself for Zen was enough for me. I was ready for Aitken Roshi's lay Zen practice—his social engagement is what really appealed to me most," the dream version of Manfred said. Then pointing to a mossy spot under a tree, he added, "You must be very tired after such a long trip. Here, stretch out under this tree and take a nap. You've got a long way to go."

I was just about to lie down when Dokyu Roshi's voice came thundering out of the tree: "Sleeping outside *zendo*, leaving cushion during sesshin—only greenhouse person do that!"

Bolting up from my foam rubber mattress on the floor and looking around the unfamiliar room, I was startled to find that I was no longer in Japan but in Hawai'i, and that Linda and a red-haired woman I hadn't been introduced to were sleeping on similar foam rubber mattresses on the floor across from me. Taking my diary and a pen from the night table, I tiptoed to the bathroom and turned on the light. Softly closing the cover of the toilet seat, I sat down and entered the dream in my diary, noting: "Despite the fact that I've broken with Dokyu Roshi and destroyed my chances for becoming a Zen professional, I'm glad I came to Hawai'i. But as this dream shows, it will take a while before I stop wanting to be a 'real monk.' I still see myself as a fugitive from a monastery. A Zen nobody who's too pure for enlightenment. Manfred says I've got a long way to go. A long way to go where, I wonder?"

Zen in Transition

I spent almost five years as a member of the Diamond Sangha in Honolulu practicing Zen with Robert Aitken Roshi. And though I will always be grateful to him and his late wife Anne Aitken for opening their doors and freely offering me the dharma, I wish I could say Aitken Roshi and I were a "perfect fit." But we were not. Even from the first day, I think it was obvious to both of us that, though we were Americans and fellow East Coasters (the Roshi was born in Philadelphia and I in New York), who loved literature and shared a career as writers, our styles couldn't be less alike. An introverted, soft-spoken, and formal "old-school" teacher who insisted on doing things just the right way, Aitken Roshi reminded me of the middle school homeroom teacher who'd recognized my sincerity and commitment to learning from him but never seemed to approve of anything I did or said. Comfortable only around equally soft-spoken, traditionally "feminine" women eager to follow his counsel, for all his social activism, Aitken Roshi was clearly not a feminist. Not if feminism meant dealing with uppity women from Brooklyn who didn't beat the drum according to his prescribed notations in the sutra chanting book during sesshin or dared to question his point of view during what were advertised as *sangha* "sharing meetings," but were really opportunities for scoring points with the roshi by agreeing with everything he said. What Aitken Roshi and I *did* share was a penchant for witty remarks and language play—though as I learned soon enough, the application of those witty remarks was unevenly balanced in his favor. Even in so-called informal encounters, I was always conscious of the Roshi's role as a teacher—not to speak of formal occasions in the zendo, where he appeared in black robes and *rakusu* (short bib-like version of a Buddhist monk's garment signifying ordination, worn on the chest), carrying his ever-present *kotsu* (short wooden wand)—Roshi's symbol of authority. The Diamond Sangha's reputation as a *Western*, egalitarian, socially engaged, nonmonastic, non-Japanese place to practice notwithstanding, I often found it more Japanese in its rituals and hierarchy than Dokyu Roshi's Soho Zendo—and certainly less relaxed. You didn't go out and have a beer with Aitken Roshi. And you certainly didn't tell jokes or raunchy stories during the well-behaved, Quakerish post-sesshin potluck gatherings held on the zendo porch. As soon as the roshi left (which he did early, saying, "Don't let me break up the party"), you could feel everyone breathe easier. Very few students would dare say it publicly, but in private, I did occasionally hear some of them refer to Aitken Roshi as "stiff." If you've read this far, you know that I'm a typically extroverted, edgy New Yorker, whose reflexive questioning of (particularly male) authority has gotten her into trouble from childhood on. So, as you can imagine, ours was an oil-and-water relationship from the start.

I did, however, love koan practice. The koans we used as meditative tools for sharpening awareness at Koko An were excerpted from ancient Chinese stories depicting supposed encounters between monks and Ch'an masters that were collected and recorded by Chinese monks centuries later. It didn't matter to me whether the stories were true or not, or whether they were Chinese or Japanese, Asian or Western, old or new; I took to the koans immediately—and still incorporate them in my own practice as well as with students. From the very first, I loved their quirky spontaneity, and the delicious moment of shared insight I experienced anew each time I engaged with one of those stories. But as time went on, the koans began to feel less like opportunities to "entwine eyebrows with the ancestors" and more like exams that had to be passed. Entering the *dokusan* room uncertain of Aitken Roshi's response to my koan presentation became onerous, and I started dreading our interviews. The original glow of insight faded, and practice became more a matter of finding the "right answers" to the questions coinciding with those printed in the official koan books piled up at the roshi's side. Even worse was having to memorize and recite, word for word, each koan as it appeared (without the answers) in my student copy of Aitken Roshi's English translations of the ancient Chinese koan collections. But even that couldn't kill my love for koan practice, and I struggled on.

Writing this now, as a Zen teacher myself, I can only imagine how difficult it must have been for Aitken Roshi to deal with me. Here he was, putting himself on the line with the Japanese Zen establishment by integrating Western "democratic" ideals into his teachers' feudal samurai practice, and a far less experienced, in-his-face student like me was trying to push him into making even more radical changes. One example: We had porridge every morning for breakfast. When my turn to be breakfast cook came around, after consulting with Manfred (who had quickly advanced after two years in residence at Koko An and was soon giving interviews as a Diamond Sangha "junior teacher"), I decided to change the morning menu. Bored by our continuous diet of porridge—which was sometimes two or even three days old—I went out to a Honolulu bakery and ordered a variety of muffins and served them the next day with jam, honey, and butter. A riot followed. Accompanied by an ad hoc committee of two, the head resident came into the kitchen immediately after breakfast to inform me that I could no longer be breakfast cook if I decided to take things into my own hands and make changes to the menu.

"The morning breakfast sutra says, 'Porridge is effective in ten ways,' not 'Muffins are effective in ten ways," he scolded.

"What? You're kidding me!" I shouted back. I was really volatile in those days, and pretty arrogant about just having come from a Japanese monastery, where I practiced "real Zen" with a Zen professional, not a layman. Brought down a peg that morning, I reluctantly gave up experimenting and went back to cooking porridge.

What I didn't realize then was that Aitken Roshi's Diamond Sangha was in the vanguard of a new American style of Zen, a transitional stage between the samurai Zen practice he'd inherited, and was in the process of leaving behind. Part of a generation raised to respect its elders even while discreetly disobeying them, the roshi was still rooted in the traditional Zen paradigm of master and student—the authority residing in the former. Our roles were therefore clearly defined from the outset: he had many years of experience and a lot to teach, and I was there to learn from him. In fact, he once hinted that if I took on his "color," I might even have hopes of teaching myself one day. I can't say for sure that's what the Roshi meant, but creating cookie-cutter versions of yourself doesn't strike me as the best way to pass on the dharma. You can't actually *teach* Zen to anyone the way you teach math, say. You can be a Zen "guide," an experienced friend who shows people how to sit and helps them along in their practice, but Zen can't be taught; it can't be learned—only experienced for yourself. The wonderful thing about Zen is that nobody holds a copyright to it. It belongs to everybody! However, in the eighties, this hierarchical, conformist mentality was (and in some Zen centers still is) the norm. I can understand how hard it must have been for a man in the early days of American Zen to free himself of the Japanese Confucian norms of male superiority drilled into him by his teachers. Conformism, as I'd learned in the monastery, was, and, as I discovered on a recent visit to Japan, still is, part and parcel of the Asian Zen tradition. Take it or leave it. Difference, or deviance, from the established dogma set by the authorities (that is, the roshis who consider themselves part of a "lineage" supposedly reaching all the way back to the Buddha himself), could only bring you grief—what Toni Packer calls "the violence of comparison, enforcement, suppression and punishment."[1] In my case, porridge was only the beginning.

Emboldened by our long discussions about democratizing Zen even further, Manfred and I embarked on what eventually resulted in our grassroots version of the practice after we'd married and moved from Honolulu to Princeton, New Jersey and started our own Zen group. The first leg of our experiment began during Rohatsu, the eight-day December sesshin commemorating the Buddha's enlightenment. To make life easier on ourselves and the other zendo residents, we had already moved out of Koko An into a nearby apartment, so, every night after the sesshin closing ceremony, we'd slip out and go home to sleep. It was the first time either of us had ever slept outside of the zendo during a sesshin. Old conditioning dies hard—even for a congenital rebel like me. I was so nervous about not sleeping in the zendo and missing the morning wake-up bell that I hardly slept at all during that Rohatsu sesshin. Every time I dozed off I'd jump up and look at the alarm clock beside the bed. In my anxiety, my old sesshin stomach troubles resurfaced, so when Manfred suggested we skip meals in the zendo and eat at home during breaks, I quickly agreed. Psychologically as well as physically, the tension lessened, and I actually began to enjoy my zazen. Interestingly, it was the first time since I'd been sitting sesshin that I didn't feel sick or "punished." Empowered by the changes we made during that Rohatsu sesshin, I looked forward to the next phase of our Zen experiment.

Aitken Roshi had given Manfred permission to offer interviews, but I was initially hesitant to go because I was afraid people might think I'd be given special treatment. Then one day I saw Anne Aitken go to *dokusan* with the roshi. If *she* wasn't worried people might think she was getting special treatment, why should I? How lucky that turned out for me. Finally getting up the nerve to go to dokusan with Manfred, I was delighted to recapture in his approach to Zen all the original freshness and vitality I'd experienced at the beginning of my koan practice. It opened me up to working with several different Diamond Sangha Zen teachers, one of whom, Father Pat Hawk, a Catholic priest, became my main teacher for a while. I spent a month sitting with him at his retreat center in Texas working on koans with him in the morning and participating with the resident Catholic monks and nuns in their some of their Buddhist/Christian services. That experience, too, offered an entirely new perspective on my Zen practice. I felt like I'd come out of a confined and stuffy closet into a vast open space and was at last breathing fresh air. The unfortunate side effect of the tonic these new teachers provided was that I no longer felt I could continue my koan practice with Aitken Roshi.

At roughly the same time, things were turning out badly for Manfred, who, in refusing formal transmission as one of Aitken Roshi's successors, had been relieved of his teaching duties and cut off from the Diamond Sangha. A private success followed by a public break-up, our Zen experiment in Hawai'i ended in an inquisitorial *sangha* "sharing meeting," and our dismissal. We had each broken the rules in our own way: I by refusing to "finish" my koan practice with the roshi and receive his imprimatur, and Manfred for refusing to be cut and baked into a cookie ready for boxing and wrapping in the Diamond Sangha lineage. In my opinion, Manfred's was the sadder story; I had nothing to give up, since, as far as I knew, Aitken Roshi had never given transmission to a woman anyway, not even some of his old-time "advanced" senior students—many of whom had left to practice elsewhere by the time I got to Hawai'i. In short, Manfred and I were publicly denounced, renounced, and figuratively run out of town. It was 1991, and there were plenty of Zen scandals and breakups and public recriminations. Ours was only a tiny, insignificant blip on the Zen radar screen—not even worthy of being written up in the Buddhist magazine *Tricycle*. A few years later, the Internet Zen gossip had it that Manfred had "gone independent" and that I'd been a "sometime student" of Aitken Roshi's. By that time, I have to say I was starting to get used to the pattern. As a woman, not only didn't I have the luxury of "going independent," but in the eyes of my teacher, I was little more than a "sometime student" who, as far as he was concerned, might as well not have existed.

9

Zen Women

Community Life at Diamond Sangha

Despite the fact that the active feminists had all left by the time I got there, I don't want to leave the impression that I didn't have anything in common with the Diamond Sangha women I met when I was living at Koko An Zendo. It was, in fact, there that I met my best dharma friend Jennie Peterson, a woman who remains as dear to me as a sister to this very day. But Jennie, like many of Aitken Roshi's senior women students, used to come around only for community celebrations, not for *zazen*. It wasn't until years later that Jennie told me that the reason she didn't sit at Koko An was that she'd studied with Yasutani Roshi in Japan and considered him, not Robert Aitken, to be her teacher. A few of the other senior women students did show up on an occasional Wednesday night for an interview with Aitken Roshi, but most led busy lives beyond the residential center and also only appeared either for memorial services or weddings, pot luck suppers, or parties for visiting roshis. During the time I was a resident at Koko An we decided to set aside one Sunday a month to cook for the homeless, and that was when several community women and their families appeared—but because of the constraints involving child care, that didn't last much longer than a couple of months, and what had started out as "family Sundays" soon dwindled to a handful of residents who did all the cooking, delivering, and serving of food to the homeless.

I did get to meet the occasional senior woman student at *sesshin*, however, which provided me with some interesting experiences, as well as the opportunity to see how Diamond Sangha women coped with the difficulty of juggling home and family life with Zen practice.

I'll never forget one hugely pregnant woman who attended sesshin the very month she delivered her baby. Charlotte (not her real name) was an elegant, extremely ladylike British woman married to a tall, stand-offish British man I'll call James. Considering that she'd never joined us for zazen and I'd only seen her once, on a Sunday when we were cooking meals for the homeless, I was surprised when she checked in for sesshin—especially at such a late stage of her pregnancy. Expressing her interest in Zen (oddly, I thought) as meeting her need for a "church experience," Charlotte cheerfully joined the crowd of women sharing one bathroom and the limited floor space of one bedroom for sleeping. I admired her for being able to sit eight hours a day in zazen, pregnant as she was; but with her special needs (which she let us know about as soon as the head resident had carried her bags into the room and unfolded her air mattress) I couldn't imagine how we would accommodate Charlotte into our schedule. To begin with, she said she needed a lot more space to sleep than the rest of us, so Pat, another woman in residence at Koko An at the time, and I squished our sleeping bags together, turning our two floor spaces into one. This still did not make enough space, and besides, Charlotte had to be close to the bedroom door because of her frequent trips to the bathroom. And she needed her flashlight.

Two women from California who were attending sesshin, Kristin and Michele, had done their best to make things easier on Charlotte and were beginning to lose their patience. At the mention of the flashlight, Kristin erupted. She was a very light sleeper to begin with, she said, and if someone turned on a light in the middle of the night, she would never be able to get back to sleep. Fortunately, someone produced a sleep mask and offered it to her. I say fortunately, because Charlotte's lips had just begun to pucker up as if she was about to start to cry. So began the first night of our seven-day sesshin.

That same sesshin also stands out for me because it was the one in which I hurt my back. With only two minutes of shower time and a line of women waiting in the bathroom, I was hurriedly scrubbing down and mindfully turning off the water before rinsing off when one of the waiting women pulled aside the shower curtain and poked her head in to hurry me along. The soap slithered out of my hand, and I bent over to retrieve it when—BAM—I felt a pain in my back that was so sharp I blacked out. Luckily, Michele, one of the California visitors waiting on line, had the presence of mind to reach out and grab me before I could fall and hit my head. She and her friend Kristin carried me, wrapped in a towel, back to the bedroom and gently laid me down on my sleeping bag. When I opened my eyes, I saw Sandra, a doctor from the Big Island, standing over me. Gently bending me forward from the waist, she palpated my back and, seeing that I wasn't hurting, she concluded that I'd only suffered a muscle spasm and recommended I remain in bed until after supper. The other women were very kind to me, too, I remember. One brought me a hot water bottle, another brought me my supper upstairs, and a third gave me two Extra Strength Tylenol tablets. I liked it that the women weren't so rigid that they couldn't break into their sesshin concentration and show their sincere concern for my condition.

As Good as It Got

At Aitken Roshi's suggestion, a few of us tried starting a "woman's group." I say "tried," not "succeeded," because although we managed to meet three or four times at different women's homes and exchanged lively stories about ourselves and our backgrounds, having never organically come into existence, our Diamond Sangha women's group soon foundered. Seeking corroboration for my opinion about the reasons for its demise, I asked one of the women why she thought we stopped getting together. "Because the roshi legislated it," she replied wryly. Apparently, I wasn't the only woman who felt like a second-class citizen at Koko An. Yet, in all the time I practiced there, I never heard any of the women complain openly about Aitken Roshi's implicit sexism. It was almost as if they had made a pact to let it remain an unspoken secret. This was partially due, I think, to the terrible sex scandals that had, and still were, rocking other American Zen centers. Known for its clean reputation, Aitken Roshi's Diamond Sangha was looked to as a model of everything Zen was not at the time. The roshi was known throughout the world for his high ethical standards. A founder of the Buddhist Peace Fellowship and respected antiwar activist who didn't drink, smoke, or abuse his students, Aitken Roshi was in fact called in as a mediator by a number of Zen centers in crisis. So, during the late eighties at least, you could say his indifference to women was a plus. And since I was his student at the lowest point for women in American Zen history, I, too, was grateful enough to overlook Aitken Roshi's sexism. The Diamond Sangha was as good as it got.

Though I eventually left the Diamond Sangha, several women who remained still stand out in my mind for their continuing dedication to Robert Aitken Roshi and the Zen community in general. Among these, I am particularly impressed by Patti Cross, who has since become a teacher at the Diamond Sangha Maui branch; Marion Morgan, who now teaches in Charlottesville, Virginia; and Vickie Stoddard, who, with her husband Don, leads the Diamond Sangha in Puna, on the Big Island of Hawai'i. These women had been practicing long before many of the men who were to become Aitken Roshi's successors even appeared in Hawai'i. Though they were given leadership roles during sesshin and were members of the sangha's governing board, and later were given permission to teach, as of this writing none of these women has yet been granted the title of roshi.

Another woman student of Robert Aitken Roshi who stands out for me is a woman I will call Sister Joyce, a nun ordained into a Buddhist order. I remember Sister Joyce especially for her wry sense of humor and her strong feminist stance. Another thing about her that sticks with me is how tough she could be in getting onto the *dokusan* line. In traditional Zen Buddhist monasteries (and convents, I presume), it's customary to make a dash for the interview line as soon as the bell announces that the roshi is ready to accept students. I've heard stories about monks getting up so fast from their meditation cushions to be first in line that they've suffered broken legs in their hurry. I also heard about those who were so reluctant to go to *dokusan* that they had to be dragged there by the head monk. Either way, there's a lot of stress and strain associated with *dokusan*, resulting from the fear of confronting the roshi's koan questions. On the other hand, there are people like Sister Joyce, who are so confident and so eager to face the roshi that they'll break your neck if they have to in order to get on line as soon as the *dokusan* bell is rung. I had a chance to see this for myself one beautiful sunny afternoon during sesshin.

It was at the end of the spring training period, and there were quite a few students from overseas. Most of them were men—at least two of them given to aggressive behavior (what my Australian friends in Melbourne like to call "battlers")—so Aitken Roshi had had his hands full keeping the peace during that training period. One battler was a woman, though. Let's call her Renee. She cropped her head almost bald in the style of a monk. Renee was always being taken for a nun. I think this annoyed Sister Joyce, who really *was* a nun and proudly distinguished herself from the rest of us by shaving her head and wearing her traditional gray nun's suit at all times. This did not stop Renee from thinking of herself as and behaving like a nun, though. It was clear that the two women didn't like each other. Though they lived and sat and ate and slept in the same zendo, they never spoke a word to each other. Everyone was waiting for the day when the two of them would clash. It finally happened on that beautiful spring day during sesshin, just as the *dokusan* bell was struck on the porch by the interview monitor.

Sister Joyce was seated close to the screen door and had leapt up from her cushion and was already on her way to opening it when Renee, who had been sitting at the farthest end of the zendo from the door, appeared like a shot at her side. Most people were still sitting facing the wall and didn't see what happened, but those of us who were turning around and getting ready to head for the *dokusan* line on the porch were given ringside seats to the battle that followed. Both women were frantically trying to occupy the same space in front of the door, but Sister Joyce soon edged her way ahead. Seeing her path blocked, Renee pushed in front of Sister Joyce and reached out for the doorknob. Striking out, a determined Sister Joyce pinned Renee to the spot with her elbow. Renee returned the favor by giving Sister Joyce such a hard push that she nearly knocked her to the floor. Restoring her balance, the undaunted Sister Joyce simply thrust Renee aside and barreled her way out the door, leaving her stunned and furious opponent standing there muttering inaudibly.

What is there about Zen practice, I wonder, that would make two spiritually committed women turn against each other like that? And in an American Zen center reputed for its nonviolent, socially engaged Buddhism, no less? Could it be the samurai brainwashing nature of Zen we inherited from our male teachers? But Aitken Roshi was no samurai. I never heard him raise his voice, and he certainly never hit anyone. If you wanted a wake-up blow from the stick during sesshin, you could silently ask for it by signaling the zendo leader with your palms placed together. If you didn't want the stick, you simply didn't ask for it. Unlike some zendos, there were never any arbitrary punitive beatings going on at Koko An.

Is violence just built into Zen? If so, how long will it take before we can shake it? There's an analogy you hear in Japanese Zen monasteries that hints at a possible answer to my question. The first thing a monk is told when he enters the front gate is to leave his shoes, and his individuality, outside. Once he starts training, he has become a potato dumped into a sack with a bunch of other potatoes that will be tossed and jostled around and shaken until every last potato will have lost all its distinguishing marks and is so shiny and clean that it can't be told apart from the others. It's a scary thing, especially for a Westerner, and a woman, to be divested of her individuality, and so roughly, too. Most of us come to Zen practice because we're looking to *find* our identity—not *lose* it. And we have had enough experience of violence at the hands of men, thank you. We don't need more from our Zen teachers.

To make matters worse, Buddhist doctrine tells us that women— whose breasts and hips even a baggy potato sack won't hide—can't get enlightened, however long and hard we are shaken. Even those of us who willingly submit to the rough treatment in the hope of becoming indistinguishable from the male potatoes are doomed to fail. On the other hand, Buddhist doctrine asserts that a man can transcend his sex entirely. Not only can he attain supreme enlightenment, but on becoming a Buddha, *his penis disappears into its sheath, never to bother him again!* I'm tempted to speculate further on this subject, but I won't. I'll leave it to a "masculinities" specialist.

Faced with such unremitting rejection for centuries, we Zen women have nonetheless refused to give up. Many of us are still experimenting with ways of breaking into the all-male potato sanctuary, even if it means getting in through the back door. What do we do to get ourselves accepted? We maintain just enough of our "femininity" to keep our male teachers interested in us. Or, if femininity is what turns them off, we mimic their "manliness." We dress up and act like men. We adopt, lock, stock, and barrel, every last vestige of macho Zen ritual and ceremony—including transmission, lineage charts, and roshi titles. When these don't exist, we make up our own. We ingeniously insinuate Zen matriarchs into the long list of patriarchs whose names, real or imagined, are recited in our egalitarian zendos headed, many of them, by women roshis.

Zen priest-in-training Sallie Tisdale, a strong advocate of adding women's names to the Zen lineage charts, offers a convincing rationale for the practice: "I think we have a right to reimagine our past. After all, it has been told to us for a long time, through the imaginations of the men who kept the records. Partly this reimagination is a way that we change our relationship to it—we learn to see the past in a different way . . . As women, so long and in some cases so utterly denied access to our factual history, we have no choice but to imagine the past—with the best of intentions, with clear eyes."[1]

Maybe the need to be acknowledged is just part of being human—even if you have to acknowledge yourself by reimagining an already imagined history that doesn't include you. Being just another jostled and shaken potato in the Zen sack, indistinguishable from the potato in front of you in the dokusan line is bruising enough for a man, so imagine how hurtful it must be for a woman. My heart is with both Renee and Sister Joyce. I can understand how going unacknowledged can be worse than being noticed for bad behavior. As for those women who try to fit in either by going unnoticed or by searching out and reciting their imagined female ancestry, my heart is with them, too. I'm no different. Though I don't any longer, for all my feminist talk, I, too, once craved to be the roshi's "special student" (what we at Koko An used to call "teacher's pet"). When you're a woman competing with men for acknowledgment, there are no limits to what you'll subject yourself to. The following observation by Toni Packer sums it all up for me: "The discipline of obeying, conforming, imitating, subjugating oneself, and marching in equal step. Why do we do this? It is practiced in monasteries and in military systems the world over . . . Tremendous feelings of comfort and safety are provided by a system in which one does everything one is told. One does not have to think for oneself, one need not question and find out for oneself. It is so much easier to follow. Does one see the danger?"[2]

Toni Packer certainly did. And so did Joko Beck, and a number of other courageous first-generation women who later went off to practice Zen on their own terms.

Good-Bye to "Superman" Zen

Toni and Joko in particular stand out for me as exemplary models of the kind of WomanZen being practiced today. Both started out as "dharma heirs" of traditional male roshis and left to found their own Zen centers. (Toni has since eliminated the word "Zen" from the name of her upstate New York Springwater Center; Joko still refers to her San Diego group as a Zen Center.) Tired of "marching in equal step" and unhampered by the need to clone themselves, both women started from scratch, each in her own way creating a radically new form of Zen practice. Rejecting the old hierarchical model of the Zen master on his high seat, neither of them call themselves roshis.

Toni refers to herself as a "co-questioner" among "friends."

Joko says, "I'm trying to take the teacher out of the superman role. The teacher is a guide but not some magical or heroic figure." Deflecting all forms of hero worship, she tells people "I'm a student just like you," and "sometimes may not sit in the teacher's place at all [but] just [will go and sit] somewhere facing the wall." An astute observer of the dependency fostered by many Zen teachers, Joko notes, "People like to project their power onto someone else . . . but I won't accept that." To students who persist, she points out, "Look, you're attributing all sorts of things to me, and you don't even know me. That does you no good, so please, let's abandon it."[3]

Relieved of the Zen authority figure role, one is free to interact with people in a much less structured, much more intimate and immediate way, custom tailoring each encounter differently according to what each individual brings, listening closely to what he or she has to say before responding. Nothing exists but that very encounter. Each one is fresh and new. There are no tried-and-true formulas, no rules in a living, spontaneous dharma exchange between equals. All teacher-student roles disappear. There are no images to guard or defend as two human beings together open up to the living radiance of the moment. As Toni puts it, "The process is always newly revealing: to sit and work together to discover what is going on in the human mind and body, to question our deep-seated assumptions and conclusions, our beliefs, traditions, and teachers, and to find out why we cling in the first place."[4]

Joko echoes Toni's thoughts on practice as "being willing to be with whatever is, at every moment. Being with our bodies. Being with the physical sensations that appear and disappear . . . and dealing with [emotions] is absolutely basic." And she's similarly committed to teaching "in a way appropriate for each person," giving equal care and attention to strong and difficult people alike. "If any life can be moved a little, become more even and steady—more 'real'—that's the most satisfying thing to me."[5]

I've noticed that, like Toni and Joko, most women Zen teachers share a strong interest in what Dokyu Roshi called "messy female emotions" and their effects on our lives and relationships. This is as radical a departure from traditional samurai Zen as it gets. I remember one friend telling me stories of monks who "never made it." An otherwise generous and sensitive person, he had coldly related several stories of monks suffering nervous breakdowns in the middle of sesshin, and of others hanging themselves in the bath house. My friend said he'd been walking the stick during these sesshin, and he proudly noted how much discipline the other monks had shown: "Not one of them stirred, even in the middle of all the commotion." I was shocked at what he was saying, but even more at the way he was saying it. My sensitive friend who'd once wanted to save the world had turned into an ice-cold samurai, ready to sacrifice his own and everyone else's life with one blow of his sword.

One wonders whether the elaborately formal structures found in traditional Japanese zendos (and imitated by those Westerners seeking to appear "authentic") only serve to bottle up dangerously "messy female emotions" that erupt into madness and suicide. One of my Zen friends at Koko An had been a monk at the late Philip Kapleau Roshi's Rochester zendo. He enjoyed watching me squirm as he talked of sitting sesshin with a knife in the sleeve of his robe, ready to kill himself if he didn't get enlightened. Toni Packer also got her training at Rochester. She, too, made her way through the "boot camp" approach to enlightenment, and must have done a good job at it, for she quickly received transmission from Kapleau Roshi and was permitted to teach. Something of her past as a half-Jewish child growing up in Nazi Germany under constant threat of exposure must have played into her initial attraction to samurai Zen. But she left, and others didn't. Why? When asked, Toni recalls:

> When we join a spiritual group or training center, there is usually a host of activities, ceremonies, etiquettes, rituals, vows, and so forth that we are expected to participate in. There's no real freedom to choose whether to participate or not. Any hesitancy is equated with "ego," while participating in what is demanded in spite of doubts is called "lowering the mast of ego." The mind quickly becomes conditioned to . . . the expected ways of relating to "teachers," "senior disciples," "advanced students," and "beginners." . . . One sees the venerated teacher participate fully and sanction what is going on . . . [Doubting any of this] is "giving way to the ego." . . . Doesn't the teacher stand for everything one has become engaged in and committed to? He or she stands for the whole past tradition! How is one going to be completely independent of the past?[6]

We all know what it's like to enter a great cathedral and be overwhelmed by the sanctified spirit of the past. Cathedrals, temples, mosques—all places of worship were carefully designed to strike awe into our hearts. We inhale the fragrance of incense, immerse ourselves in the silence or the chanting and, instinctively, we bow our heads and are humbled. Religions have orchestrated just such a response for centuries. Even a heretic like me still gets shivers up her spine the minute she takes off her shoes and enters a zendo—any zendo, anywhere in the world. The same reverential hush comes over me every morning as I approach my little altar, light the incense, and prepare the cushions for zazen. Ritual is fine, if I perform it gently. But not if it becomes compulsive—in this regard I have to keep myself in check. Especially when I'm being watched.

My father was constantly putting me through little testing rituals. At breakfast, even before I'd picked up my glass to drink my orange juice, he'd pose a math problem or a mental teaser or ask me to name five characters in five different Dickens novels—things like that. Like a quiz show host, he was constantly poised to press the buzzer and tell me I was wrong. It wasn't that he didn't love me (or I him), it was that he saw in me a mirror of what he felt he'd lost the chance of becoming. Demanding perfection, he was always ready to criticize the way I did things, like dry the dishes or cut a slice of bread. So I rebelled against everything my father said and did; deliberately giving the "wrong" answers and doing things the "wrong way" became reflexive for me, a form of *offensive* defense.

The same thing happened during sesshin when I served as interview monitor and had to hand over the incense stick to Aitken Roshi at the altar before his dharma talk. I'd always manage to hand it to him the wrong way no matter how many times he would demonstrate the right way to do it. Okay, so it was a mark of my inattentiveness, my scattered mind, my ego stubbornly resisting the teaching. No harm in a little ritual slippage now and then, I say.

What about bowing? Like most Western Zen students uncomfortable with bowing, I, too, had been assured that I was not bowing *to* any person or thing but "lowering the mast of ego." I've always preferred my aikido teacher's explanation that I was actually acknowledging the Buddha Nature in myself and everyone else every time I bowed. I still instinctively perform *gassho*—putting my palms together and briefly lowering my head to acknowledge the Buddha Nature in everyone and everything. When taking a walk on the beach I sometimes spontaneously *gassho* to the ocean—or to a tree, or a flower, or a bug, or a friend. But it always felt strange offering full prostrations to Aitken Roshi on entering the *dokusan* room, especially since Dokyu Roshi had eliminated the practice. It seemed so un-Zen-like, so heavily *Buddhist*. The Zen I'd been attracted to was embodied in free and irreverent spirits like Pu Hua, the Chinese clown who wouldn't join a monastery but preferred chanting, ringing bells, and performing somersaults in the streets; and the Japanese Emperor's illegitimate son Ikkyu, a composer of sexy poems celebrating his love for Lady Shin, a blind singer; and the Chinese monk Tanka, who burned the wooden statue of the Buddha on his altar to keep warm on a freezing winter's night. (Manfred and I even wrote a book about these "Crazy Clouds.")

But how much is too much? How far do you take your rebellion against your father or your teacher before the whole structure comes falling down and there's no longer any form or place to practice in? I like the way Joko Beck has handled this issue. She seems to have struck a reasonable balance between authoritarianism and anarchy in the way she's set up her zendo. The Zen Center of San Diego is administered by a board of which Joko is not a member. She can be voted out as teacher by the full membership at any time, and has no power over decisions regarding the day-to-day administration of the zendo. Her decisions relate strictly to areas having to do with practice, such as the length of sitting periods, interviews, and dharma talks, which include open discussion and questions and answers. Joko candidly comments, "I'm not saying we don't need teachers, center, or techniques. We need them very much. But when we think that something except ourselves and our own correct effort is going to effect some sort of transformation in our life, we're deluding ourselves. Any teacher is there simply as a guide so that you can get in touch with the wisdom that you already are."[7]

I'll *gassho* to that.

10

Getting Personal

What "Self" Are We Talking About?

I just read what I wrote in the last chapter and realized that I've painted a very narrow picture of my relationship to my father. Of course, there's always more than one side to every story—and every relationship. But that's what the self (or ego) likes to do most: nail down a permanent image—in this case, of me as victim, and my father as oppressor. I could have chosen an entirely different set of images to characterize our relationship. I could have said that my father was also generous and intelligent and had a beautiful smile. That he instilled in me a lifelong love of books and films, music and art. That we read Dickens and Shakespeare and the Sunday comics together, or that he took me to the movies every week, and that we both identified with heroes like Ivanhoe. Or that when I was five, he walked me to the neighborhood library, lifted me up to the checkout counter, and proudly showed the doubting librarian that I could not only read but sign my name in script to prove to her that I deserved a library card. The images themselves aren't the problem—it's the attachment to them that plants the seeds of suffering as is the notion that we carry around of a "self" in here, defending its turf against everyone else's "self" out there.

The fact is there is no permanent self. When we speak of self-realization in Zen, we're indulging in yet another paradox. What we're realizing when all the old images of who and what we are drop away, is *freedom* from that narrow little self we've placed at the center of everything: *Oh, is that the way it is? How could I not have seen it when it was there all along? Nobody there. What a relief!* It's not that we don't physically exist, but that we're constantly changing, so there's never a moment when the self we thought we were a minute ago hasn't become something new. Our busy mind with its continuously running narrative—*I like this. I hate that. I'm this kind of person and she's that kind of person; I can't stand her*—presents us with the illusion of a solid, fixed entity. The trouble comes when that entity is threatened—not by something really dangerous, like a tiger, which the body/mind instinctively knows to run away from—but by the endless chatter about imagined dangers to the self we've lavished so much time and attention fabricating.

We all do this—whether we're "enlightened" or not. The important thing is to remain alert and attentive to our own tendencies and not fall prey to the idea that our self is more special than anyone else's. Anne Aitken just popped into my mind as the perfect example of what I'm talking about.

Caring

Though never officially given dharma transmission, Anne Aitken was a natural-born Zen teacher. In fact, it was she who kept me coming back to the *zendo* when things got really tough. She didn't have to say much. Our conversations were casual and had less to do with Zen than with her love for Häagen-Dazs chocolate ice cream, or with how much she enjoyed swimming in her apartment building's pool every morning. (With a mischievous twinkle in her eye, she once leaned over and whispered in my ear that some of the women swimming alongside her were "ladies of the night.") Seeing Anne wave through the window of her cottage kitchen or sitting on the zendo porch steps in her long flowered muumuu poring over the latest L.L. Bean catalog was inspiring enough. When Anne died in 1994, Manfred and I paid a condolence call to Aitken Roshi. It was our first contact with him in three years. Since then we still occasionally stop in to visit with the roshi when we're in Hawai'i. Anne may be gone, but her caring practice of reconciliation is as strong as it ever was when she was alive.

By "caring," I don't mean caring *about*—that kind of caring is associated with outcomes. Nor do I mean caring in the sense of "caretaking"—as in being responsible for a person, or a garden, or a building. I'm talking of caring *for* what is manifesting right now, as this very moment. Such caring begins with an understanding of who we are, of how our body/mind works, attending to our reactions and feelings as they arise, and not separating self-observation from what's going on or dissociating ourselves from others. When we're truly caring, our minds reflect everything that appears. Letting this reflection sink in, actually *becoming one* with the reflection itself, we meet the moment—uncluttered, unadorned by the usual images, projections, and fears that normally accompany us as we make our way through the day.

Sitting itself is caring. So is walking. And eating. And sleeping. And swimming. And reading the L.L. Bean catalog. There's no need to hold a knife in your sleeve to "get enlightened" in order to become a caring person. A Zen focused on killing yourself is exactly the opposite of caring. That knife-wielding punisher sitting there with you on your cushions is incapable of experiencing the caring that comes with a loving Zen practice. It drives you to hate yourself for failing. It leads directly to more suffering and more pain, inflicted not only on yourself, but turned outward on others—your parents, your teachers, friends, lovers, bosses, foreigners—all those other "selves" that you mistakenly believe are standing in your way.

As soon as we come face to face with our attachment to that image of a permanent self, caring for the moment happens naturally. Suddenly all the rage and frustration give way to openness, to the realization that all things are interdependent, that we're not disconnected from anyone or anything else. We don't have to struggle to push away or dissociate or alienate ourselves from rising thoughts, feelings, and conditions—whatever they may be. Letting go isn't easy. But awareness, attention, and caring provide the energy to keep from acting on those destructive impulses or to just ignore them altogether. It's not a question of instrumental change; caring isn't a tool, or a machine that will automatically work to get us results. There will always be setbacks, phases when we find ourselves in a desert, dried up and lifeless. In times like these caring manifests itself as perseverance. Just taking one step after the next. Caring for the moment, dry and lifeless as it may be, will reveal the oasis in that desert. A place where we can accept ourselves just as we are—warts and all. But first we have to put down that knife.

"Imperfectly Perfect"

It isn't only Zen students who have to be careful of getting caught in self-aggrandizing images of what it is to be an "enlightened person." It's a trap for Zen teachers, too. Jan Chozen Bays urges teachers to set an example by openly admitting their own imperfections, making it clear from the outset that they themselves are not "fully enlightened, actualized [beings], but just another human being who will make mistakes."[1] I'm in favor of that. Yet, for me at least, there's a disconnect between the kind of open-hearted humility and ordinariness Jan advocates, and the austere, solemn vision of a woman roshi in black monastic robes performing elaborate ceremonies.

Acknowledging weakness, flaws, and ordinariness isn't the usual way of Zen masters. And no matter how approachable a woman might be, once she's got that "roshi" title and all the monastic accoutrements that go with it, she's still far from ordinary. Feminists who emphasize gender differences would say it doesn't matter what a woman is wearing, that even under the black robes and shaved head, she's still locked into her feminine gender role. They'd argue that because women have been so immersed in the caretaking and nurturing activities associated with what Joko Beck calls "everyday Zen," we have an easier time of appearing ordinary—regardless of what we're wearing. But I wonder about that. Is there really anything especially "female" about acknowledging your weaknesses, flaws, and ordinariness? In other words, once a woman is sitting there with people who've come to practice with her, regardless of whether or not she calls herself a roshi or shaves her head or wears black robes, is it really easier for her because she's a woman to acknowledge that she isn't perfect? I can imagine my former women's studies colleagues cringing at the essentialist nature of the question I just posed. Assuming anything like a grand truth about stereotypical female or male behavior is the cardinal sin among academic feminists.

The Zen experience of "no-self" also reveals that there's no difference between male and female, me and you—there is only oneness.

But that's only half the story—what the old Chinese Zen masters called a one-eyed view of reality. Seeing the whole picture means realizing that, as the Heart Sutra states, "form is emptiness and emptiness is form." We are both mysteriously one with all beings and brilliantly, marvelously, uniquely different at the same time. (This is another one of those Zen paradoxes that has to be experienced rather than figured out.) To illustrate this "difference" perspective, Yasutani Roshi once observed that the duck's legs are short and the crane's legs are long, and that both are perfect as they are. I'm very fond of Yasutani's observation, because I have short duck legs and it helped me stop envying my cousin Maxine for inheriting our maternal grandmother's long crane legs. Likewise, in writing this book, I've come to appreciate the differences in the way men and women Zen teachers deal with being perfectly imperfect.

Let's go back to the question of whether women teachers are more likely to *publicly* share their vulnerabilities with their students than men teachers, even in formal dharma talks during *sesshin*. Remember San Francisco Zen Center's Blanche Hartman sharing with students her experience of pain and the whole train of thoughts charging in on her *zazen?* Here, in another dharma talk, Blanche goes even further and shares a classic anxiety dream she had the night before she was to officiate at a monastery ceremony.

In the dream, Blanche appears in public wearing nothing but her black robe. She starts her dharma talk by offering her interpretation of the dream, describing her discomfort at being "completely exposed." Then she goes on to describe to her listeners how a group of people (presumably her students) interpreted her dream. One student says Blanche wasn't exposed but "maybe . . . was hiding something behind the robe." Another says it could be that she "had no other business except to wear this robe—that all the other layers of clothing or roles or identities had dissolved and there was only this one." Now really opening up to the "difficulty . . . [she has] in . . . how to teach," and acknowledging that she needs "to make more of an attempt to teach," Blanche fully reveals her fallibility. Again, standing "completely exposed" in front of her students, she presents them with a second dream in which she's at the Green Gulch Farm affiliate of the San Francisco Zen Center "circling" an "impenetrable wall" in search of a way over it. After many frustrating failed attempts, Blanche discovers "a hole in

the wall" revealing "the entrance [she] was looking for." Though she
resolves the problem, this dream, too, shows Blanche in an uncertain
position as a Zen teacher. Beautifully weaving together the theme of
both dreams, she concludes that the solution to her anxiety lies exactly
"where I was standing, right in the middle of the imperfectly perfect
anxiety itself."[2]

Susan Murphy also shares a dream of ambivalence about being a
Zen teacher with her students during sesshin. Susan's richly symbolic
dream is about a woman traveling in a "pitch-black palanquin" who
makes her way out of confinement into the light only to be com-
manded by the four silent men on whose shoulders she's been traveling to "fold herself back into the pitch-black palanquin," and let
herself be carried out of the light back into the dark forest from which
she came. At the end, Susan lets the dream speak for itself, asking her
students rhetorically, "Is it a dream? Who is the unknown woman?
When will we have another chance like this?"[3]

Set in the context of a talk about all the unknown women in a lineage that celebrates only men, Susan's dream echoes Blanche Hartman's ambivalence about being acknowledged as a Zen teacher. Both
women are dressed in signifiers of authority—Blanche in black
priestly robes, and Susan in the red dress of a noblewoman. But
Blanche has nothing on under her robes, and despite her noble status,
Susan is virtually dumped out of her palanquin and forced to crawl
around on the grass, "utterly dazed" by the light. Clearly, both dreams
express the inadequacy so many women Zen teachers feel in assuming
traditional male authority. But the fear of being exposed as somehow
unworthy isn't what interests me here. We all, male or female, have
performance anxiety. It's the fact that these women can be so bold in
confessing their anxiety, whisking away the trappings of their long-
sought authority and standing exposed before their students that im-
presses me most.

Bold Girls and Authentic Female Voices

Rejecting "any of those lineages [that] are not able to include and accept the particularly female expression of life," Zen teacher Trudy
Goodman is disarmingly honest in admitting the "reticence [she bat-

tles in herself] about assuming a leadership role." Speculating on the possibility that her battle may be rooted in "simple unfamiliarity or in old self-doubts," Trudy ultimately concludes that her reticence "is not a bad thing . . . It brings more level communication and dialogue, more circles and councils. There is more truth-telling of the kind girls are bolder at." She is less interested in creating images of external authority than in establishing the "wise voicing of . . . inner authority, and genuine openness, [of] unapologetic, strong vulnerability. This combination feels like an authentic female voice."[4]

Again, at the cost of provoking the derision of my academic feminist colleagues, I'd like to explore the existence of a truly "authentic female voice," attributed by Trudy to bold, truth-telling girls. Presumably the girls Trudy is referring to are prepubescent, between seven and ten years old. Such a girl, in my mind, is always nine. She's the one you see peddling madly down the street on her bicycle, yelling for you to "Watch out, I'm coming through!" She may travel with one or two other girls. But she's usually happiest on her own. She enjoys her own company immensely and is never bored. Even at airports, when she's waiting around, usually six steps away from where her mother is sitting watch over her younger brother or sister, this bold, nine-year-old girl finds interesting things to do. Or think about. She's maybe telling herself a story in which she's the conquering hero, dispelling wicked demons or obnoxious boys with a sharp word or a well-placed pop on the head. Sometimes, accompanied by her own voice, humming a tune or singing lyrics of her own composing, she's dancing. Or flying through the air in a grand jete. Or walking a tightrope fifteen feet off the ground. Or twisting her rubber-limbed, flat-chested body, she's performing humanly impossible gymnastic feats at the center ring of the Cirque de Soleil. She's the one Mary Pipher writes about in her best-selling book, *Reviving Ophelia*. We've all been this nine-year-old girl at one time or another. Many of us still are. I know I am. So what happens to her that causes her to lose her bold "authentic female voice?" Why does she start to become apologetic, self-doubting, and reticent? Why does she fear taking authority over her own story, her own life?

Volumes have been written in an attempt to answer these questions, but in my opinion, Pipher's book still hits closest to home. Though I don't agree with all of it, I admire her for taking a more moderate stance than the biological determinists currently cornering the market who place the blame for the girl's loss of confidence strictly on hormones. According to this argument, coming into reproductive age, sprouting breasts and underarm and pubic hair mark the death of our nine-year-old hero in preparation for her rebirth into marriage and motherhood. Thus, the girl, once smarter and more articulate than any boy in her class, now withdraws in silent, grinning idiocy when called upon by her teachers. Her once varied and colorful vocabulary is reduced to fourteen phrases liberally peppered with "likes" and "ohmygods." Her two great obsessions are boys and being fat. These, and nothing else, equally preoccupy her day and night. She no longer makes up stories or sings or reads but compulsively sends text messages on her ever-present cell phone when she is not shopping until she drops. And on, and on, and on.

Let me state right here that I don't agree with the reductionist argument of the biological determinists—on this or any other subject. Nor do I go along with the strictly social constructionist school of thought, either. It isn't simply a question of hormones or social conditioning but probably a combination of both—plus luck, plus karma and a whole lot of other intangibles and unknowns that are responsible for turning bold girls into pliant, fearful women. What we're dealing with here, in relation to Zen, is about a woman speaking in her own, authentic voice, retrieving it from wherever she lost it, regardless of when or why, and fearlessly expressing the wisdom of her own inner authority. Not looking to the Zen patriarchs for permission to speak or sing or dance or teach or lead a *sangha*.

Though it takes a certain kind of courage to be vulnerable in public, I still worry about the self-effacing language women use in describing their feelings about assuming spiritual leadership. For example, Zen priest Reverend Teijo Munnich, a dharma heir of Dainin Katagiri Roshi, echoes Trudy Goodman's focus on vulnerability, candidly admitting, "I do this practice because it helps me find my heart. I want to be a genuine person and that is why I throw myself into the practice again and again. Difficulties come, and like an idiot I keep throwing myself back into the fire."[5] Teijo proves that even monastic women with transmission from authentic Japanese Zen masters will refer to themselves as idiots and use characteristically "feminine" metaphors of love and self-sacrifice, like "finding my heart" and "throwing myself back into the fire" to describe their practice.

"Difference feminists" like Carol Gilligan would agree that women's language is more emotionally expressive, more relational, and "heart-felt" than men's. And that women are more likely to care about the effects of what they say on others. Not wanting to offend, women therefore tend to be self-deprecating in discussing subjects they feel strongly about. I'm not saying that this isn't the case; but I question how much of this relational emotionality is inherently female and how much of it is learned. Going back to the ancient Chinese Zen women—surely products of an oppressively misogynist Confucian society—might prove helpful in figuring this out. Granted, the action and the dialogue exhibited in the following koans featuring Layman Pang's daughter Lingzhao and Iron Grinder Liu have been sketched and put into these women's mouths by men. But even this can't hide the fact that these two were formidable and fearless Zen women who needed no man to corroborate their vast spiritual insight.

Here's Lingzhao, daughter of the renowned lay Zen Master P'ang responding when her father challenges her worthiness as a dharma companion: "I have looked for the essential qualities of men and women and cannot find them . . . The Buddha said that no one is really a man or a woman. Such things neither exist nor do not exist."

And here's Iron Grinder Liu on a visit to her ailing old teacher Guishan:

> "Old cow, I see you've come," said Guishan.
> "Tomorrow there is a great feast on Mount Tai. Will you go?" . . .
> At her words, Guishan lay down, sprawling on the floor. The Iron Grinder turned and left, without another word. No need to talk about it anymore.[6]

These Zen women undoubtedly had no choice but to be tough, confronted as they were by the horrific sexism of a society that, at best, viewed them as chattel and, at worst, murdered them in infancy for being born female. They certainly could never have survived the patriarchal Chinese monastic world without putting up a fierce battle in dharma combat with their male Zen partners. Nevertheless, I doubt that either Lingzhao or Iron Grinder Liu would have tempered her language or expressed her vulnerability even if she were practicing Zen in the more tolerant climate of the West today. Nor do I think that hormones had anything to do with how fearlessly these bold Zen women faced all challenges to their insight.

Circles, Lines, and Mothers

But words aren't the only way bold Zen women express their insight. As Iron Grinder Liu showed by walking out on her teacher Guishan, silence is another good way. And so is a wordless gesture. Or an image. In one koan, for example, a group of monks are on pilgrimage together when one stoops down in the center of the road and draws a circle in the dust. This sets off a playful drawing contest among his fellow travelers that turns out not only to be an enjoyable diversion from a long, hot day of walking, but an opportunity for each of the monks to express his Zen insight. Taking their cue from this playful Chinese monk, many of today's women Zen teachers have expanded the image by actually sitting among their students in a circle rather than above them at the head of two or more long straight rows, as traditional Zen masters do.

Toni Packer and Joko Beck were among the earliest to change the linear seating configuration in the zendo to a circular one. More recently, Wendy Egyoku Nakao, first woman abbot of the Zen Center of Los Angeles, was so determined to get her *sangha* to stop focusing entirely on the teacher that as soon as she assumed her position as abbot, she "[sat] the *sangha* down in circles." As Wendy charmingly puts it: "I sat in the circles, too, like everyone else. At first that was confusing to people, and when they spoke, they'd look at me, as if I were the authority in the room. But we've all learned together, and now they don't pay any special attention to me. It's wonderful for me . . . because I can have a practice, too, and people can see that . . . When we sit in a circle, there's a flattening of the hierarchy. Everyone gets heard, and everyone realizes the tremendous wisdom and compassion that is inherent in every single person, not just the teacher. We have learned that our diversity is not a problem, it's our strength."[7]

Another dramatic innovator of circular space as an expression of intimacy and equality is Joan Halifax Roshi. Uncomfortable "standing
before a thousand people and lecturing," and only finding her "real
nourishment from very deep, concentrated contact with a few people
at a time," Joan not only sits among her students in a circle but has deliberately chosen to build her entire New Mexican desert Upaya Zen
temple complex in the shape of a circle. Joan proudly asserts that her
circular Zen temple, the first of its kind, is thoroughly "grounded in a
female vision."[8]

I find it interesting that these women teachers express their
uniquely "female vision" of Zen practice in the form of circles. But
I'm still not exactly sure what they mean by it. What makes a circle female, I wonder. Like Trudy Goodman's "authentic female voice,"
Wendy's and Joan's "female vision" compels me. Yet I hesitate to follow. Why is a circle any more female than a straight line, I want to
ask. Is it because a pregnant woman's belly is round rather than
square? (So are big male beer bellies.) Is it because women's breasts
and hips are circular? (Well, some of them are. But so are some
men's.) Or is it because the male priests who created the symbols of
our ancient religions decided that circles were female and straight
lines were male? Did women have anything to say about it? Or are we
just unquestioningly accepting these so-called universal images of
maleness and femaleness created and handed down to us by men?

As feminist historian Gerda Lerner has pointed out, women have
been missing from history for so long that we don't even have a language or images of our own with which to name, let alone construct,
our social, political, sexual, cultural, aesthetic, and religious stories
and symbols from scratch. Piecing together the shreds of thousands of
years of a "herstory" that has been totally ignored or deliberately destroyed strikes me as an impossible task. That is unless, as Sallie Tisdale advises, we reimagine patriarchal Zen in matriarchal terms
or—using the only (patriarchal) language available to us—invent it
ourselves. I have to say, though, that I'm not comfortable with elevating either gender. I've had enough of gods—and goddesses—to last
me a thousand lifetimes. Anyway, visions of divine beings, called
makyo in Zen, are seen as obstructions to meditation rather than a

means to higher states of consciousness. We're advised to ignore them, and they'll go away. That's what the old teachers meant when they warned their students to kill the Buddha if they met him.

Then again, maybe Trudy Goodman, and Wendy Nakao, and Joan Halifax, and Sallie Tisdale have a point. Maybe we do need to supply our own missing female authentic voices and visions, if even temporarily, to the strictly male voices and visions that have dominated Zen for so long. Hopefully, filling in those missing female authentic voices and visions and "flattening the hierarchy" will insure that "everyone gets heard." Perhaps only then will women and men be able to sit down together in a big circle and finally do away with *everything* that divides us.

The biological determinists, of course, have already settled the problem. Their ready answer to the question of whether such a thing as an authentic female—or male—vision exists is that women's brains are wired to envision the world holistically (circles), while men are wired to apprehend the world by breaking it down into discrete, linear forms (lines). Oh, so that's the reason you find so few women in the Zen Master's High Seat!

I don't buy it for a minute. Unscientific as it is, I much prefer the intuitive approach of Barbara Rhodes, another woman Zen priest who doesn't hesitate to reveal the distinctly "female vision" that inspires her practice. A successor of Korean master Seung Sahn and head teacher at the Kwan Um School of Zen in Providence, Rhode Island, Barbara says:

> I lead a lot of meditation retreats and I feel so gratified that men come in for their koan interviews and there doesn't seem to be any thought of whether I'm less than or different; there's just a nice sense of flow back and forth. Sometimes people do say, "I'm glad you're a woman," because maybe I spent a little more time with them, or I said, "Oh you look sad," when one of our male teachers might not have said that. Sometimes I think that's a gift, but sometimes I think one of our male teachers might have given a sharper interview that would have been just as or more helpful . . .
>
> So there is some difference. I think I have rounder corners than a lot of male teachers and that can be a blessing sometimes. When my daughter was little, I would pick her up all the time, and I think I pick up my students in a way—not physically, but with that same sense of patience and loving their weaknesses if they're vulnerable, just feeling that and going into it.[9]

I really like what Barbara has to say, but it bothers me that a woman who's so obviously comfortable with herself as a Zen teacher can doubt her "gift" of empathy, her ability to "flow back and forth" with her students. Totally overlooking the praise she gets for being a woman—presumably from both her female *and* her male students—Barbara even goes so far as to demean her feminine handling of students in *dokusan* by contrasting it with the "sharper interview" style of her male counterparts. Why does she think her softly flowing "rounder corners" (circles, again) are any less effective than the male Zen teacher's "sharper," penetrating lines? What's wrong with loving weakness and vulnerability? Are we embarrassed about loving weakness and vulnerability because they've been so continuously denigrated by generations of macho Zen men?

I realize I'm contradicting myself here. But I still haven't made up my mind (and my heart) about this "female vision" thing. Stay with me a while longer . . .

Hoping that an endorphin rush would help me sort out my thoughts, I saved what I just wrote, closed my computer, and went to the gym. It was a good decision, but not because of the endorphin rush. Letting go and trusting the moment rather than trying to figure it out, I was rewarded by one of those marvelous synchronicities you hope for but can never force. It happened like this.

I entered the crowded Friday afternoon tram on my corner (which was even more crowded than usual because of the ongoing Melbourne Commonwealth Games) and luckily found the last empty seat. Three university students in their early twenties, two male and one female, were standing alongside me arguing over who among their women friends was "feminine" and who was not! Straining to listen to their conversation above the noise and chatter on the tram, I heard the following exchange:

First young man: "[Inaudible name] is very feminine."
Young woman: "She's more feminine than I am. [Pause] But I'm feminine."

Second young man: "Yeah, Sarah is very feminine—given to
   irrational crying jags as she is . . ."
Young woman: [Defensively] "I'm not that feminine, come to
   think of it."
All three laugh.
I reach my stop.

As I'm getting off the tram it suddenly dawns on me that "feminine" is a *pejorative* word!

Now I know why I am uncomfortable when I hear those women
Zen teachers talk about an "authentic female voice" or an exclusively
"female vision." It's because it isn't good to be feminine. Feminine
means being given to irrational crying jags. Being taken advantage of.
Being too soft with your students. (The loathsome chair of the writing
program at the university where I once worked as an adjunct called
me a "patsy" for encouraging rather than failing students who had difficulty writing. Interestingly, he, too, was a Zen teacher!) You'd think
in our era of gender bending, gay marriage, male parenting, and paternity leave, we'd have gotten over it! But we haven't. Well, not altogether. Softness and round corners are in these days—at least where
motherhood is concerned. Celebrities can't wait to get pregnant.
There's at least one mother-to-be movie star on the cover of every supermarket tabloid and monthly woman's magazine. Maternity clothes
are skin tight, designed to show off rather than hide. Beaches are
clogged with women at advanced stages of pregnancy proudly wearing skimpy bikinis. The bigger the belly, the better.

I've heard several theories about this latest obsession with motherhood. One that's currently popular with sociologists is that it has
something to do with 9/11 and the ensuing global war on terror. They
claim that people tend to have more children when they're at war.
Some feminist theorists say it reflects the influence of Christian con-
servatives in the United States and their emphasis on "the family."
Others point to the increased popularity of childbearing as a triumph
for the "pro-life" movement, calling it a reflection of the backlash
against feminism. But even among Zen women who think of themselves as feminists motherhood is seen as a positive thing. Maybe
they're responding to traditional Buddhism's negative take on motherhood, which equates it with the suffering that accompanies all at-

tachment, including even the loving bond between a mother and her child. Women are, after all, supposed to be more conflicted than men about parental responsibilities and dedication to their Zen practice. Whatever the reason, like Barbara Rhodes, most women Zen teachers see their motherly role in a positive light—even as a distinct advantage in the way they relate to their students.

Jacqueline Mandell shares this view of the nurturing role of motherhood and practice. Contrasting her life as a monastic with her current status as the mother of twin daughters, she says, "When I lived in monasteries, I felt superior . . . The monastic system is a great gift for the preservation of Buddhism . . . But it also involves hierarchy, with the male monk at the top, and laypeople and mothers hovering somewhere on the bottom. Through sharing my experiences of having been both a mother and a monastic, I try to dispel that dualist conception . . . Mothering, for me, means being undividedly with my children, fully in the present."[10]

I admire these women for their creative ingenuity in turning a spiritual disadvantage into an advantage. After all, isn't the central message of Mahayana Buddhism all about selflessness? And who's more selfless than a mother? What else is a bodhisattva for, if not to keep on being reborn in this world and giving birth to the many beings she's vowed to save?

San Francisco Zen Center's Jiko Linda Cutts also refers to the mother/child relationship in describing the interaction between teacher and student, but she offers a unique twist on the subject. Comparing the face-to-face encounter between Zen teacher and Zen student to the "gaze between mother and child," Linda recalls psychologist Heinz Kohut's emphasis on "the importance for children to have someone reflect back to them, mirror back to them all their interest, their love and excitement about their various activities and states of mind. Someone there looking at the child eye to eye is pivotally important for developing a stable sense of self." She concludes, "This mirroring, the 'gleam in the mother's eye,' is not dissimilar to the face to face reflecting back and forth between teacher and disciple. The same caring and intimacy is there . . . Seeing that face reflecting back to you, mirroring you, you don't see all the distinctions of ugly or beautiful, this or that. There's just this face-to-face transmission, reflection back and forth."[11]

It's astonishing how Linda manages to turn her own dharma transmission ceremony—conducted by a male roshi, and possibly the most solemn and elaborate (some would say pompous) hierarchical ritual invented by the Zen patriarchs—into the blissfully intimate encounter between mother and child! It makes you wonder if we haven't already entered the new postpatriarchal age of Zen predicted by Buddhist feminists like Rita Gross—a time when "egoless and detached" childrearing "would seriously and positively undercut [motherhood as] one of the most unattractive aspects of femininity as constructed in patriarchy."[12]

So, to return to my original question: Do women practice differently from men? Or put another way, is gender an illusion? I think the majority of women Zen teachers, and women practitioners in general, would definitely say yes to the first, and no to the second. Lesbian feminist Kate O'Neill puts it this way: "[Women] especially need to value our experiences, so that we have the possibility of seeing them more clearly . . . The key point, I think, is to acknowledge and honor women's relational orientation in approaches to Buddhist practice . . . There is a long history of perhaps unconscious, perhaps unintentional, patriarchal bias skewing the teachings toward men's experiences. Historically there have been many fewer women teachers. It is time these assumptions changed . . . in order to continue to feel our human connectedness, we need to recognize our differences with open eyes."[13]

What, exactly, is this "relational orientation," and what role can it play in Zen practice? Unlike other spiritual traditions, which foster worshipful relationships with teachers, Zen is bent on getting people to stand on their own two feet, to value their own experiences, and, most importantly, not to take the finger pointing at the moon for the moon itself. In this context, it could be argued that the relational orientation of women poses a danger to the student's self-confidence. After all, if you've got a Zen mother to pick you up every time you fall down, one who loves your weakness and vulnerability and cares enough to "go into it," why not just take it easy? Indulge yourself a little. Let her take the burden of investigating the great matter of life and death off your shoulders for a while. I find this happening with my Zen students every time I give way and let myself become too "motherly." Particularly with the more "vulnerable" students there's a tendency, if I'm not careful, to let the interview turn into a therapy session. I can think of several occasions when I've been side-tracked into discussing a student's family or health problems instead of focusing on her (or his) Zen practice. And in every case I can think of, the student stopped sitting when I refused to get caught in a motherly role. So, as soon as I find myself tilting off lopsidedly into mothering my students, I swing over and become less rounded and more sharp. Sometimes too much so: I know this when students tell me I'm pulling my "samurai Zen" persona on them. It's a question of finding the middle way—which is, after all, what Buddhism is all about.

But Kate O'Neill is right; it's true that women's experiences have been pushed to the back while the men were given front and center stage. And motherhood is perhaps the most problematic of women's experiences when it comes to practicing Zen. One woman in particular comes to mind in connection with this issue—the late Maylie Scott, a Zen teacher from Berkeley. We met at a conference on women and Buddhism in San Rafael, California, in 1990. I loved Maylie on sight. She was a tall, thin, very smart, and very funny woman in her early sixties whose honesty and wit in describing her experience as a first-generation American woman Zen practitioner had a profound effect on us all. I'll never forget sitting beside Maylie in a small circle of women listening to her relate her story. She'd grown up in a strict Episcopalian household and had always wanted to go the way of her sister, who became an Anglican nun, but had somehow ended up married and pregnant in her early twenties. Maylie was already the mother of two young children when she met the legendary Shunryu Suzuki Roshi, founder of the San Francisco Zen Center. Like so many of her generation, she was immediately drawn to this charismatic Japanese Zen master and enthusiastically dived into her practice with one of his successors in Berkeley.

Maylie's domestic situation, however, was not conducive to the demands of the strict monastic practice of her Zen community. She described the many occasions on which she had to choose between attending sesshin and remaining at home with a sick child, how torn she was between taking a leadership position at the zendo or going to a child's soccer match, and how draining it was to be faced with these continuous choices—not to speak of the guilt she experienced every time she chose one over the other. Never in her talk did Maylie refer to her husband. And since she didn't, none of us dared to ask. (As I learned later, they were divorced well after the children were grown.) Maylie concluded her story by admitting that she had put her Zen practice on hold while her children were growing up and that she hadn't really begun to devote herself fully to Zen until they had both left home. She had made her choice—motherhood over Zen—and, she wistfully informed us, she wasn't sorry that she had to wait until her sixties to become a Zen teacher.

The saddest part of the story is that Maylie died not too long afterward.

Never having been a mother myself, I can't really comment on what I would have done in her place. The responsibility for raising a child strikes me as formidable. But so is taking responsibility for your Zen practice. I wonder if perhaps the old Buddhists had a point: motherhood and the spiritual path may indeed be mutually incompatible because they both demand the same gut-wrenching commitment. The same self sacrifice, if you will. I don't know. I'll leave it to all the amazing Zen mothers who are still working on this monumental life koan to find out.

The "A" Word

It may be relatively easy for women to acknowledge their imperfections and their weaknesses and vulnerabilities. But what about their anger? Until women themselves forced the issue, the "a" word wasn't even whispered in Zen communities, let alone expressed publicly. I remember sitting through endless Diamond Sangha sharing meetings discussing how pernicious and destructive anger was, and how unsuited being angry was to maintaining a dharmic attitude toward the world. Really advanced Zen students, it was believed, were never angry. They never raised their voices. Especially if they were women. Those meetings got me so angry, I would sit there ready to explode. Why were the women talking so low that you could barely hear what they were saying? Or not talking at all? Were they trying to impress the roshi with how well they'd learned to control their anger? What were they so afraid of? "What about Yasutani Roshi?" I wanted to call out (but didn't). "Didn't he talk about the healthy expression of 'righteous anger'?" For that matter, wasn't our entire Zen practice based on koans about masters beating and yelling at monks? Or killing cats? Or calling the Buddha a shit stick? Was anger reserved only for "enlightened" Chinese and Japanese male Zen masters? And how could you tell "enlightened" anger from "unenlightened" anger, anyway?

Buddhist social activist Anita Barrows expresses the same frustration in encountering similar attitudes toward women who express their anger against war and injustice: "Here we go again, I thought. Now we are using Buddhism as a way to deprive ourselves of what we're feeling . . . Rather than using our practice to boil down our anger, why can't we use it to explore it, to honor it, to give it amplitude, to restore its vitality, its usefulness, its freedom from destructiveness?"

Anita worries that by trying to eliminate anger, women practitioners in the West will, "squeeze the juice out of our feelings." Becoming "good," that is, acceptable as "enlightened beings," we'll revert to the stereotype of the Victorian angel in the house, mild and serene and nonconfrontational.[14]

Buddhist writer and feminist activist Sandy Boucher also suspects that wearing the soft face of Buddhist compassion while suppressing angry feelings can be dangerous for women. Concerned that social gender stereotypes "are so pervasive that we are especially sensitive when the subject of nurturance or service to others arises," Sandy advises that we must first acknowledge our resentment before giving "to *ourselves* the love, the understanding, and forgiveness that can make us whole. The compassion for others comes then from this strong, fulfilled sense of oneself."[15]

The other night, while watching the evening news, I was rudely reminded of just how dangerous it can be when a woman suppresses her anger under forced compliance for too long. Members of the Palestinian Hamas party had taken to the streets and were celebrating their election victory by shooting off guns in the air. When the television cameras focused in on the specific object of their celebrations, I was stunned to see a woman in traditional Islamic robes and headscarf addressing the cheering crowd of masked, gun-toting men. Despite the fact that she had no political experience, the woman had just been elected as a parliamentary representative simply because she had trained three of her six sons as suicide bombers and sent them off to kill Israelis. The woman was proudly informing her constituents that she had three more sons she was training as suicide bombers, and would eagerly send them off to die and kill Israelis as well. Her murderous speech was awful, but even worse was that she spoke without raising her voice and had a gentle motherly smile on her face! And all in the name of religion!

It's hard to understand how a woman who thinks of herself as a religious person could be proud of training her sons to die and kill others. But isn't that what women have been doing for centuries, sending their sons off to war to die and kill others? And now—thanks to women's liberation—their daughters? You'd think the point of *any* religion is not to condone violence but to infuse compassion into a world overflowing with anger and hatred. But compassion doesn't appear just because our religions preach it. It comes only after we've faced up to the anger fueling our responses to the oppression, injustice, and suffering we heap on ourselves or experience at the hands of others. When anger is unacknowledged and left to fester, it invariably becomes destructive. As Zen teacher Diane Rizzetto says: "The key is to know whether the anger motivates actions that benefit the well-being of ourselves or others, or if it motivates actions that are hurtful to ourselves or others . . . Life-centered anger has the power to be open and transformative . . . It rises and falls quickly and is never held on to . . . What makes anger self-indulgent is the fact that we use it, *and hold on to it,* to maintain our identity or dream of self."[16]

That is why we spend years, lifetimes of meditation practice, acknowledging whatever rises out of the depths of the conditioned self. With practice, all our emotions—including anger—begin to flow through us simply as energy. In their new form our emotions are neither to be obsessively clung to because they give us pleasure, nor violently plucked out like "an eye that offendeth" because they cause us pain.

11

Getting Physical

This Very Body Is the Buddha

Takuan, the sixteenth-century Zen master to the shogun, urged his warrior-monks to practice *zazen* (sitting meditation) so they could die or kill without flinching. He taught that everything in the universe was "empty." A man's neck about to be cut by a sword, the enemy wielding the sword, and the sword itself—they were all illusory. Life and death were not real, so there could be no distinction between them. The only reality was emptiness. Geared to inculcate fearlessness in the face of death, Takuan's samurai Zen clearly had little use for the body. Takuan might have been considered a great Zen master in the shogun's day, but his embrace of death was based on a dangerously one-sided view. Substitute the word "emptiness" for "paradise," and you've got the same rationale for waging "holy war" as that suicide bomber's mother. It shows how misleading distinctions between spirit and matter can be: Take any rigid position, and you will suffer. Get stuck in emptiness, or idealizing a teacher, a spiritual practice, a religion, a philosophy, or a social movement, and you're bound to bump into disappointment. Takuan was wrong in exhorting his students to go beyond killing and giving life. No matter how insubstantial the self is, for a time, at least, we occupy a body, and the neck bared to the sword will bleed, one embodied human being will die, and another embodied human being will be responsible for killing him. And since zazen itself is physical, rooted in the body, even Takuan couldn't deny that one needs a body in order to practice Zen.

Emptiness doesn't mean that nothing exists—but that everything is just as it is. This is what the Buddha realized when he stood up after meditating under a tree, saw the morning star, and got enlightened. Everything just is. Suffering just is. War just is. Misery just is. Poverty just is. But that doesn't mean we aren't called upon to do something to alleviate them. Without idealizing the Buddha's realization of "everything just is" or wringing our hands over it, we have to engage one hundred percent in life such as it is. When we do this, we become truly filled with the realization of interdependence. Killing another becomes synonymous with killing oneself. It's not a question of, "Gee, there but for the grace of God go I, I'd better not kill that person." Awakening to interdependence reveals that there's no "that person" out there and "me" in here; that cutting some else's throat is cutting your own throat. It is the opposite of Takuan's samurai killing message of "emptiness." Zen is no rationale for violent and destructive behavior but the practice of compassionate action in this very moment. We don't know why or where this compassion flows from, and there's no need to ask. We just do, we just help. There's no mystery, no secret; it's right there, it's who we are.

If we are to establish a sense of place, a home in the moment, we also have to establish an awareness of our bodies, our physicality. Buddha, says Hakuin, the great eighteenth-century Japanese Zen reformer and founder of Ryutakuji monastery, is lodged right here in our bodies. Nevertheless, in his early days as a Zen monk, even Hakuin couldn't overcome the tendency to see his body as an obstruction to his spiritual practice. Like the Buddha before finding the middle way, Hakuin, too, indulged in extreme ascetic austerities. His penchant for meditating naked out in the woods all night and letting himself be bitten by mosquitoes until he was sitting in a pool of his own blood by morning gives me the shudders. It's not the young ascetic Hakuin who appeals to me, but the older, mellower author of the Song of Zazen who wrote: "This very body is the Buddha. This very place is the Lotus Land."

Women Zen practitioners generally don't deny the connection between embodiment and enlightenment, but they're still dealing with problems stemming from centuries of shame, inferiority, and even disgust for women's bodies. Women have only just begun to acknowledge their embodiment as manifestations of the Buddha. The ascetic and the woman who hates her body share the same mistaken notion that the body stands in the way of something they desire—enlightenment, in the first case, and love, in the second. Regardless of what motivates them, both have a very troubled relationship with the body. How does this play itself out in the way women approach their Zen practice?

My oldest woman Zen friend, Hetty Baiz, is a founding member of the Princeton Area Zen Group and a gifted artist. For over twenty years, we've been talking about the connection between Zen and her artwork and how it represents her feelings about her practice as a woman. I recently asked Hetty if she'd share her latest thoughts on the subject so I could include them in my book. This is what she wrote:

Dear Perle,
I have been thinking of writing about zen and art. I sat down this morning and started to type. I wanted to share this with you. I hope this will give you some start in your book. It's very rough but that is the way it came out . . . for now . . .

During the fall semester, I applied to and was accepted into the Princeton Atelier, something started and directed by Toni Morrison, where guest artists are invited to the [Princeton University] campus to collaborate with students to produce multi media (intermedia) works. I participated this past semester and made a lot of artwork inspired by the African novel *My Life in the Bush of Ghosts* by Amos Tutuola and Pac Man the video game (yes . . . that is what this workshop focused on!).

As part of this process, I collaborated with one student to make masks for his Noh-inspired performance art piece. To do this, I researched both Noh and Yoruba masks. Then I made imprints of his face using plaster and gauze and painted and collaged them.

For my own individual project I decided to make a figure . . . a "ghost" inspired by the rich imagery in Tutuola's novel (I've been doing figures over the past several years). To do this I made plaster and gauze imprints of members of the Atelier and of myself, and assembled the "body parts" in my studio where I then made body collages (in many cases these look like fragmented bodies). I was particularly inspired by the images in Tutuola's novel of gold, silver and copper ghosts . . . ghosts without arms, legs, hands . . .

I then wondered what would happen if I enclosed the "ghost" in architectural space. Would it change the space? Would it change it in any way? Would the experience of this ghost-like figure be different than if it were just hung on a wall? To prepare I researched African painted houses and Pac Man design grids (surprisingly they look African!) I got permission from the Buildings department at Princeton and installed [the structure I made] on the Princeton campus. I plastered the outside walls like the women do in Africa and then dug designs (Pac Man-inspired) into the walls along with quotes from the book and other African-inspired motifs.

In any case, in writing about these pieces, how they were made, what I was experiencing in the process, I realize they are very influenced by my experience with zen . . . by my years of sitting. It just comes out and through the work. It is an integral part of the work. It cannot be separated. It's how I see and experience the world. The world of "ghosts" for me is the transitory quality of all life, impermanence. It's not something that I find horrific but rather an integral part of what it means to be human. In making figures, I am trying, through direct expression, to imbue these pieces with this very dichotomy and reality . . . broken, transient bodies, evolving/devolving from nothingness . . . yet substantial, right there in front of the eyes, made from wet paper and gauze, torn tissue and paint . . .

The process of creating the figures involves making imprints of the body in plaster and gauze and then tearing and ripping the parts (legs, arms, hands) and recombining them to make a "body." I paint and stain and collage the parts as well. I try to end up with an integrated whole. I often use my own body to make imprints. I call these works "body collages in mixed media." They are all life size. When I make these imprints, I sometimes use just tissue paper and paint in lieu of plaster and gauze. I like the transparent quality of tissue. When I work with tissue, I sometimes put down many layers and then peel back and tear away at it until the form that I want has evolved . . . until the true "self" reveals itself.

In the tradition of the ancient Chinese and Japanese Zen artists, Hetty accompanies her "body collages" with verses like the following:

This figure of plaster and gauze
Imprint of your body
Imprint of my body

I rip and break the hands, arms, neck
I tear away at the face
Peel back skin
Till almost nothing is there
Combining your foot with my leg
My groin with your breast
A new body, one body
Emerging from traces.[1]

Hetty's "body parts" rendition of her Zen practice is humorously and affectionately self-deprecatory—but not self-hating. Using traditional koan imagery in very nontraditional ways, her work slyly manifests the true comic spirit of Zen art. Those looking for a sign of Zen wisdom in the otherworldly features of a blissfully meditative Buddha are likely to be disappointed. Zen artists portray themselves in more eccentric guises—like the book of Japanese art I once read that contained a scroll painting depicting the Buddha as a bullfrog sitting on a lotus throne, delivering a sermon to an audience of monkeys, cats, foxes, and rabbits dressed as monks! The same spirit of fun and tender humility pervades Hetty's work. Like her Pac Man video game, the Japanese Zen scroll painting reveals that there's no event or creature or image too trivial or base to provide an opportunity for discovering that we are all embodied "ghosts" in this world "clinging to bushes and grasses"—just passing through, simultaneously physical and ephemeral, form and emptiness both.

I especially love the way Hetty lambastes the seriousness people usually associate with Zen practice: the image of bald monks in black robes lined up in rows, sitting stiff-backed, facing the wall. The way she celebrates her woman's body, all women's bodies, by combining them groin on breast, to create a "new body, one body/Emerging from traces" . . . she's telling us we need to lighten up, to stop being so serious about our condition. She's prodding us to acknowledge that our women's bodily experience of the world is as spiritual as a monk's—maybe even more so, because monks are so removed from the everyday experience of the world. Anyway, male or female, we're all bound to break up "till almost nothing is there." So why not accept ourselves as we are? Why not love our bodies—temporary and broken as they may be.

Not Feeling Well

Illness and disability are perhaps the most potent reminders that we occupy bodies. It's when we're sick that we usually start paying attention to our bodies, too often as adversaries. But it doesn't have to be that way. Darlene Cohen was well along in her Zen practice when she developed a severe case of arthritis. Her illness only served to deepen her mindfulness of every moment, regardless of what it brought. She writes:

"Changing my posture was a dramatic event in my life. I needed to heed every little sensation in my legs and feet in order to go from sitting to standing . . . Most importantly I learned from my study of Zen to be less attached to things . . . It is very difficult . . . to have a strong functional body displaced by a painful helpless one. It shakes up our very identity . . . We must penetrate our anguish and pain so thoroughly that illness and health lose their distinction, allowing us to just live our lives."[2]

Darlene's positive attitude toward illness as an aid to the practice of mindfulness doesn't have too many precedents in the Zen we Westerners inherited from Japan. Influenced by the samurai ethos of masters like Takuan, our monastic Zen teachers were never very patient with physical or mental illness. Recall how my friend felt about monks who "never made it." Or, for that matter, Sadaprarudita, the ancient Indian bodhisattva who mauled and mutilated himself in hope of attaining supreme enlightenment. And yet, I can think of several inspiring koans depicting how some of the ancient Chinese masters—whose gentler, kinder Zen preceded the onset of the Japanese samurai influence—dealt with sickness, old age, and death. One of my favorites is about an abbot who is lying on his deathbed, surrounded by his grieving monks, when a squirrel suddenly runs across the roof. Mustering his last bit of strength the master points up at the roof and offers the monks his final teaching: "There it is! Nothing else! Just this!"

Today's women Zen teachers are similarly using personal experiences with illness and acceptance of their own mortality as a teaching tool. Joan Iten Sutherland, for example, describes how she discovered new depths of practice in coping with debilitating chronic fatigue syndrome. Combining the concentrated attention to "what was happening to [her]" with the "visceral . . . intuitive . . . kinetic intelligence" of koan practice, she says she became truly intimate with her body "as substance, matter, flesh and blood" . . . [manifesting] . . . buddha-nature."[3]

Embracing the moment—even the moment of illness and death—doesn't require ascetic forbearance. Self-torture isn't what Zen is about, yet many women I've talked to have a hard time understanding this. Equating zazen with pain, they avoid the practice. American women especially hate the idea of anything that will cause pain or injury to their bodies—except, that is, in the name of vanity. They spend more money, for example, on cosmetic surgery than any other women in the world. You could call that a strangely inverted form of asceticism, but it really harks back to the desire to stave off aging and is a reflection of what they fear most—namely, death. And that's the opposite of Zen.

Wanting to be healthy is another thing, though. Women Zen practitioners are no exception; they want to be healthy, too. But what happens when we aren't healthy? Is it possible to continue to have an active life in Zen when we are sick or disabled? And if so, how do we work with our body's new, and sometimes debilitating, condition? This is where women's nonjudgmental acceptance of weakness and vulnerability has resulted in some of the most radical changes in Zen attitudes toward disability. Joan Tollifson, who was born without a right hand, provides a dramatic example. After years of painfully trying to adapt to rigidly formal monastic practice with a male Zen teacher, Joan began working with Toni Packer. In the open and accepting environment she encountered at Springwater, Joan "learned . . . beyond any shadow of a doubt that real meditation can happen in any clothing, in any position, in any place, in any body . . . It is simply being here . . . Everything is happening on its own."[4]

Following in the footsteps of innovators like Toni Packer, instead of turning away people who are chronically ill or disabled, more Zen centers are not only acknowledging and accepting them, but are going out of their way to accommodate them. Relaxing sitting schedules, allowing people longer breaks, and in some cases, even letting them get up and leave the *zendo* during sitting periods. Without sacrificing the discipline required for a strong zazen practice, many Zen centers, often headed by women teachers, have incorporated yoga, tai chi, and other exercise programs in their *sesshin* schedules. Recall Maurine Stuart, who started the trend by massaging her student's shoulders to keep them awake instead of beating them with the traditional stick. Since then a number of women Zen teachers have taken these gentler forms of practice even further by bringing professional shiatsu therapists in to massage participants who sign up for them during sesshin breaks; or by scheduling dance and movement periods between sittings; or by providing wheelchair ramps for the disabled, and one-on-one zazen instruction tailored specifically for the elderly and infirm.

During sesshin at our Princeton zendo, for example, members spend the first half hour before morning zazen in a free-exercise period and the afternoon break in informal individual walking meditation outside the zendo. We also provide chairs for people with physical conditions that don't allow them to sit in traditional zazen posture on floor cushions. And we've even had people with serious back problems doing zazen stretched out flat on their backs in a side alcove of the zendo.

This emphasis on keeping the body healthy rather than torturing it has even spread to Japan, where the abbot of one well-known Zen monastery has his monks do early morning jogging in sweat suits and sneakers through the streets of town in place of slow formal *kinhin* (walking meditation) around the zendo.

The practice of caring for the moment extends to caring for moments we usually want to turn away from—like illness. As our practice deepens, we come to know that there really isn't any distinction between the illness moment and the body that's experiencing it. Body, illness, disability, Buddha Nature—they're all of a piece. You can't pry them apart. Realize this, and you'll no longer see your body as an obstruction to your spiritual practice.

How Do I Look?

When I was teaching women's studies at Illinois State University, I came across a sociological study of the differences in the way college men and women handle failure. Unsurprisingly, men expressed their anger and frustration at losing a game or a girlfriend or failing a course or not getting into graduate school by kicking furniture or punching the walls or moodily slinking off to the nearest bar for an extended session of beer drinking. But when women experienced what they perceived as failure—whether in love, or at school, or in friend-ships—the first thing nine out of ten of them did was go to the mirror and scrutinize their physical flaws. In other words, the men who saw themselves as failures externalized their frustrations while the women blamed it on their appearance.

Women Zen practitioners may not run to the mirror after experi-encing failure, but they still anguish over their appearance. They just handle it differently. I think what worries them most is that they don't fit the image of what a "real" Zen practitioner looks like—that's be-cause, until the twentieth century, a "real" Zen practitioner was a man. And if a woman wanted to fit the image of a "real" Zen *master*, she'd not only have to be a man, but a bald-headed, black-robed Asian man. Before the advent of sex-change surgery that wasn't possible, so the best she could do was make herself look like a man by shaving her head and wearing black robes. She might have done a fairly good job in passing, but inside, she always felt like an imitation, never the real product—like one of those irregular sweaters with the half-cut-out designer labels you pick up at discount stores like TJ Maxx or Filene's Basement. Faced with the challenge of fitting into a physically de-manding spiritual practice designed for male warriors, many women gave up practicing Zen altogether. Even a brilliant and feisty feminist Buddhist scholar like Rita Gross could write of hating her body throughout her childhood as "the impediment to the human being I wanted to become" until she got older and realized that it wasn't her body but the "system that is wrong."[5]

Despite the strides we've made, why, I wonder, do women still feel so unequipped to practice simply by virtue of being born into a female body? Could it be all those centuries of misogynist Buddhist propaganda? After all, in ancient times a woman didn't have to un-dergo sex-change surgery or shave her head and dress like a monk in order to get enlightened. If she was sufficiently spiritually developed, she could simply will herself to assume the body of a man. The Bud-dhist sutras are filled with stories about women magically turning into men in order to prove themselves worthy of enlightenment. That's because the traditional Mahayana Buddhism of which Zen is an off-shoot has it that you could only be enlightened in a man's body. I suppose the monks who wrote those sutras had to offer some rationale for all those enlightened women around the Buddha in India, and later in China, Japan, Korea, and Tibet, so they came up with the brilliant idea of having those women magically turn themselves into men. One famous story perfectly illustrates my point. I've selected it because it involves a bold preadolescent human girl rather than a goddess, or a water sprite, or any of those other mythical women with supernatural powers who populate the magical sex-change sutras.[6]

The Sutra of the Dialogue of the Girl Candrottara was written somewhere around the fourth century as part of the famous Sutra of the Teaching of Vimalakirti; Vimalakirti was a brilliant lay bodhisattva whose liberal attitude toward women pervades all his discourses. The story is about Candrottara, Vimalakirti's daughter. Born a Buddhist prodigy, the preadolescent girl is already famous for her fabulous sermons and has thousands of followers when we first meet her. After many marvelous adventures and visionary experiences on her way to meet the Buddha, Candrottara encounters a group of male bodhisattvas who challenge her for trying to become a Buddha in a female body. You can almost hear the men sniggering in the background as one of them, Amoghadarsana, comments sarcastically: "Candrottara, one cannot become a Buddha while being a female. Why don't you change your female sex now?"

Candrottara replies, "Good son, the nature of Emptiness cannot be changed or altered. This is also true for all phenomena. [Consequently] how could I change my woman's body?"

A lengthy philosophical dialogue between Candrottara and her male challengers ensues in which they each call her momentous spiritual accomplishments into question. All the heavy spiritual talk is, of course, an ill-disguised cover-up for the bodhisattvas' core challenge, namely, that, despite her momentous spiritual accomplishments, being a woman negates Candrottara's potential Buddhahood. I'll spare you the details and cut to the chase. On meeting the Buddha and hearing his prediction that she will indeed become a Buddha, Candrottara is "ecstatic, leaping in the air countless times to the height of seven Tala trees. Resting on the seventh tree, the girl changed her female body, transforming into a boy"—whereupon she attains supreme perfect enlightenment.

Why, you might ask, after such a lengthy dialogue spent in convincing the male bodhisattvas that being female or male has nothing to do with supreme enlightenment, does Candrottara turn herself into a boy? I have no idea. It might have something to do with the fact that Candrottara refused to get married. At least that's the reason offered by Diana Paul, the feminist Buddhist scholar who translated the story: "Receiving the prediction that she will become a Buddha, Candrottara, nevertheless, changes her sex, in spite of the discourse she has just delivered, perhaps as a concession to the fact that rejection of marriage in society at that time was virtually impossible for a woman unless she entered the religious order of nuns. Restrictions upon a woman because of family responsibilities to marry and to become the mother of sons resulted in restrictions upon a woman's religious roles. Candrottara changes into a male to avoid these restrictions."[7]

There seems to be no end to what women will do to prove themselves "one of the lads," as Maura O'Halloran put it. Remember how I cropped my hair in the hope that Dokyu Roshi would find me worthy of becoming his monk. A desperate measure? Yes, but not nearly as radical as actually turning yourself into a man! Today's version of Candrottara's magical sex change is a bit more subtle. Women in Western Zen centers do it by being ordained as lay Buddhist priests who wear black robes and shave their heads. Fran Tribe, for example, honestly admits her "desire to join the ranks of the patriarchs" as the reason for becoming a Buddhist priest at the San Francisco Zen Center. I admire her for the way she dealt with the tensions between her life as a priest and her role as a wife and mother. When her life beyond the zendo caught up with Fran, she realized that she and her nine-year-old daughter both had to cope with the same crushing demands "the system" places on women for occupying female bodies. Wandering through department stores shopping for clothes with her daughter, Fran "experienced again and again the hatred of my body I had felt as an adolescent, and the hatred I imagined my mother felt." Happily, Fran gave up trying to become one of the patriarchs and eventually grew her hair back and stopped wearing her robes while still maintaining a strong Zen practice. She even reached the point where she could humorously observe, "I hope [my robes] are not embarrassed to share space with the silk negligee I save for special weekends with my husband."[8]

It's interesting that Fran sees her robes as "embarrassed" to be hanging in the same closet as her sexy silk negligee. She's right; the two don't really go together. Any woman who's tried so hard to erase everything "feminine" about herself—her "messy female emotions," her hair, her clothing, her voice, her body language—will experience coming back into her body as a failure. But even a woman who is comfortable with her robes and bald head can't escape being regarded as a distraction to men who would otherwise be chastely focusing on their meditations and not fantasizing about her breasts. At one Zen center, I once heard a prominent visiting Zen teacher talk about his difficulty restraining his urges to *rape* (he didn't say "have sex with," he said "rape"!) every woman sitting in the zendo. No surprise that he was later involved in several messy sex scandals and a paternity suit lodged by one of his female students. But that didn't stop him from continuing to function as a Zen leader. Nor did the superiors in his respectable Zen lineage censure him. In fact, they promoted him to *roshi*. I doubt that kind of tolerance from the Zen establishment would be extended to a woman; even if she didn't have sex with her students, being a lesbian would be enough to condemn her. Jisho Warner, a Zen priest and dharma heir of Dainin Katagiri Roshi, would agree. She states matter-of-factly: "Most Buddhist lineages would repudiate me first as a woman and again as a lesbian." But Jisho refuses to let society mold her "life as a lesbian," or to "look to my Dharma lineage, to the sutras and commentaries, or to the Vinaya for models of how to be me as a priest." Called upon to continuously reinvent herself within the parameters of her liberal Zen lineage, she asserts, "In the Dharma it doesn't matter one whit what I call myself . . . all Dharma practice is embodied practice . . . true practice is with our bodies, not with our ideas about ourselves . . . including my ideas of being a particular thing called a lesbian. Or a particular thing called a priest . . . My job is . . . attempting to love the world no matter what kind of reception I get."[9]

Not trying to get anywhere. Or prove anything. Responding to the world with love, caring, and compassion—but not without first recognizing our anger and loving ourselves and our bodies as we are: this is the "female vision" of women currently reshaping Zen practice.

Again, I think Toni Packer puts it best, so I'll give her the last word on the subject: "About twenty years ago, sitting in a zendo, trying to be a good meditator way into the night, I noticed clearly for the first time how every once in a while in the midst of quiet, unconcerned sitting, the brain would click in with the question: 'Am I doing all right?' 'Am I getting somewhere?' When the 'am I doing it right' tape became transparent, it was also clear that I don't have to know how I am doing. Sitting quietly is not knowing . . . Not knowing, the body is at ease."[10]

12

Zen "Ox-Herding" for Women

The Ten Ox-Herding Pictures

The image of the ox as an embodiment of the divine goes as far back as the origins of civilization in ancient Babylon. Still used in traditional agricultural societies throughout the Middle East and Asia for plowing, transportation, food, and fuel, the ox continues to stand as a symbol of divine beneficence for millions of people today. Ancient Indian traditions based on the Vedic *Upanishads* (400 B.C.E.) used the metaphor of the ox and herdsman to characterize the search for spiritual enlightenment. In the eighth century of the common era, Chinese Ch'an (Zen) Buddhists extended the Indian ox metaphor to create *The Ten Ox-Herding Pictures*. Accommodating the allegory to their own cultural environments, Japanese, Korean, and Vietnamese Zen Buddhists transported the original Chinese version of *The Ten Ox-Herding Pictures* to their homelands shortly after. The Chinese Ox-Herding texts were translated and brought to the West by Buddhist scholars in the nineteenth century, but it was not until the American Zen boom of the mid-twentieth century that they began to enjoy the popularity that has been associated with them ever since. As a result, this eighth-century Chinese allegory is probably the best-known collection of Zen art in the world today.

Comprised of ten ink drawings, each accompanied by a poem, *The Ten Ox-Herding Pictures* depicts the adventures of a boy ox-herder as he makes his way along the difficult path of self-realization. In the first panel, we see the ox-herder searching for his missing ox. In the second, he locates the ox's traces. In the third, he finds the ox. In the fourth, he catches the ox. In the fifth, he tames the ox. In the sixth, he rides the ox home. In the seventh, the ox is forgotten and the herdsman remains. In the eighth, both ox and herdsman disappear. In the ninth, both ox and herdsman return. In the tenth, the herdsman rides his ox into the marketplace with "gift-giving hands"—filled with compassion and totally one with the world.

From its inception in the eighth century, the collection of Chinese Zen drawings and verses known as *The Ten Ox-Herding Pictures* has been the subject of innumerable interpretations. All Zen artists, poets, and commentators nonetheless agree that each of the ten ink drawings, set at the center of a thick black circle, corresponds to a stage in the practice of *zazen*—sitting meditation. So, for centuries, the adventures of the herder in search of his ox were presented as a series of progressive stages marking the way to self-realization. Needless to say, all the commentaries on the ox-herding pictures were made by men. That is, until now.

A Zen Woman's Commentary on the Ox-Herding Pictures

To begin with, instead of tracing a linear progression leading in stages to an endpoint, I read *The Ten Ox-Herding Pictures* holistically. As is more often the case in everyday life (which is far "messier" than these lovely, but relatively static, depictions), there are no clear-cut boundaries marking off the stages of Zen practice. The spiritual path doesn't always take a straight course leading from one point to the next. Like life, it loops, progresses, doubles back on itself, and moves forward again. Zen, too, is a dynamic process, allowing for times when even the most experienced meditator regresses back to stage one. So rather than follow the chronological order of the ten original ox-herding pictures, I don't stick strictly to the sequence. Rather, I approach the linear stages of meditation practice portrayed by the ox-herding pictures and poems in circular ("female") fashion, as they dovetail with the open-ended, ongoing process of ripening into Zen as a life practice.

I take the ox-herding pictures as not only pictorial and poetic representations of a woman's journey to self-realization but as living koans embodying the Zen experience itself. So uniquely do these picture/poems capture the gamut of expressions, emotions, and physical sensations entailed in koan practice that no amount of rendering or interpretation can dim their original luster. With each reading, I feel I am seeing these koan picture/poems for the first time. Incorporating them into my zazen, I can enter each koan and become one with its every detail.

The original Chinese ox-herder is a young boy. Mine is a bold preadolescent girl who is not only responsible for protecting the ox when she leads it out to pasture to graze, but also for overseeing its grooming, health, and general well-being. She's slight but strong enough to lead the ox by a halter attached to a ring in its nose without being trampled. The girl is standing in the middle of a wilderness, looking around. She is surrounded by mountains and coniferous trees and shrubs. A little stream runs nearby, its banks strewn with rocks and lined with boulders. The landscape is wild and deserted but beautiful, in its own way. The girl ox-herder is the only human being we see. There she stands, in the middle of this craggy wilderness, looking around, obviously searching for something. From the empty halter she carries in her hand, it's clear that she has lost her ox and is wandering about in the hope of retrieving it and leading it back home. The girl looks around with a mixed expression of anxiety and hope. Her body speaks of isolation, dismay, even of desperation. She's just standing there, bewildered. She isn't even actively searching, just looking around, toying with the empty halter in one hand and holding up the other to shade her eyes from the setting sun. Perhaps she has stopped here because she has a hunch that the ox is somewhere in the area. At this point, even a glimpse of it will do.

We Zen women are all ox-herding girls who at one time or another find ourselves standing in this craggy, inhospitable male-centered wilderness, looking around with an empty halter in our hands, trying desperately to find the ox. Bemused, puzzled, a little fearful of having ventured out so far alone, we wonder what to do next. We're looking for something, yet we don't really know what it is. We've searched for it a long time, making our way deeper and deeper into the thickets of our thoughts, emotions, images, hopes, memories, dreams, and projections. The object of our search, the thing we want most—enlightenment, self-realization, peace of mind, understanding, clarity, contentment—is nowhere to be found. And yet, there's something that drives us on. Could it be the high-pitched song of the cicadas singing in the trees—evidence that we are not alone on the path—that gives us the courage to continue searching?

What are all these bushes, trees, and boulders—this wilderness in which we find ourselves? They are nothing more than the context of our search, be it a less than satisfactory job or a tense relationship with our male Zen teacher. Too often, however, we lose ourselves in the scenery and begin to wander off. Haunted by the search for special experiences, extraordinary moments, we start objectifying the landscape of our lives. We fantasize about quitting our job, leaving our partner, and running off to a monastery: "How much simpler my life would be if I were a Zen monk rather than a woman tied up in a relationship and a nine-to-five job." We're so busy concocting images of the ox and its whereabouts that we don't see that we're headed straight for a muddy swamp. We're spending so much effort in escaping the moment that we're left confused and exhausted. We're so intent on looking around for our elusive "ox" that—paying no attention to the ground under our feet—we suddenly find ourselves knee-deep in that muddy swamp. What is this place that we enter without even noticing? Why are we stuck there? Think about it. We have all experienced this condition from time to time, so we all know the answer to this question.

Not contented with ourselves as we are, we languish in our imagined world. Captured by ideals and preconceptions about the ox, our own lives inevitably fall short. It's so easy to lose ourselves in this craggy wilderness of thoughts, hopes, and wishes—a perfect hiding place for the ox. Our discontent thickens the underbrush and blocks the path with boulders. Straying further and further, we lose ourselves in searching for a "he-ox" whose body and experiences have nothing to do with our own. At times we might convince ourselves that we've arrived at our ideal condition. Lying down among the fragrant grasses under the setting sun—settling into our zazen—body and mind drop away and we experience one of those magical moments: "Oh! I know what the ox is. It's this wonderfully peaceful state of mind." Okay, now, what? No sooner have we experienced that wonderfully peaceful state of mind than it's gone. "Where did that terrific feeling go? My back stopped hurting. I stopped thinking about the chewing out my boss gave me at work. Or about the five pounds I must have put on last night after eating all that chocolate because I was depressed. I had a few minutes of pure peace. I want it back!" And the chase resumes.

We slog our way through the mud in search of the ox. Now we're even more lost. The dusty regions of our mind, of our existence—the familiar landscape—recedes ever further from view. Maybe the ox has no shape, no form or substance at all. Maybe that's what's meant by "emptiness." This whole experience could be nothing but a dream, an illusion. One brief moment of bliss, and the ox seems further away than ever. We take a step forward and unexpectedly find ourselves entangled in a thicket we've mistaken for the path that will lead us to the ox. Suddenly we remember we're carrying a halter. What about that halter? Do we really need it in order to find what we're looking for? How did the ox slip out of it? Why were we so careless?

Oops! Now we've gotten ourselves more deeply entangled. If we stay in this thicket long enough, we grow even more confused and anxious. Eventually we start chastising ourselves for having taken up such a futile search. This thicket of self-doubt is the place where everything is up for questioning. It's a really tough place to get out of. How do we go about it? Should we lasso the nearest branch with the halter and pull ourselves out? Or should we just stay where we are?

None of the above. We just come back to the breath. We stop worrying about the ox. We stop trying to find it. Most important, we stop chastising ourselves for losing the way. There's no use trying to flee through the escape hatch of memory, either. Stop thinking about yesterday. It's gone. Just attend to this breath, this moment—right here, amidst all the doubt and confusion.

If we stop to listen, we'll realize that there is never a moment when those cicadas aren't singing—in the trees, in the stars, in the supermarket, even in the midst of an argument with the *roshi*—in that very same bushy, dappled place where we're standing, even though we're scratched by thorns and mired deep in mud. It may be faint at first, but that song keeps us going. We may be exhausted, on the verge of giving up. But that's a good sign, because it means we're starting to let go, that our fingers are starting to loosen around that halter; our determination to find that ox and tie it down so that it will never again run away is starting to weaken. The struggle has served to loosen the hold of our womanly fears of unworthiness. It has helped us understand, if even for a moment, that there's no way we're going to catch that ox by trying to transform ourselves into men. Perhaps the only way to find it is by dropping all our notions about what a Zen ox should look like in the first place. Could it be that we're running after the wrong animal? Who says we have to find a "he" ox? Maybe we'd be better served if we searched for a "she-ox"—like the Native American White Buffalo Woman—female symbol of the redemptive power of compassion. Just because the old Zen patriarchs say the ox-herder and the ox are both male doesn't mean it has to be so.

Knowing that other women have been here before us, and that they have carved a path through the underbrush, bolsters our confidence. As we adapt to trekking around in the male-centered wilderness we might even find one of these women to guide us. But even experienced wilderness trekkers get bitten by mosquitoes, and sometimes even by snakes. We still have to deal with the mud and the fever on our own. Losing our sense of direction, we may even want to give up. Or hoping for rescue, wanting to be taken back into the fold, we may set off flares. Taking refuge in patriarchal Zen lineage charts, black robes, bald heads, and transmission ceremonies, we fill the sky with flashing lights—and are disappointed when nothing comes of it. Once again, we've reached a dead end, with nowhere to go. We're right back where we started. It's unfair. Here we are, crying, pleading, hollering: "Where are you, ox? Didn't I do everything I was told to do? I sat regularly, attended every single *sesshin*, answered all the roshi's koan questions the way he wanted me to—and here I am, still searching for that damned ox."

The ghost bushes and grasses through which we make our way may be dense, making it difficult to see where we're going. Or they may be thin, allowing us a full view of she-ox traces to follow. Either way, the resolve we are confronted with every day of our lives is, "I will keep searching for her no matter what happens." And we are rewarded by a passing glimmer of awareness, the knowledge that she is with us—right here, in the bushes and grasses we're clinging to so tightly. The berries on those bushes—all those days, all those intermingled tastes and transient experiences that confront us—may be sweet or bitter, but they are none other than the she-ox herself.

If it weren't for the sound of those cicadas singing in the trees, we'd have given up long ago. In the evening, right there, when everything is quiet, we know, deep inside, that there's something about this search that is worthwhile. We don't know exactly what it is, but we know it, because we can hear those cicadas singing. Even when we're knee-deep in mud, thoroughly lost, we know the way; mindfulness and caring have made us more adept at thinning out the underbrush of fantasies, dreams, and memories that block our entry into the moment. It's not that we cut off those mental thorns forever; we still get scratched. But those scratches no longer cut as deep.

Over time the landscape changes. It may happen slowly, but change does happen along the way. Not one, but many changes happen. We know those subtle changes, we experience them in our daily lives, when we go to the office, or clean the house, or read a book. Something has changed in our interactions with the world. What is it? Perhaps it's our attitude toward change itself? No longer resisting, no longer doomed to a life of interminable searching, we merely let change happen. Losing, finding, taming the she-ox and riding her into the marketplace, we know that she was never lost. She is always standing right here, where we are—an honored guest in her own home. No matter how far up the mountain she may climb, she cannot escape. She has no place to hide. Her traces are everywhere.

Nothing Holy, Nothing Special

When Bodhidharma, the founder of Zen in China, had his first and only audience with the emperor, a devout Buddhist, he declared that nothing, not even Buddhism, was holy. Seeing the emperor's blank expression, Bodhidharma asked him if he understood what he meant. The emperor said he didn't understand, so Bodhidharma left. Like the emperor, most people wouldn't consider searching for an ox a holy undertaking. But, as Bodhidharma said, there's nothing holy about Zen. In fact, it's pretty earthy. Oxen aren't the cleanest animals on the farm, either. They tend to leave big piles of dung after them as they move along. So, the first thing an experienced ox-herder would be likely to look for is a spoor trail. What is a spoor trail, and why is it relevant here? In Africa, or even closer to home in the forests of

North America, hunters track game by following the dried dung animals leave in their wake. Native Americans pursued deer and bison by following spoor trails across the most difficult terrain. Indigenous people all over the world, who live close to the soil and depend on animals for food, clothing, and housing materials, are all experts at discovering the whereabouts of animals from such spoor trails. Any ox-herder worth her salt would therefore be looking down at the ground for traces of ox dung. Why? Because she knows that "holiness" is as far away as you can get from the ox. Unlike the Chinese emperor who interviewed Bodhidharma, the ox-herder isn't so busy looking up at the heavens that she'll ignore the little trail of spoor ahead of her and lose the ox altogether. Pity the poor emperor. The very precious goal of his pursuit was right there in front of him, and he missed it because it appeared to be too low, too insignificant. It was dirty. It stank. And who knows, it might even have been contaminated. Besides, it was beneath the Son of Heaven's dignity to kowtow to a human being—not to speak of bending over to mindfully investigate a pile of ox dung!

Like the emperor, we, too, sometimes think we're above looking at that little trail of dried ox dung. We recoil in horror at the first whiff of its scent. Ashamed of our she-ox's animal nature, we deny her. And in so doing, we blunder. I did, the first time I came across the koan about the Chinese Zen master Yun-men who called the Buddha "a dried shit stick" (the ancient Chinese equivalent of a "shit-smeared piece of toilet paper"). I was mortified. I came to Zen as a Platonist, my head filled with dualistic notions of a transcendent soul and a base body. It didn't seem possible that enlightenment could have anything to do with ordinary human functions, let alone trivial or material things. I thought enlightenment, the manifestation of true Buddha Nature, couldn't be anything but a heavenly experience, transcending nature. It was the same when I first read *The Ten Ox-Herding Pictures*. My ox had wings and flew through the clouds, like Pegasus, the magical flying horse in the Greek myths. I certainly didn't imagine a shit-producing, smelly ox like the kind you find in a barnyard. In fact, so glorified and ethereal was my idea of Zen, that it was inconceivable to me that an enlightened Zen master, or Buddha, or bodhisattva would have any human qualities at all. I thought that the practice would have refined such a person to the point where one was never angry, never constipated, nasty, or cranky. I was convinced that a woman who was truly in touch with her ox would be smiling, blissful, and lovely—all the time. One whose heart would be open to the world and continuously spilling forth loving-kindness and compassion. But that was before I actually started practicing Zen.

Round and round we go, caught up in our illusions, notions, fantasies (harbored for who knows how long) about the true nature of the ox. The ox of perfection: once we find it, we promise ourselves, we'll never leave that mountain peak. Once we've attained nirvana, all our flaws will drop away and we'll be supremely enlightened Buddhas. We will never again grasp at anything, never need anything. The material world will melt in front of our feet as we glide six feet off the ground like the sex-changing women in the Buddhist sutras, bestowing benevolence wherever we go. This condition is not only time consuming, but dangerous. We can sit down to rest in that withered ghost bush for years. Hypnotized by male-created images of the ox, a woman can remain in that dead-end place for her entire life—never noticing that her "she-ox" is right there with her all along.

Invidious Comparisons

Another dangerous trap awaits the ox-herder when she starts comparing herself to other women. We all do this: "Lots of women are on this path, but I'm going to be the one who finds the ox." We've been conditioned to compete with others, wanting to get there first. But where, exactly, is *there*? Some Zen masters used to encourage this kind of one-upmanship by parading people who experienced *kensho* (awakening) through the *zendo* during sesshin, announcing their great achievement by making a big ceremonial display of them. Needless to say, this only resulted in enhancing the envy of all the "un-awakened" sitters in the room. Fortunately, the increasing democratization of Zen is putting an end to such practices. In substituting egalitarian circles for the hierarchical Zen pyramid with the roshi on his high seat and eliminating the glorified race to the enlightenment prize, women are largely responsible for these salutary changes.

Sometimes, perhaps as a result of having read too many Zen books, we set unrealistic goals for ourselves. Inspired by great Zen masters of the past, stories of their vast enlightenment experiences, we start blowing things out of proportion. The very ordinariness of Zen becomes extraordinary when we aim at nothing less than a big-bang experience, a total transformation. We get so caught up in following our fantasies of becoming great Zen masters that we lose our sense of direction. Where were we headed? North? South? We stand gazing at the empty halter in our hand, suddenly realizing that our she-ox has vanished. Even her little spoor trail is gone. This is a sure sign that we missed a turn somewhere and have strayed right back into the trap of our preconceptions.

Wondering where we went wrong, we start rehearsing all the old stuff about what a she-ox must look like. Given steam by all the books we've read, the stories we've heard, we torture ourselves with invidious comparisons. "So-and-So is an expert at the tea ceremony, and she's a roshi; I'm going to take up the practice of tea." Or, basking in vicarious glory of our women Zen idols, we hang around them all day trying to make ourselves indispensable. Following that pseudo ox trail in our head is so confusing. We thrash around for a while. Then we give up. It finally hits us that there's no use worrying about other women's accomplishments. There's only one way to find that ox—and that's *our* way, no matter what happens or how long it takes.

Finding herself at a crossroads, having to make a choice about which way to go, the ox-herder appears to waver. It's almost as though she's prodding herself on, retracing the original questions that made her start searching in the first place. Does this search apply to all women, or am I just some kind of freak? Think about it. In your own family, or at school, or at work, or in the social or religious community you were brought up in—how many women have you known who were looking for the ox? How many do you know who have found it? Does the ox-herder's plight truly reflect your own?

The underlying assumption of Buddhism is that everyone—male or female, aware of it or not—is looking for this ox, for the meaning of life and death, of suffering, of relationships. With its emphasis on meditation, Zen Buddhism goes directly to the heart of existential questions like, "Who am I?" "What am I doing here?" "What is my purpose?" Yet, despite our experience of life's brevity and pain, most of us choose not to answer, but to divert ourselves from such questions. Telling ourselves we might as well pack it all in now, since it's all going to be over with soon anyway, we chase after perfunctory, fugitive pleasures. In a futile attempt to stave off aging, sickness, and death, we dive headfirst into an obsessive quest for fame, wealth, and eternal youth. It's especially sad to see this among young women today, who don't seem to have the slightest shred of social consciousness—not to speak of spiritual hunger. For example, at the university where I taught, many of my women's studies students unashamedly admitted that they were only getting a degree in order to get a high-paying job. But they were not the only ones; showing this attitude to be widespread, one CNN poll reported that more than half the college students in the United States expect to be multimillionaires before turning forty. Notice they don't say they *hope*, but *expect*, to be not millionaires but *multimillionaires* before they're forty. Unfortunately, theirs is the most common way of looking for the ox in today's world.

Another way of avoiding the ox is by satisfying ourselves with ready-made, second-hand answers. We seek refuge from our questions by relying on "the wisdom of the ancients"—religious scriptures, faith, promises of salvation, reward in heaven, or punishment in hell. Judging from the worldwide resurgence of religious fundamentalism, this seems to do it for millions of people who cut off their search for the ox by refusing to start out at all. Content to live vicariously through the experiences of other spiritual seekers, they simply plop themselves down in a ghost bush and stay where they are.

Commitment

Probably every woman at one point or another in her life has pursued the ox—however briefly or unknowingly. The difference between those who get a glimpse of it and those who give up searching is that the first group are willing to shoulder the responsibility for themselves, while the others are either too afraid to search or would rather let someone else shoulder the responsibility for them. It's not that a woman who practices Zen is a superior being, a member of a spiritual elite. The distinction between the many and the few marks the difference between those who take the easy way by latching onto a quick and easy answer without assuming responsibility for the search, and those who will settle for nothing less than an actual, intimate confrontation with that she-ox, even if it takes years of slogging through that obstacle-ridden terrain.

A committed Zen practitioner who is resolved never to stop until she finds her ox, our herder picks up the halter and continues walking. North side of the mountain . . . south side of the mountain . . . Through the valleys, through sickness, boredom, pain, joy, delusion, bliss—through all these, it's about having the grace, the courage to go with your gut instinct that there's only one way. You follow your she-ox's scent, even when it grows very faint, even when it seems that her spoor trail may not have been there at all, that it was just another illusion. "What am I doing sitting on this cushion for five days with my legs tucked under me, my back breaking, not allowed to speak, wondering who that woman is sitting in the interview room. Why am I talking about my most intimate experiences on the cushion to someone I see only four times a year? What is this practice about, anyway? I'm getting nowhere. I was getting more out of sitting home in my comfortable armchair listening to inspirational tapes."

Yes, it's true, getting out there and actually looking for your she-ox is infinitely harder than relaxing in your favorite armchair and listening to inspirational tapes. You don't get blisters on your feet or cricks in your neck or poison ivy crawling through imaginary tall grasses and spiky ghost bushes, for one. But it isn't possible to find your she-ox any other way. Simply resting there isn't going to cut it. At some point you'll have to get up and make a move. You'll have to plunge into that wild and craggy terrain if you want to find her.

Here the ox-herding girl becomes your companion, appearing just when you need her. She's telling you not to worry. Hers is the voice inside that whispers benevolently, "Go on. Go on. Take courage. Know that on the Great Way of light and darkness, of pleasure and pain, of suffering and joy, everything is as it should be. This very place is the Lotus-Land. This very body is the Buddha." This very path, along which everything ceaselessly comes and goes, is the only way there is. *Knowing that makes everything okay.* Finding the ox, not finding the ox—the search itself is all that matters.

The Ox-Herder's Smile

In the manuscript collection of Shokokuji monastery in Kyoto, a fifteenth-century Japanese illustration of the third ox-herding picture, "Glimpsing the Ox," shows the little ox-herder running after the ox. All we see is the animal's rump. Its big tail is sticking out, practically wagging in the ox-herder's face, but its head and horns aren't visible. The ox-herder is smiling. This charming picture of the gleeful ox-herder running barefoot after the ox is perhaps the most comic illustration in the series. That smile signals the way out of the ghost bush.

During sesshin, or even perhaps during an evening of zazen, you enter a stage—sometimes only for an instant—where your preoccupations simply drop away and everything is okay as it is. This experience is often accompanied by a warm feeling in your stomach, and a sense of wonder at the moment, whatever it might be presenting: just breathing, or seeing a ray of sunlight on the floor in front of you, or hearing the whistling wind outside. However ordinary, that moment deeply touches you. It doesn't have to be a moment on the cushions. It's possible to glimpse that she-ox anywhere, at any time—even right in the middle of work. But it's always unexpected. You can't make it happen.

You're sitting at your desk, in the middle of preparing a report, and the telephone rings. You pick it up and say "Hello," and suddenly, right there, in the sound of your own voice answering the phone, it hits you: "That's it! I couldn't be doing anything else, I couldn't be anywhere else, just right here! Talking!" And it feels really good. It's this good feeling that makes you smile. Like the ox-herder, your face lights up with a joyous smile. You experience a rush of gratitude—not directed at anyone or anything in particular, not a person or an object, or a state or condition—you're just feeling gratitude for its own sake, for being there talking on the telephone, perceiving the moment for its own sake. Or, though you may have seen it every day, one morning on your way out of the house, you happen to catch a glimpse of the locust tree in the yard, or you see a bird hopping onto a telephone wire, and you spontaneously break into a smile at the wonder of it all. That's what glimpsing your she-ox is about.

An old Chinese Zen poet captured it best when he said: "To be mature in Zen is to be mature in expression." The ability to embrace the moment—just as it is—is the stage where Zen becomes mature. We simply express ourselves. Whoever we are, whatever we happen to be doing—whether it's nursing a baby or loading the car trunk with bottles and taking them to the recycling bin—the act is itself already the perfect expression of the goal. Means and ends are no longer distinct. In other words, action and aim have become one. There is no thought coming between them. All thoughts of a goal have, in fact, vanished.

It's interesting that the ox-herder's smile is the same smile we see on the face of Kuan Yin Bodhisattva on her pedestal in the Honolulu Art Academy. And that Vietnamese Zen teacher Thich Nhat Hanh speaks of doing zazen with a "half smile" on your face. I'd prefer a full smile, a big, generous grin. Why? Because it's the perfect expression of peace of mind, of contentment, of joy in being alive, of the vibrancy and vitality we experience that doesn't need anything special for it to appear—because everything is already special. Opening the door of the refrigerator and cleaning it out is a joyful event (believe it or not), simply because it's what we happen to be doing at the moment. That's what a woman's maturity in Zen is about: living encounters with her she-ox—over and over again.

There's a saying in Chinese Zen that describes enlightenment as awakening to the fact that the willows are green, the flowers are yellow, the sun shines—everything is just as it is. No adornments, no commentaries or evaluations are necessary. The she-ox pervades the whole universe. Every breath we take is filled with her presence. She is as much part of us as salt is part of seawater.

The sun shines warmly on our skin. We feel the breeze wafting through the green river willows, and we are filled with joy. Just the breeze, the warmth of the sun on our skin, the slam of the door down the hall, the bark of the neighbor's dog in the yard, a woman in a muumuu sitting on the steps reading the L.L. Bean catalog: that's it! Once we truly realize that the she-ox has no place to hide, we experience the end of suffering. We make complete the practice of Zen.

Of course we can't make that condition permanent. But that doesn't stop us from trying to, from chasing after it again and again to no avail. This is where the power of our Zen practice comes in. Rather than letting the dualistic mind greedily chase after that glimpse again and again, we can just come back to the moment. We can come back to the breath, or to whatever it is we're doing. We go on playing ping pong, cleaning the refrigerator, throwing out the garbage, making the bed, calling our friend, going out for dinner, sitting zazen—and suddenly, unexpectedly—*"Whoa! Here she is! What a collision!"*

Longing for Permanence

The ox-herder is smiling, blissful, yet she's running after the ox's disappearing hindquarters as fast as her feet will carry her. There is effort, strain, self-consciousness in her desire to catch up with the ox again. She has just glimpsed the ox. She's overjoyed. So, why is she so frantically running after it? Let's explore this paradox.

As soon as we experience that luminous instant of "just being," our dualistic mind can't help but jump into action. "Hey, that felt good. What was it? It must have been *samadhi*—the blissful absorption I'm supposed to experience in meditation, the peace of mind that comes from glimpsing my she-ox. It had to be *samadhi*, then. Uh . . . I was there, right?" At that moment, the gap is opened; our she-ox is running away, and all we see is her generous rump and curly wagging tail. Our first impulse is to run after her. Prompted by the dualistic mind, we want to grab hold of that joyous moment we've just experienced. We want to tie it down, make it permanent, and that's where the suffering starts.

Run as we may, we will never catch up with her. That's because the joyful experience of glimpsing the she-ox isn't something happening outside us. It has nothing to do with changing conditions, with whether we had a good day or a bad one, whether we felt happy or unhappy, whether the movie we watched was thrilling or boring, for, each and every one of these changing conditions is itself the she-ox, right there in the flesh. What widens the gap between her and us is the attempt to make permanent the peace of mind that descends on us unexpectedly when we see that "everything just is."

It's important to remember that we can't *force* a glimpse of the she-ox; it only happens unexpectedly, when we're not self-consciously running after it. Aitken Roshi used to say, "We can't make the accident happen, but through zazen, we can make ourselves accident-prone." That is, we greatly enhance our chances of glimpsing her when we sit zazen. It's a very important part of training for the event. And let's not forget that Zen practice is a form of training, a way of life. We can't expect to glimpse the she-ox without zazen. So, it's essential that we keep to a regular schedule of sitting meditation. Unlike Zen professionals for whom zazen is part of their daily life in the monastery, as women living, working, and raising families out in the world we have to be especially careful not to give in to the tendency to let our practice slide. We wouldn't dream of not taking a shower for three weeks. And yet, for some reason, we tell ourselves we're too busy, make all sorts of excuses for not sitting zazen, sometimes for even longer than three weeks. Glimpsing the she-ox is what makes our practice real, in that we begin to understand that any moment is a wonderful opportunity for us to express who and what we are—in that very moment—without any reservations. And meditating is the best way to go about it.

There's a koan in the *Mumonkan*, the thirteenth-century collection of koans and verses by the Chinese Ch'an master Mumon, that also involves an ox—a water buffalo, actually. I like to think of Mumon's water buffalo as White Buffalo Woman. She's extraordinary because, despite her great size, she can pass through a window. Her head, horns, hooves, massive body, and hind legs all get through—yet her tiny little tail cannot. Why? Because her passage is still not complete. It can never be complete. That's the point. For completion is just another barrier, another concept we put in our heads that keeps us from glimpsing her. For some reason, we think completion is what we're here for. We create all sorts of notions about it. We're so disappointed when the "real moment" doesn't measure up to the one we've created that we fall headlong into the pit of despair.

Zazen is our way out of that pit. It allows us to let go of those notions and see them for what they really are. We detach ourselves from the need to paint a "complete picture" of the she-ox, and suddenly there she is with her great head and majestic horns, popping out of the underbrush, wagging her curly tail. Still not fully through that window, but that's okay.

The Heart-Ox

I was initially puzzled by a reference in the eighth-century Chinese version of the ox-herding pictures to the "heart-ox." Since I didn't see the association between the words "heart" and "ox," I wondered why the poet put them together. At first I thought it might be a mistranslation. But then I remembered that the Chinese words for "heart" and "mind" use the same characters. The implication is that there is no distinction between heart and mind, emotion and thought, so it's possible that the "heart-ox" represents the mind/self and emotion/self. As mind, it produces thoughts; as heart, it produces feelings. Self-realization reveals the true nature of the ox as "Buddha-heart/mind." It collapses the heart and mind into one, obliterating all distinctions between emotion and intellect, subject and object, self and other. We divide heart and mind when we talk about the world of distinctions—colors and forms, hot and cold, day and night. But the heart-ox is neither male or female, black or white, tall or short, fat or bony, for all distinctions vanish as soon as the ox-herder catches a glimpse of it.

This experience of interdependence (recognizing the other as no other than oneself) is where loving-kindness enters quite naturally into Zen practice, leading us beyond empathy or pity to the most reflexive acts of compassion. Thus, while not devotional, Zen can truly be called a practice of the heart. We find this in the relationships that develop over years of practicing together as a *sangha*, a Zen community. People spontaneously and unselfconsciously perform compassionate acts in what appear to be the most ordinary ways. It happens all the time in our Princeton Area Zen group. One member created a brochure and a Listserv to make it easier for us to get together via e-mail. Another taped our dharma talks and discussions. Another created the group's website. A member who is a professional accountant handles our accounts free of charge. Two donate their family beach house for sesshin. If one member can't make it as timekeeper on a Sunday evening of zazen, there's always someone to fill in. And of course there's our fabulous cook to feed us delicious vegetarian meals during sesshin. Nobody has to ask. As reflexively as the Bodhisattva Kuan Yin reaching over for her pillow in her sleep, these acts of compassion speak to an essential quality of Zen practice that is intimately related to the experience of glimpsing the heart-ox.

When the heart-ox pervades our lives, we find that good works are no longer duties that have been imposed upon us. Social action is neither an ethical imperative nor a religious commandment designed to make us feel guilty. It is simply the heart-ox manifesting itself in the moment of ladling soup for the homeless or staying after school to talk to that kid who is being bullied. Repeated glimpses of the heart-ox become the basis for our Bodhisattva Vow to save the many beings of this world instead of merely seeking our own enlightenment. Most of us aren't full-fledged bodhisattvas yet, but that doesn't matter. Even the Buddha himself is said to be still practicing. And like the Buddha, we just keep at it. Despite all the greed, hatred, and ignorance besetting us, we try our best to be mindful of slipping up and not behaving like a bodhisattva. It helps to know that, even when we're not glimpsing her, our heart-ox is always there.

As we become more mindful of the heart-ox, we begin to manifest compassion in every area of our lives. The instinct to ameliorate suffering is inherent in all of us; there's no need to think about it. It's the natural, unselfconscious activity of the heart/mind. No roshi or god or Buddha can teach it to us. We don't have to learn it; it's already there.

But before we become too saintly, let's remember that no matter how many times we catch a glimpse of our heart-ox, that's not our permanent condition. Nothing is permanent—not even enlightenment. This may be hard for us to grasp, because we all come to spiritual practice with the hope of not merely glimpsing her, but of never losing sight of her again, and that isn't possible. There is no end to glimpsing and then losing sight of her. It is part of the ongoing, dynamic process called life. The ox-herding picture/poem koans are like that, too. Entering them doesn't happen in linear stages leading us from point A to point Z or from "delusion" to "nirvana." Interpenetrating and dovetailing into one another, they're a dynamic, ongoing process that never ends.

When we think of the heart-ox in the context of social engagement—the way we see, relate to, and interact with others—we get a much clearer idea of why there is so much conflict and misunderstanding the moment she disappears into the bushes. We experience this very clearly during sesshin, where one twenty-five-minute period of zazen feels like heaven and the next feels like hell. It's not that the practice takes you further toward becoming a saint. Remember what Jan Chozen Bays says about flawed human beings who—especially if they are spiritual teachers—have to openly acknowledge that they're no different from all the rest of the many beings occupying our messy, dynamic world of love and hate, of violence and beauty. The point of being a bodhisattva is not to become perfect, but to work continuously to bring more heart-ox activity into that messy, dynamic world.

The great majority of today's women Zen practitioners are not monastic. Nor are they even Buddhists. For example, I'm a Zen teacher who guides people in meditation. I'm not a priest or a roshi, and I don't perform any clerical functions. In a way, this makes it easier for my students to see that Zen isn't about professional accomplishment. My practice is about diligence—not flawlessness. It's not about beating up on yourself for not being perfect. Nor is it about eliminating thoughts. "Sweep as you will, you cannot sweep out the mind," as one koan has it. So what is it that we're trying to do here? We're giving the heart-ox a free hand, letting her manifest herself in every form, voice, image, and activity of our lives.

Why do we sit? What has the search for our she-ox got to do with zazen? Isn't our searching itself manifesting her presence? We sit because it's incomparably easier to find her when we make space for her than if we tried to do it without a meditation practice. This is especially evident after sesshin, when we notice that—like the smile lighting up the ox-herder's face—the "sesshin glow" continues to illuminate our daily lives. Things are sharper. We are more centered, more settled, not as easily rattled by events. We're gentler with ourselves and others, less driven to accumulate—fame, money, comforts—whatever it is we're driven to accumulate. We're more contented to just *be* than to be doing something, running after some goal.

Like the time Manfred and I had just come out of a seven-day sesshin in Hawai'i and were driving home when our car suddenly stopped dead in the middle of a busy street: normally, I'd be frustrated and complaining, but on that day I was uncharacteristically calm about the whole thing. Without a word, I just got out of the car and helped him push it all the way to the nearest garage, which was almost a mile away. I could even laugh at myself as we made our way through the streets. Not even the high repair bill could unsettle me. That most certainly would not have been the case if I hadn't just emerged from sesshin.

Just let the willows be green; let the gentle breeze blow through your hair; let the warm sun shine on your skin. You have to stop in order to experience it. If you keep running after your heart-ox, she'll never reveal herself.

The ox-herder opens her eyes, takes a look, and sees herself. She sees herself in her neighbor, her cat, even in that difficult teenage daughter asking for a tattoo. It takes a deep degree of commitment and a willingness to perceive the heart-ox in the world of the many beings. It is only when we turn the mind away from its habit of splitting off the self from everyone and everything else that she turns up. How can we help but smile when this happens? All we have to do is open up to the world of the ten thousand things, and the heart-ox will appear on her own. Don't try to make it happen. Simply open up to the moment and let the cicadas in the treetops trill her out of hiding.

Postscript

The True Woman of No Rank

The great Chinese T'ang Dynasty Master Lin-chi (Rinzai) was fond of gathering his monks in the meditation hall and throwing out a question or a phrase in the hope that someone would come up with a worthy Zen response. Sitting before the assembly one day, he challenged the monks with what was to become one of the most famous koans in the history of Zen.

Picture this wild old "Crazy Cloud" glowering down at the standing crowd of terrified monks from his Zen master's high seat, proclaiming in his thundering voice: "Upon this lump of red flesh is a true person of no rank who continuously goes in and out through the eyes, ears, nose, and skin of your face. Those who have not recognized this person, watch out! Watch out!"

Nobody dares move.

Then, from somewhere in the middle of the crowd, there's a rustling as a wiry, jug-eared little monk steps forward and makes his way toward Lin-chi. Stopping only a few inches from the master's seat, the trembling monk clears his throat and, in a high-pitched, piping voice, asks, "What is the true person of no rank?"

The monks all hold their breath.

Lin-chi suddenly descends from his teaching seat. Like a tiger swiping its prey, he grabs the monk by the collar of his robe and roars, "Speak! Speak!"

The monk hesitates for a split second.

Lin-chi thrusts him aside shouting, "What a shit stick this true person of no rank is!"

Then flourishing the long black sleeves of his robe, the master departs the meditation hall leaving the monk standing there with his mouth agape.

Of course Master Lin-chi didn't actually use the word "person" but "man" in delivering his famous Zen challenge. I did. Now, in ending this book on an appropriately feminist note, I'll go even one step further and change the word "person" to "woman" before throwing the question out to you.

"What is this true woman of no rank who continuously goes in and out through the eyes, ears, nose, and skin of your face?"

As they say in Zen, "Hesitate!—and all is lost." Or, "Blink!—and the arrow has already passed Korea."

Unlike the monk who hesitated for only a split second before Lin-chi had done with him, I spent years hesitating before discovering the answer to that question. I was too distracted by my womanly wounds, too bitter and resentful to notice that the true woman of no rank had been there all along. I needed a good dose of serious Zen practice to help me clear my mind and invite her in. Once I stopped hesitating, old Lin-chi's challenge no longer fazed me at all. The true woman of no rank continuously goes in and out of my face. In fact, she made her appearance only last week at an academic conference where I was the only woman participant. I had just finished delivering a paper on women and religion. Before the moderator could open the question period, a white-haired Japanese professor, obviously incredulous, blurted out, "Is there such a thing as a feminist Buddhist?"

Never hesitating for a moment, the woman of true rank replied, "You're looking at one!"

To my delighted surprise, she was greeted with collective murmurs of approval, and even applause, from the men.

This true woman of no rank has countless faces that she is continuously coming in and out of. To the Tibetan Tantrist, she appears as a multicolored *dakini* (female deity) with a thousand heads and arms. To the Hindu Yogi, she comes as Kali, the demon killer. To the Kabbalist, she is the divine Shekhinah. To the Sufi, she is Fatima, the Prophetess. The Christian mystic sees her as the wise Sophia. And the Buddhist as Kuan Yin, the bodhisattva of compassion. But she needn't appear in such exalted forms. The truth is that she most often does not. If you look closely enough, you'll see her in the Chicana driving the bus, or in the old woman leaning on her cane in front of you in line at the museum. Many's the time I've seen her in the bag lady wheeling her shopping cart down the street. No one form can contain her, for she is as varied and unique as those to whom she appears.

The best way to know this true woman of no rank is through meditation. I'll even go so far as to say that the *only* way to truly know her is through meditation. For it is in the still, silent spaces of every woman's heart that she reveals herself most clearly.

After centuries of patriarchal Zen, we're so lucky in having so many wonderful women teachers around to guide us in the uniquely "female vision" of meditation practice alluded to in this book. We women are only at the threshold of a new century, yet it is already clear that we're well under way in creating a practice that is uniquely our own—a wide and generous Zen practice to which all true women—*and men*—of no rank are welcome.

I deliberately emphasize including men because I strongly disagree with separatism of any kind. Despite having been demonized and excluded as a woman, I refuse to give in to the impulse to demonize and exclude men. Gender stereotyping can be very satisfying—even for women. That's because it divides us up into neat little categories and always contains a grain of truth. Women are from Venus and men are from Mars. That's the way it is. Subject closed. Okay, so Zen isn't known for its femininity; but let's not forget that "grandmotherly kindness" is part of Zen, too. One of my favorite koans is about an elderly Chinese Zen master entering the monks' dining hall carrying two heaping buckets of rice he's cooked himself. After setting down the buckets, the old man does a little jig and sings out, "Come, little bodhisattvas and get your rice!" Then gathering the monks around him, he lovingly ladles the rice into their outstretched bowls one by one. That's what I call grandmotherly kindness. It shows that Zen teachers can be gentle and nurturing even when they're men.

The truth is, stereotypes about the way men and women are supposed to behave get us into ruts. They focus too much attention on the battle of the sexes and too little on what we share as human beings in search of a meaningful life. Zen women will never get anywhere if we see all men as competitors, or even worse, as opponents. It's a terrible thing when human beings can't—or won't—talk the same language. Remember the Tower of Babel? It began as a great spiritual experiment. Wanting to see God face to face, people started building an enormous tower toward heaven. God didn't like the idea and suspended the operation on the spot by inventing different languages. Suddenly finding themselves unable to communicate with each other, the people were forced to stop building the tower. As I see it, the lesson of the story is that what distinguishes us is less important than what we share in common. For example, when we breathe, are the inhalations "female" and the exhalations "male?" When we walk, is that step we're taking "masculine" or "feminine?" When we're really doing something without thinking about it, all categories drop away. There is just this breath. Just this step. Yet, it's precisely because we come into the world as male persons and female persons that we can raise our shared spiritual energies without labeling them "male" or "female."

How to experience the "sameness in difference" that supports a true dharma friendship between any two people, woman or man? Being one-hundred-percent present is a good way to start. It helps thin the boundaries between self and the other. It allows you to feel another person's condition as intimately as you do your own regardless of his or her gender. Be present long enough and you will get really good at detecting the subtle cues; you'll soon find yourself anticipating each other's needs in silence. Communication borne of mutual surrender to shared spiritual experience is a by-product of meditation. As you go deeper into it, moving from watching your breath to just breathing, you become increasingly aware that what you thought of as "me" inside and "you" outside are really one and the same.

But to get to this point in your practice you've got to be flexible. Soen Roshi had a lovely way of describing this. He said it was better to be a bamboo than an oak, because the bamboo could sway with the storm and survive, while the fixed oak tree could be split right down the middle. That kind of bamboo flexibility is vital to a relationship in which there are no masters and disciples—just friends. As equals, we have to be able to shift roles from moment to moment, ready to teach or be taught, to lead or be led, as the situation demands.

Zen master Dogen said: "To find the Self, you must lose the self."
Losing the self (the ego) is hard enough when you're practicing alone.
It's even harder when you are interacting with people in a community;
so it's essential to start on level ground. Power-sharing must replace
old hierarchical patterns. And that can't happen in a Zen friendship
that doesn't entail role plurality. We all play many different roles in
our lives. And we all have our strengths and weaknesses. In some
roles, we are called upon to lead; in others, we have to follow people
with more experience or expertise. Women have had an easier time
accepting this; but men, too, are learning to be receptive, willing to
assume different (dare I say, more "feminine") roles in shifting situa-
tions, and to let go of preconceived, petrified hierarchies that threaten
to undermine the fluidity of human interaction.

One way to establish role plurality in a *sangha* is by having women
and men working mindfully together on mundane chores like washing
and drying dishes. Or gardening. Or child care. Here the *sesshin* work
practice (*samu*) model comes in handy. Our Princeton Area Zen
Group membership is small, so sometimes, in addition to rotating
tasks, each participant has to double up and perform two or more of
them. This means that the *zendo* leader might also have to serve as
kitchen cleanup helper after meals. Or that the teacher washes her
own dishes. Sesshin multitasking has worked out very well not just for
the individual members of our Zen group but for their partners, too.
Over the years we've noticed this role flexibility carrying over into our
lives beyond the zendo. One of our members, for example, told me
that she and her husband had renewed their relationship by consciously exchanging chores like driving the kids to school and mowing
the lawn. Best of all, they started cooking dinner together as a form of
meditation in action.

Switching roles is a really good way of practicing detachment. It
helps loosen our dearly held notions about ourselves. When we're
flexible, we don't have to wait for emergencies to slip into new roles to
see how resourceful we really are.

Another helpful way of fostering flexibility in our Princeton Area
Zen Group is by going over the "sesshin cautions." At the outset of
every sesshin, we all gather around the kitchen table and the zendo
leader reads a list of cautions outlining the procedures for carrying
out a smooth-running retreat. The cautions range from introducing

sesshin leaders and assigning tasks to explaining zendo protocol, iden-
tifying the schedule of *zazen* and walking meditation periods, interviews, dharma talks, mealtimes and breaks, and, most importantly,
enumerating the basics of sesshin: silence, mindfulness, and consider-
ation for fellow participants. It doesn't matter whether you're a
teacher, or an experienced Zen sitter, or someone entirely new to the
practice—you listen to and absorb the cautions anew each time
they're read. Having entered the receptive, flexible state of "beginner's mind," you fall naturally into sesshin mode.

It's easy to be mindful within the safe enclosure of a sesshin, away
from home, family, and job with nothing to protect, and where your
dharma friends are meditating alongside you eight hours a day. When
you return to your everyday relationships, however, you're no longer
as sharp—but mindfulness is even more important then. Why? Because when we're attentive, everything we touch, see, smell, taste, and
hear is radiant in its ordinariness. Even a trip to the supermarket becomes a ceremonial occasion. Of course we can't be expected to maintain that receptive, flexible beginner's mind every single minute of our
life—but I can assure you that it does come easier the more you practice it.

Flexibility also demands that we develop a sense for knowing
when to be encouraging and when to offer correction. Take the interactions in the *dokusan* room, where each person plays what Crazy
Cloud Lin-chi called "guest" and "host." Now playing host, the
teacher serves up a word or a question, or a shout, or, on some occasions, sits in silence, and the student is the guest, responding in kind.
Now they change places. When things are going really well, both
reach a point where it's impossible to tell who is host and who is guest.
Or who is teacher and who is student. I think of these *dokusan* encounters as "dharma dancing." Our best performances are the least elaborate, reflecting us at our most vulnerable, when we're shorn of our
ego's defenses. Equally shared, that vulnerability is based on our mutual commitment to dharma dancing. Sometimes we step on each
other's toes. This doesn't mean we stop dancing. We correct the break
in our rhythm and continue on—supporting each other as we go. And
since that correction might come in the form of a sharp, well-timed
shock, it's important that we trust each other. Unlike ordinary dancing, dharma dancing is less about relying on our instincts than it is

about being mindful. Mindful of the changing rhythms of the practice, good dharma dancing partners are adept at tailoring their interactions to the demands of the moment.

It takes a mutual decision to transform Zen "masters" and "disciples" into spiritual friends, and the daring to experiment with fresh, untried ways of practicing together—as equals, friends and partners—each slipping into the role of student or teacher as the situation demands. As this partnership model evolves, the very stuff of our daily life encounters becomes an expression of our Zen maturity. In fact, the boundary between formal practice and ordinary activity disappears altogether. This, I feel, has been the greatest gift women have contributed to Zen.

Notes

Introduction

1. See Joan Halifax Roshi's "Women Ancestors Hymn to the Perfection of Wisdom," http://www.upaua.org/htmls/ ZP _Lit_Women Ancestors.html.
2. See James C. Dobbins, *Letters of the Nun Eshinni: Images of Pure Land Buddhism in Medieval Japan* (Honolulu: University of Hawai'i Press, 2004); and William Bodiford, *The Role of Women in Medieval Soto Zen,* available at http://www.columbia.edu/cu/ea/ac/imjs/programs/1998-fall/Abstracts.
3. See, for example, Bernard Faure, *The Rhetoric of Immediacy: A Cultural Critique of Chan/Zen Buddhism* (Princeton: Princeton University Press, 1991); and Stuart Lachs, "Means of Authorization: Establishing Hierarchy in Ch'an/Zen Buddhism in America," http://www.darkzen.com/Articles/meansofauthorization.htm.

Chapter 1

1. Blanche Hartman, "Pain as a Teaching: Sesshin Lecture Day II," lecture given at the Tassajara Zen Monastery, reprinted from the *Wind Bell,* Volume XXX, No. 2, Summer, 1996, 1, 3–4, available at: http://www.intrex.net/chzg/hartman.htm.
2. Linda Ruth Cutts, "Breaking Through the Concrete," in *Being Bodies: Buddhist Women on the Paradox of Embodiment,* ed. Lenore Friedman and Susan Moon (Boston: Shambhala Publications, 1997), 106–8.
3. Linda Ruth Cutts, "Breaking Through the Concrete," in *Being Bodies,* 108.
4. Charlotte Joko Beck, "Our Substitute Life," in *Being Bodies,* 233.

Chapter 2

1. See Diana Paul, *Women in Buddhism: Images of the Feminine in the Mahayana Tradition* (Berkeley: University of California Press, 1985).

2. Paul, *Women in Buddhism*, chapter 4.
3. Paul, *Women in Buddhism*, chapter 4.
4. Brigid Lowry, "EMBODIMENT," *Mind Moon Circle: Journal of the Sydney, Australia Zen Group*, Spring 2006.
5. Susan Murcott, *The First Buddhist Women: Translations and Commentary on the Therigatha* (Berkeley: Parallax Press, 1991).

Chapter 3

1. See Paula Kane Robinson Arai's excellent account of life in a contemporary Japanese Zen nunnery, *Women Living Zen: Japanese Soto Buddhist Nuns* (New York: Oxford University Press, 1999).
2. Susan Murcott, *The First Buddhist Women: Translations and Commentary on the Therigatha* (Berkeley: Parallax Press, 1991), 40.

Chapter 4

1. http://www.angelfire.com/realm/bodhisattva/mo-shan.html, for example, offers a detailed history of the first Zen matriarchs.

Chapter 5

1. Roshi Jiyu Kennett, *The Wild White Goose*, vol. 1 (Mt. Shasta, CA: Shasta Abbey, 1997), 25–26.
2. Sallie Tisdale quoted in *Our Great Matriarchs* (Practice Supports), Clouds in Water Zen Center, available at: http://www.cloudsinwater.org/matriarchs.htm, 13.
3. An excellent book on the subject of Zen and militarism is Brian Victoria's *Zen at War* (New York: Weatherhill, 1997).
4. Natalie Goldberg, *The Great Failure: A Bartender, A Monk, and My Unlikely Path to Truth* (San Francisco: HarperSanFrancisco, 2004), 123.
5. So many books and articles have been written on this subject that it would be redundant for me to go over the same ground. Natalie Goldberg's *The Great Failure* is the best, in my opinion. Foremost among the accounts of the sex scandals from an interested writer who does not practice Zen is Michael Downing's *Shoes Outside the Door: Desire, Devotion, and Excess at San Francisco Zen Center* (Washington, DC: Counterpoint, 2001). In contrast to Downing's serious investigative stance, Jessica Roemischer's article, "Women Who Sleep With Their Gurus . . . and Why They Love It," *what is enlightenment: redefining spirituality for an evolving world* 26 (August-October 2004), presents the phenomenon from a decidedly third-wave-feminist, Sex-and-the-City point of view. Religion scholar Rita Gross, one of my favorite Buddhist

commentators, argues against the moralism of spiritual people searching for the perfect teacher in her online piece, "Guru, God and Gender," *Shambhala Sun Online*, http://www.shambhalasun.com/
revolving_themes/Women%20in%20Buddhism/gross.htm; and, finally, for a scholarly sociological exploration of the subject in a Western Buddhist context, I suggest Charles S. Prebish and Kenneth K.
Tanaka, eds., *The Faces of Buddhism in America* (Berkeley and Los Angeles: University of California Press, 1998).

6. Lenore Friedman's excellent book, *Meetings With Remarkable Women*
   (Boston: Shambhala, 1987), contains a typically honest and straightforward version of the story from Maurine herself. So does Roko
   Sherry Chayat's edited collection of Maurine's sesshin talks, *Subtle
   Sound: The Zen Teachings of Maurine Stuart* (Boston: Shambhala, 1996).
7. Maurine Stuart, *Subtle Sound*, ed. Roko Sherry Chayat, 25.
8. *Subtle Sound*, 87–88.
9. *Subtle Sound*, 68.
10. *Subtle Sound*, 99.

Chapter 6

1. The information in this section comes largely from the following
   sources: Heng-Ching Shih's online article, "Women in Zen Buddhism:
   Chinese Bhiksunis in the Ch'an Tradition," available at: http://www.
   geocities.com/zennun 12_8/chanwomen.html? 20053; Mountain Source
   Sangha online publication available at: http://www.angelfire.com/
   realm/bodhisattva/mo_shan.html; and Sallie Tisdale quoted in Clouds
   in Water Zen Center's lineage chart, "Our Great Matriarchs," available
   at: http://www.cloudsinwater.org/matriarchs.htm.
2. Miriam Levering quoted at: http://www.angelfire.com/realm/bodhi-
   sattva/mo_shan.html.
3. For a full account of the story of Layman P'ang and his daughter, see
   Perle Besserman and Manfred Steger, *Crazy Clouds: Zen Radicals,
   Rebels, and Reformers* (Boston: Shambhala Publications, 1991).
4. See Sallie B. King's edited translation of Myodo's inspiring story, *Passionate Journey: The Spiritual Biography of Satomi Myodo* (Boston: Shambhala, 1987).
5. *Passionate Journey*, 107.
6. *Passionate Journey*, 111.

Chapter 7 Notes

1. *Maura Kannon, (A Brief History)*, translated by Shiro Tachibana, in
   *Pure Heart, Enlightened Mind: The Zen Journal and Letters of Maura
   "Shoshin" O'Halloran* (New York: Riverhead Books, 1995), 301.

2. The quotations cited here are all from *Pure Heart, Enlightened Mind.*
3. Quoted in Ranyini Obeyesekere's *Portraits of Buddhist Women: Stories for the Saddharmaratnavaliya* (New York: State University of New York Press, 2001), 12.
4. Ruth Benedict, *The Chrysanthemum and the Sword: Patterns of Japanese Culture* (New York: Mariner Books, 1989).
5. Robert C. Christopher, *The Japanese Mind: A Reinterpretation* (New York: Pantheon, 1983), 39, 43.
6. *The Japanese Mind,* 54.
7. *The Japanese Mind,* 62, 160.
8. Nan Shin (Nancy Amphoux), *Diary of a Zen Nun* (New York: Dutton, 1986), 24–25.
9. *Diary of a Zen Nun,* 46.
10. *Diary of a Zen Nun,* 183.
11. *Diary of a Zen Nun,* 213–214.
12. *Diary of a Zen Nun,* 221–222.

Chapter 8

1. Toni Packer, *The Work of This Moment* (Boston: Shambhala, 1990), 54.

Chapter 9

1. Sallie Tisdale, *Women of the Way: Discovering 2,500 Years of Buddhist Wisdom* (San Francisco: HarperSanFrancisco, 2006), 23.
2. Toni Packer, *The Work of This Moment* (Boston: Shambhala, 1990), 54.
3. Joko Beck quoted in Lenore Friedman, *Meetings With Remarkable Women* (Boston: Shambhala, 1987), 113.
4. Toni Packer, *The Work of This Moment,* 10.
5. Joko Beck quoted in Lenore Friedman, *Meetings With Remarkable Women,* 112–119.
6. Toni Packer, *The Work of This Moment,* 11.
7. Joko Beck quoted in Lenore Friedman, *Meetings With Remarkable Women,* 125.

Chapter 10

1. Jan Chozen Bays, "Can This Practice Be Saved?" in *Not Turning Away: The Practice of Engaged Buddhism,* ed. Susan Moon (Boston: Shambhala, 2004), 213.
2. Blanche Hartman, "Right Where You're Standing," reprinted from the *Wind Bell,* Volume XXX, No. 2 (Summer, 1996), 1, available at: http://www.intrex.net/chzg/Hartman2.htm.

3. Susan Murphy, "All the unknown women," reprinted with permission from *Mind Moon Circle*, Sydney, Summer 1998/99, available at: http://www.zendo.org.nz/pages/alltheunknownwomenarticle.html.

4. Trudy Goodman quoted in *Women's Buddhism Buddhism's Women*, ed. Ellen Banks Findly (Boston: Wisdom Publications, 2000), 173.

5. Rev. Teijo Munnich, http://www.main.nc.us/greattreetemple/about-teijo.htm.

6. Sallie Tisdale, *Women of the Way: Discovering 2500 Years of Buddhist Wisdom* (San Francisco: HarperSanFrancisco, 2006), 131, 141–142.

7. Wendy Egyoku Nakao, in *Not Turning Away: The Practice of Engaged Buddhism*, ed. Susan Moon (Boston: Shambhala, 2004), 135–136.

8. Joan Halifax Roshi quoted in *Women's Buddhism Buddhism's Women*, 381.

9. Barbara Rhodes quoted in "Women's Liberation: Four women talk about why they sought liberation through Buddhist teachings, what it means to be a woman dharma teacher, and how they see Buddhism in America change," *Shambhala Sun Online*, 4, available at: http://www.shambhalasun.com/revolving_themes/Women%20in%20Buddhism.html.

10. Jacqueline Mandell quoted in *Buddhism Through American Women's Eyes*, ed. Karma Lekshe (Ithaca, New York: Snow Lion Publications, 1995), 52–55.

11. Jiko Linda Cutts, "Face to Face: The Meaning Comes Alive," reprinted from *Wind Bell*, Vollume XXXI, No. 2 (Summer, 1997), 3, available at: http://www.intrex.net/chzg/LindaC.htm.

12. Rita M. Gross quoted in *Buddhist Women Across Cultures*, ed. Karma Lekshe (New York: State University of New York Press, 1999), 289.

13. Kate O'Neill quoted in *Buddhist Women on the Edge: Contemporary Perspectives From the Western Frontier*, ed. Marianne Dresser (Berkeley: North Atlantic Books, 1996), 25, 31, 33.

14. Anita Barrows quoted in *Buddhist Women on the Edge*, 53, 55–56.

15. Sandy Boucher, *Opening the Lotus: A Woman's Guide to Buddhism* (Boston: Beacon Press, 1997), 127.

16. Diane Rizzetto, *Waking Up to What You Do: A Zen Practice for Meeting Every Situation With Intelligence and Compassion* (Boston: Shambhala, 2005), 148, 153.

Chapter 11

1. Hetty Baiz, personal correspondence, 15 December 2005.

2. Darlene Cohen, "The Only Way I Know of to Alleviate Suffering," in *Being Bodies: Buddhist Women on the Paradox of Embodiment*, ed. Lenore Friedman and Susan Moon (Boston: Shambhala, 1997), 11–13.

3. Joan Iten Sutherland, "Body of Radiant Knots: Healing as Remembering," in *Being Bodies*, 9.
4. Joan Tollifson, "Enjoying the Perfection of Imperfection," in *Being Bodies*, 22, 23.
5. Rita M. Gross, "Anger and Meditation," in *Being Bodies*, 97.
6. The information for this section comes from Diana Y. Paul, *Women in Buddhism: Images of the Feminine in the Mahayana Tradition* (Berkeley: University of California Press, 1985), 166–246.
7. *Women in Buddhism*, 193.
8. Fran Tribe, "Piecing Together a Life," in *Being Bodies*, 88, 90, 91.
9. Jisho Warner, "What Do Lesbians Do in the Daytime?" in *Being Bodies*, 112–114.
10. Toni Packer, "Tracking the Two Bodies": A Conversation Between Toni Packer and Lenore Friedman, in *Being Bodies*, 182.

Glossary

akema (Jap.) evil spirit

Amoghadarsana (Skt.) male Bodhisattva who challenges Candrottara to transform herself into a male in The Sutra of the Dialogue of the Girl Candrottara

Ananda (Skt.) The Buddha's nephew and compiler of the Buddhist teachings, famous for his prodigious memory and his support for women wishing to join the Buddhist order

Avalokiteshvara (Skt.) early Indian Buddhist male bodhisattva of compassion

Blue Cliff Record (*Hekigan Roku*, Jap.) eleventh-century compilation of koans by eminent Sung dynasty Ch'an master Hsueh Tou Ch'ung Hsien

Bodhidharma (Skt.) legendary sixth-century Central Asian prince who brought Zen to China

Bodhisattva (Skt.) (*Bosatsu*, Jap.) Mahayana Buddhist archetype of compassion; one who puts off entering nirvana in a vow to save the many beings

Bodhisattva Vow recitation chanted by Zen Buddhists after meditation

brahmin (Skt.) member of the Hindu priestly caste

Buddhist Precepts the ethical guidelines of Buddhism, such as not killing, stealing, and so on; essence of Zen ethics

Ch'an (Chin.) (Zen, Jap.) original practice of Mahayana Buddhism in China, placing emphasis on meditation and direct experience of self-realization; the "teaching beyond words and scriptures"

daishi (Jap.) women's quarters in a Zen monastery

dakini (Skt.) Tibetan Buddhist female deity

dharma (Skt.) Buddhist teachings

Dharma Heir a Zen master's chosen successor

dharma talk (*Teisho*, Jap.) lecture given by a teacher during a Zen retreat or an evening of meditation

dharma transmission a ceremonial occasion during which a Zen master declares a dharma heir

Dharmodgata (Skt.) bodhisattva, teacher of Sadaprarudita, hero of the Lotus Sutra

Dogen Kigen thirteenth-century Japanese Zen master who practiced Ch'an
    for several years in China before returning to Japan and founding the
    Soto Zen sect
dokusan (Jap.) private interviews with a Zen teacher devoted to koan or other
    practice related matters
gaijin (Jap.) foreigner
gassho (Jap.) gesture in which the palms are placed together in respectful
    acknowledgment of the Buddha Nature inherent in all things
Great Vows another name for the Bodhisattva Vow.
Gudo Uchiyama Japanese socialist peace activist and Soto Zen master, publicly
    executed for protesting against Japan's militarism during World War II
Hakuin Ekaku eighteenth-century Japanese Zen reformer, compiler of
    Rinzai koan curriculum, author of The Song of Zazen and founder of
    Ryutakuji monastery
Hakuun Yasutani twentieth-century Zen master and founder of the lay
    Sanbokyodan lineage, teacher of American *roshis* Robert Aitken and
    Philip Kapleau
han (Jap.) wooden board and mallet hung outside a *zendo*, struck to announce
    daily activities
Heart Sutra a brief but extremely significant Zen Buddhist scripture
    declaring the essence of Mahayana Buddhism: "form is emptiness;
    emptiness is form"
Hui Ko (Chin.) legendary one-armed first successor of Bodhidharma,
    founder of the Ch'an sect in China; referred to as the second patriarch
    of Zen
Hui neng (Chin.) originally an illiterate rice polisher, he became the sixth
    Zen patriarch, one of the greatest in Zen history
Jizo Buddha (Jap.) the bodhisattva of healing and protector of children
Joshu (Jap.) (Chao chou, Chin.) beloved Zen master of the T'ang Dynasty
    who appears in many significant koans and is said to have lived to be one
    hundred and twenty years old
Kabbalist Jewish mystic
Kali (Skt.) Hindu warrior goddess
Kao-an-Ta-Yu (Chin.) teacher of first Chinese Zen matriarch Mo-shan Liao-
    Jan
karma (Skt.) Buddhist concept of the law of cause and effect
kensho (Jap.) seeing into one's essential nature; another expression for *satori*
kinhin (Jap.) walking meditation
koan (Jap.) Zen meditation technique employing vignettes from ancient
    exchanges between master and disciple as a focus for concentration; a
    nonintellectual means for penetrating through dualistic thinking to the
    Absolute

kotsu (Jap.) short wooden wand, traditional symbol of Zen master's authority

Kuan-chi-hsien (Chin.) Mo-shan Liao-Jan's student, first monk to study with a female Zen master

Kuan Yin (Chin.) (Kannon, Jap.) Chinese female bodhisattva of compassion, originally referred to as the male Avalokiteshvara in her early Indian Buddhist incarnation

kyosaku (Jap.) traditional long wooden stick used to awaken meditators or adjust posture

Lin-chi (Rinzai, Jap.) the fiery Chinese T'ang Dynasty Zen master after whom the Japanese Rinzai Zen sect is named

Ling zhao (Chin.) daughter and traveling Zen companion of the famous eighth-century lay teacher P'ang Yun

Liu Tiemo- "Iron Grinder Liu" (Chin.) eighth-century Zen nun reputed for her tough style of teaching

Lotus Sutra Mahayana Buddhist scripture written somewhere between 100 and 200 C.E. that is somewhat favorable to women

Mahapajapati (Skt.) the Buddha's aunt and foster mother; founder of the first Buddhist order of nuns in India

Mahayana Buddhism (Skt.) the "Greater Vehicle" northern sect of Buddhism emphasizing the bodhisattva ideal of saving the beings of this world. In contrast to the more otherworldly Hinayana ("Lesser Vehicle")—with its roots in India and Southeast Asia—Mahayana Buddhism was adopted in China, Korea, Japan, Tibet, and to some degree in Vietnam. Hinayana is called Theravada Buddhism today.

makyo (Jap.) visions or hallucinations that may come up as distractions during meditation

miko (Jap.) Shinto female shaman/medium

Mo-shan Liao-Jan (Chin.) eighth-century woman Zen master, the first woman documented to have received dharma transmission from a male Zen master.

mu (Jap.) (*wu*, Chin.) "no" or "nothing," the first koan used for meditation in the Rinzai Zen sect, based on Master Joshu's reply to a monk's question about whether a dog had Buddha Nature or not

Mumonkan (Jap.) thirteenth-century Chinese koan collection by Zen master Mumon

Myoshinji (Jap.) one of the head temples of the Japanese Rinzai Zen sect

Nansen (Jap.) (Nanquan, Chin.) renowned Chinese T'ang Dynasty Zen master, teacher of Joshu, famous for a koan involving a cat

Nirvana (Skt.) literally, "extinction"; goal of the Southern School of Buddhism, the end of suffering when one is permanently freed from the wheel of birth and death

P'ang Yun (Chin.) illustrious wandering T'ang Dynasty lay Zen master
  accompanied by his daughter, Ling zhao, one of the earliest
  "matriarchs" of Zen
rakusu (Jap.) shortened version of a monk's garment worn by lay Zen
  Buddhists as a sign of their commitment to the Buddhist Precepts
rinpoche (Tib.) high-level Tibetan Buddhist spiritual teacher
Rinzai Roku (Jap.) recorded sayings of the Zen master Rinzai
Rinzai Zen (Jap.) Japanese Zen sect taking its name from the T'ang Dynasty
  Chinese master Lin-chi; traditionally associated in Japan with the
  military training of samurai warriors.
Rohatsu (Jap.) eight-day commemorative *sesshin* ending on December 8, the
  day of Buddha's enlightenment
roshi (Jap.) literally, "old man," "old boss"; Zen master
Ryonen Gesho (Jap.) seventeenth-century Japanese Zen nun renowned for
  her beauty, who mutilated herself in order to be accepted as a student of
  Haku-o, a prominent Zen master of the time
Ryutakuji (Jap.) monastery in Mishima, Japan, founded by the eighteenth-
  century Rinzai Zen reformer Hakuin
Sadaprarudita (Skt.) young Indian prince, hero of the Lotus Sutra, which
  details his adventures on the way to becoming a bodhisattva
Sakra (Skt.) ancient Indian mythical king of heaven appearing in the Lotus
  Sutra
samadhi (Skt.) meditative state of concentrated absorption
samu (Jap.) work practice; part of Zen training in monasteries and residential
  centers. *Samu* is also scheduled between meditation periods during
  sesshin.
sangha (Skt.) Buddhist community
seiza (Jap.) sitting on one's knees on the floor or on a cushion, a posture
  common in Japan that is used in *zazen*
sensei (Jap.) teacher
seppuku (Jap.) ritual suicide by self-disembowelment practiced by members of
  the samurai caste
sesshin (Jap.) literally, "to draw in" or "concentrate" the mind; a Zen
  meditation retreat
sheikh (Arab.) Muslim mystical master
shekhinah (Heb.) female face of the godhead in Jewish mysticism
Shin'ichi Hisamatsu (Jap.) twentieth-century lay Zen master whose
  "fundamental koan" is at the core of the teaching of the contemporary
  school of Zen he founded
Shinto (Jap.) the indigenous animist, shamanic religion of Japan
Shobogenzo (Jap.) one of thirteenth-century Zen master Dogen Kigen's
  philosophical treatises on Zen

Shusogi (Jap.) instructions on Zen protocol by Dogen Kigen

Song of Zazen poem by eighteenth-century Rinzai Zen master Hakuin recited during *sesshin* in Rinzai monasteries and training centers

Sophia (Gr.) female face of the Holy Spirit in Christian mysticism

Soto Zen (Jap.) the largest Zen sect in Japan; associated with farmers and lay people as opposed to Rinzai Zen's samurai heritage. Unlike Rinzai Zen, Soto does not rely primarily on koans but emphasizes *shikantaza*, sitting meditation for its own sake.

Sufi (Arab.) Muslim mystic

sutra (Skt.) Buddhist scripture

Sutra of the Dialogue of the Girl Candrottara a section of the early Indian Buddhist Vimalakirti Sutra narrating the enlightenment story of the bodhisattva Vimalakirti's daughter Candrottara

Sutra of the Perfection of Wisdom a section of the Lotus Sutra

tabi (Jap.) split-toed white socks worn with wooden or straw sandals

takuhatsu (Jap.) alms begging performed seasonally by Zen monks in towns and cities

Tantrist (Skt.) practitioner of Tibetan Tantric meditation focusing on erotic visualizations involving female deities

Tassajara mountain monastery affiliate of the San Francisco Zen Center

tatami (Jap.) plaited rush floor matting used in traditional Japanese rooms

Theravada Buddhism (Pali) earliest Indian form of Buddhism; originally called Hinayana by Northern Mahayana Buddhists who broke away from their Southeast Asian roots

Therigatha (Pali) poems by the first Indian Buddhist women (sixth century B.C.E.)

toku (Jap.) spiritual merit toward gaining enlightenment and teaching others

Transmission of the Lamp eighth-century Chinese collection of enlightenment stories

Tsung chih (Chin.) first Zen matriarch, the only female successor of Bodhidharma, founder of Zen in China

unsui (Jap.) "cloud over water," a metaphor for the homeless life of a Zen monk

Upanishads (Skt.) earliest Hindu scriptural texts (400 B.C.E.).

Vimalakirti Sutra Mahayana Buddhist scripture outlining the teachings of the illustrious lay Bodhisattva Vimalakirti (third-fourth century C.E.)

vipassana (Skt.) insight meditation, a psychologically oriented form of Theravada Buddhist meditation widely practiced in Southeast Asia and the West

wabi (Jap.) the austere minimalist aesthetic associated with Zen culture and art

zabuton (Jap.) a large, square padded mat used in Zen meditation
zafu (Jap.) the smaller round meditation cushion placed on top of a *zabuton*
zazen (Jap.) sitting meditation
zendo (Jap.) meditation hall
zoris (Jap.) thong sandals

Selected Bibliography

Aoyama, Shundo. *Zen Seeds: Reflections of a Female Priest.* Translated by Patricia Daien Bennage. Tokyo: Kosei Publishing Co., 1990.

Arai, Paula Kane Robinson. *Women Living Zen: Japanese Soto Buddhist Nuns.* New York: Oxford University Press, 1999.

Bays, Jan Chozen. *Jizo Bodhisattva: Modern Healing and Traditional Buddhist Practice.* Boston: Tuttle Publishing, 2002.

Beck, Charlotte Joko. Edited by Steve Smith. *Everyday Zen: Love and Work.* San Francisco: Harper and Row, 1989.

_____. *Nothing Special: Living Zen.* San Francisco: HarperSanFrancisco, 1993.

Besserman, Perle. *Owning It: Zen and the Art of Facing Life.* New York: Kodansha, 1997.

Besserman, Perle and Manfred Steger. *Crazy Clouds: Zen Radicals, Rebels and Reformers.* Boston: Shambhala, 1991.

Besserman, Perle and Manfred Steger. *Grassroots Zen.* Boston: Tuttle Publishing, 2001.

Boucher, Sandy. *Opening the Lotus: A Woman's Guide to Buddhism.* Boston: Beacon Press, 1997.

_____. *Dancing in the Dharma: The Life and Teachings of Ruth Denison.* Boston: Beacon Press, 2005.

Clores, Suzanne. *Memoirs of a Spiritual Outsider.* Berkeley, CA: Conari Press, 2000.

Christopher, Robert. *The Japanese Mind.* New York: Fawcett Columbine, 1983.

Courtois, Flora. *An Experience of Enlightenment.* Wheaton, Ill: Quest Books, 1986.

Dobbins, James C. *Letters of the Nun Eshinni: Images of Pure Land Buddhism in Medieval Japan.* Honolulu: University of Hawai'i Press, 2004.

Dobisz, Jane. *The Wisdom of Solitude: A Zen Retreat in the Woods.* San Francisco: HarperSanFrancisco, 2004.

Downing, Michael. *Shoes Outside the Door: Desire, Devotion, and Excess at San Francisco Zen Center.* Washington, D.C.: Counterpoint, 2001.

Dresser, Marianne, ed. *Buddhist Women on the Edge: Contemporary Perspectives From the Western Frontier.* Berkeley: North Atlantic Books, 1996.

Erlich, Gretel. *Questions of Heaven: The Chinese Journeys of an American Buddhist.* Boston: Beacon Press, 1997.

Feldman, Christina. *Woman Awake: Women Practicing Buddhism.* Berkeley: Rodmell Press, 2005.

Findly, Ellison Banks, ed. *Women's Buddhism Buddhism's Women: Tradition, Revision, Renewal.* Boston: Wisdom Publications, 2000.

Friedman, Lenore. *Meetings With Remarkable Women: Buddhist Teachers in America.* Boston: Shambhala, 1987.

Friedman, Lenore and Susan Moon, Editors. *Being Bodies: Buddhist Women on the Paradox of Embodiment.* Boston: Shambhala, 1997.

Goldberg, Natalie. *Writing Down the Bones: Freeing the Writer Within.* Boston: Shambhala, 1986.

_____. *The Great Failure: A Bartender, A Monk, and My Unlikely Path to Truth.* San Francisco: HarperSanFrancisco, 2004.

Gross, Rita M. *Buddhism After Patriarchy: A Feminist History, Analysis, and Reconstruction of Buddhism.* New York: State University of New York Press, 1993.

_____. *Feminism and Religion.* Boston: Beacon Press, 1996.

_____. *Soaring and Settling: Buddhist Perspectives on Contemporary Social and Religious Issues.* New York: Continuum, 1998.

Hopkinson, Deborah, Michele Hill, and Eileen Kiera, Editors. *Not Mixing Up Buddhism: Essays on Women and Buddhist Practice.* New York: White Pine Press, 1986.

Ital, Gerda. *The Master, The Monks, And I: A Western Woman's Experience of Zen.* Translated by T.M. Green. London: Thorsons Publishing Group, 1987.

Kaza, Stephanie. *Hooked: Buddhist Writings on Greed, Desire, and the Urge to Consume.* Boston: Shambhala, 2005.

Kennet, Jiyu Roshi. *The Wild, White Goose,* vols. 1 and 2. Mt. Shasta, CA: Mt. Shasta Abbey, 1997–98.

King, Sallie B., tr. and annotator. *Passionate Journey: The Spiritual Autobiography of Satomi Myodo.* Boston: Shambhala, 1987.

Kramer, Jacqueline. *Buddha Mom: The Path of Mindful Mothering.* New York: Tarcher/Penguin, 2003.

Larkin, Geri. *Stumbling Toward Enlightenment.* Berkeley: Celestial Arts, 1997.

Moon, Susan, Editor. *Not Turning Away: The Practice of Engaged Buddhism.* Boston: Shambhala, 2004.

Mountain, Marian. *The Zen Environment: The Impact of Zen Meditation.* New York: Bantam Books, 1983.

Murcott, Susan. *The First Buddhist Women: Translations and Commentary on the Therigatha*. Berkeley: Parallax Press, 1991.

Murphy, Susan. *Upside Down Zen: a direct path into reality*. Melbourne: Lothian Books, 2004.

Obeyesekere, Ranjini. *Portraits of Buddhist Women: Stories from The Saddharmaratnavaliya*. New York: State University of New York Press, 2001.

O'Halloran, Maura "Soshin." *Pure Heart, Enlightened Mind: The Zen Journal and Letters of Maura "Soshin" O'Halloran*. New York: Riverhead Books, 1994.

O'Hara, Nancy. *Just Listen: A Guide to Finding Your Own Voice*. New York: Broadway Books, 1997.

_____. *Work From the Inside Out: 7 Steps to Loving What You Do*. New York: Three Rivers Press, 2001.

Packer, Toni. *The Work of This Moment*. Boston: Shambhala, 1990.

_____. *The Wonder of Presence and the Way of Meditative Inquiry*. Boston: Shambhala, 2002.

Palmer, Martin, Jay Ramsay, and Man-Ho Kwok. *Kuan Yin: Myths and Prophecies of the Chinese Goddess of Compassion*. San Francisco: Harper Collins, 1995.

Paul, Diana Y. *Women in Buddhism: Images of the Feminine in the Mahayana Tradition*. Berkeley: University of California Press, 1985.

Phillips, Kathy J. Photographs by Joseph Singer. *This Isn't a Picture I'm Holding: Kuan Yin*. Honolulu: University of Hawai'i Press, 2004.

Prebish, Charles, and Kenneth K. Tanaka, Editors. *The Faces of Buddhism in America*. Berkeley: University of California Press, 1998.

Rizzetto, Dian Eshin. *Waking Up to What You Do: A Zen Practice for Meeting Every Situation With Intelligence and Compassion*. Boston: Shambhala, 2005.

Salzberg, Sharon. *A Heart As Wide As The World: Stories on the Path of Lovingkindness*. Boston: Shambhala, 1999.

Sher, Gail. *One Continuous Mistake: Four Noble Truths for Writers*. New York: Penguin, 1999.

Shin, Nancy (Nancy Amphoux). *Diary of a Zen Nun*. New York: Dutton, 1986.

Smith, Jean. *The Beginner's Guide to Zen Buddhism*. New York: Bell Tower, 2000.

Smith, Patrick. *Japan: A Reinterpretation*. New York: Pantheon, 1997.

Stuart, Maurine. *Subtle Sound: The Zen Teachings of Maurine Stuart*. Edited by Roko Sherry Chayat. Boston: Shambhala, 1996.

Tisdale, Sallie. *Women of the Way: Discovering 2500 Years of Buddhist Wisdom*. San Francisco: HarperSanFrancisco, 2006.

Tsomo, Karme Lekshe, Editor. *Buddhism Through American Women's Eyes.* Ithaca, NY: Snow Lion Publications, 1995.

_____, Editor. *Buddhist Women Across Cultures: Realizations.* New York: State University of New York Press, 1999.

_____, Editor. *Buddhist Women and Social Justice: Ideals, Challenges, and Achievements.* New York: State University of New York Press, 2004.

Tworkov, Helen. *Zen in America: Profiles of Five Teachers.* San Francisco: North Point Press, 1989.

Acknowledgments

I want to thank Bill Boyle, the current resident teacher, and all my dear friends at the Princeton Area Zen Group, in Princeton, New Jersey, for fifteen years of deeply rewarding grassroots Zen practice. I could not have asked for a more perfect group of crazy cloud dharma dancing partners. My heartfelt thanks to Lucy Gay, Ti Manicas, Leialoha Apo Perkins, Jennie Martinez Peterson, Kathy Phillips, and Sigrid Tokuda, the wonderful women in my Honolulu Hui Na Wahine O Honua—"Earth Women's Collective"—for always being there for me no matter how far away I wander from home. Thank you, Adele Ne Jame, for our Kapiolani Park walks and Portobello mushroom sandwich poetry lunches. May peace reign in our troubled ancestral lands. Thanks to my women Zen friends in Australia, Kathy Shiels and Kiya Murman, to Helen Summers, president of the Melbourne Interfaith Centre, and Mary Cunnane, and Helen Caldicott for your warm welcome to Oz. The women to whom I dedicate this book have kept me going through thick and thin: Hetty Baiz, Brigid Lowry, Jennie Martinez Peterson, and Kathy J. Phillips—you are all Kuan Yin. My editor at Palgrave, Amanda Moon—another manifestation of the bodhisattva of compassion—is the answer to every author's prayers. And what would I do without Emily Leithauser, who always finds perfect solutions to my impossible requests; Yasmin Mathew, who, undaunted, tracks me across the globe; and Amanda Fernandez, who so patiently and meticulously corrects the work of this technically challenged author?

My gratitude to Manfred Steger, my companion on the Great Way, is boundless.